THE AUTOBIOGRAPHY of WILLIAM ZECKENDORF

with Edward McCreary

ZECKENDORF

First Edition

Designer: Berry Reavis-Eitel

Parker Publishing Company

info@parkerpub.co

www.parkerpub.co

**To dear Marion
for many, many reasons**

Contents

Sixteen pages of illustrations follow page 152.

One

▪ Prologue

LATE ON FRIDAY afternoon, May 7, 1965, I asked my chauffeur to drive me down to Wall Street for one more visit with my creditors. After that there would be the blessed relief of the weekend.

As we were traveling down the East River Drive, my car phone rang. I picked it up. It was a reporter from *The New York Times* asking, "Is it true that Webb & Knapp is going into bankruptcy?"

I said, "My boy, somebody is pulling your leg. Webb & Knapp is not going into bankruptcy. We are paying our debts and will continue to do so."

I put down the phone. It rang again. This time it was Larry O'Donnell of *The Wall Street Journal*. He asked the same question. Again I said no, but now I knew something concrete must be causing these rumors. I called my office. They knew of nothing. A few seconds later, however, the office called me back. The Marine Midland Bank, as trustees of an old 8.5-million-dollar Webb & Knapp bond issue, had just called in this note. Webb & Knapp was *being put* into bankruptcy.

The note the Marine Midland was calling in was signed years ago when we bought 120 Broadway, for which we had paid more than eight million dollars in cash plus 8.5 million dollars in notes. Under what is called the boiler plate (the standard small print of any contract) there was a particular clause which stated that Marine Midland could demand full payment of the note before its maturity date if Webb & Knapp could not meet its obligation as due—in other words, they could collect the 8.5 million dollars whenever they wished, once they learned Webb & Knapp had not paid one of its other creditors.

Ironically, we were not in arrears either as far as interest or principal on the Marine Midland note, but there was no defense against the statement that we were not meeting other obligations. For more than three years I had been maneuvering to keep a suddenly greatly overextended Webb & Knapp from actually falling over the edge of the cliff. To this end I had gone into deep personal debt, often by countersigning the notes necessary to keep the company going. We had, of course, curtailed expansion, and we were liquidating assets and retiring debts as rapidly as possible. Knowing what we had accomplished in tight corners in the past, as well as our capacity for making money, our creditors had been riding with us. With just a little more time to capitalize on one project or perhaps salvage another, we would have been able, I believe, to make it to safety, but on that Friday afternoon in May time ran out. The directors of the Marine Midland, as trustees of an 8.5-million-dollar note, felt vulnerable about stockholder suits if they did not act, so they acted. They pulled the cord. Twenty-six years of work, plus what remained of Webb & Knapp, were now moving down the chute.

There was nothing at all I could do now for Webb & Knapp on Wall Street. I told my driver to take me back to our 383 Madison Avenue office. This is where I had started Webb & Knapp's climb, and here I would stay with it to its fall.

When I had joined Webb & Knapp as a partner in 1939, it was a management company, a caretaker of other people's property. Gradually I moved the firm into wider and more complex fields. By 1942 the company controlled assets of two million dollars. By 1945, after the end of World War II, our assets were seven million dollars. By 1951, when the company went public our holdings had swelled to a net worth of forty-two million dollars, and kept growing from there. By then, we had acquired all manner of properties. We had accumulated strategic acreage such as the site of the UN, Roosevelt Field in Long Island, the 63,000-acre Indian Trail Ranch in Florida, and Mountain Park in Los Angeles. We had bought television studios, warehouses, and the Chrysler Building. In the 1950's, Webb & Knapp, the property company, underwent a further change in character. In some part this "change" was a logical result of our growth, but in large part it was a matter of my own personality: I like to build. After envisioning a given property's building and architectural potentialities, the challenge always lay in making these potentialities come true. I had ideas, all kinds of ideas, that nobody else was willing to carry out, so I carried them out myself. I knew where to find partners and backers, and because of its excellent business record, Webb & Knapp had access to plentiful financing. In time I found a gifted architect, I. M. Pei, and I talked him into leaving Harvard to work with us.

We were off.

Actually, Webb & Knapp had moved rather modestly into construction work, by erecting office buildings. These were enormously successful. Then we branched off in several directions at once. In Long Island we created Roosevelt Field, the first of the giant suburban shopping centers. At the same time, we were pushing the Rip Van Winkle city of Denver into the twentieth century through the creation of Mile High Center, an office complex, and by putting up a new department store and hotel on the site of Denver's Court House Square. Webb & Knapp started a Denver building boom that has greatly improved and drastically altered that town's skyline and history. The same is true of Montreal, where we built Place Ville-Marie, a midtown office and shopping complex that has become the new heart of a refurbished city. As urban-redevelopment laws were passed by Congress to encourage rebuilding in America's cities, Webb & Knapp moved into this field. We fathered the southwest Washington, D.C., redevelopment area whose five hundred acres are now one of Washington's most prestigious office and residential areas. We designed and built the Society Hill towers and townhouse complex that is the centerpiece of Philadelphia's revitalized city core. We conceived and created University Towers in Chicago. We built in Pittsburgh, and in New York we created Kips Bay, built Lincoln Towers and Park West Village. With the possible exception of that extraordinary man, Robert Moses, Webb & Knapp was the largest urban redeveloper in the nation. We placed twice as many bids as we finally won, and in doing so, Webb & Knapp made Title I respectable. Time after time it turned out that our decision to bid was what drew other builders out to bid as well. Invariably, in these encounters, it was our designs that set the planning and architectural standards others had to meet.

Throughout this period we were also buying land and properties, putting up individual buildings in various cities, creating a string of new shopping centers and industrial parks across Canada, and drilling for oil off the coast of Surinam. The secret of any great project is to keep it moving, keep it from losing momentum, and this, for me, meant a constant flow of telephone calls and trips, often by company plane, to Montreal, Chicago, Washington, Cleveland, Philadelphia, Denver, and points west. Meanwhile, there were ceremonial as well as promotional presentations to be made; to President Eisenhower for our work in southwest Washington; to the Queen of England, in Montreal, for Place Ville-Marie, and to bankers and backers in board-rooms across the country for many other projects. In New York, and in every town where we had interests, there was a constantly chang-ing skein of contracts, agreements, and trades to be kept in motion.

As it turned out, unexpected and phenomenal delays (especially in urban-renewal projects) between the start and actual finish of our building programs greatly increased carrying and interest costs for these projects. However, we had committed ourselves, and the eventual return from these projects promised to be so great that we carried on. At the same time, Webb & Knapp's profits from the purchase and sale of lands and buildings were so great that we had no financial worries. Once, when I was talking to Billy Reynolds of Reynolds Aluminum, I asked, "What's your company's net per year?"

"Around nine million dollars," he said.

"My God, I pay my shylocks more than that!"

I have never been afraid of debt, because debt is what gives you leverage, and I also knew our projects were excellent ones. So, one day when the head of Morgan Guaranty stuck out his hand at a gathering of bankers and said, "Bill, you look like a million dollars," I could crack back, "I'd better—I owe you three million."

At the time, we all laughed, but in May, 1965, no one was laugh-ing. Webb & Knapp had been wiped out.

We had been loaded down by too many projects that were taking too long to be realized, and we could no longer control the direction we were going in. Like a doomed father on a raft who throws his children to shore when approaching the rapids, I had thrown some of our most cherished properties, such as Place Ville-Marie and Century City, to the trustworthy hands that I knew would bring these projects to fruition. This lightening of the load helped. For more than three years I was able to maneuver Webb & Knapp through the rapids. Then, a combination of trends and events, which I shall mention in more detail later, finally piled up and smashed the company. They almost did the same to me. In fact, there were moments after the breakup when I found myself all but in the wreckage bobbing along-side me.

Actually, once Webb & Knapp had completely gone under, there was an almost welcome stillness. For month after month we had been hectically working to raise cash, to make one last deal, to fend off or pay off creditors. Now, all action ceased. Even our phones were disconnected. When I tried to use my car phone, the operator refused to place my call. Once declared bankrupt, Webb & Knapp was out of the reach of individual creditors and in a fiscal limbo where no one could do business with us. In any event, since Webb & Knapp would now be in the hands of a trustee, I could no longer act for the company. I became, in effect, a bystander at the wake, and an official nonperson, a role both unfamiliar and unenjoyable. At the office, where my associates and I showed up to be of all the help we could, we had the dubious pleasure of watching appraisers come in to evaluate and tag all company fixtures and furniture for bankruptcy sale. Meanwhile, downtown, the New York Real Estate Association posted my son and me for nonpayment of dues. My membership, maintained by Webb & Knapp, was not a detail about which I would normally concern myself. The association board members and officials knew this, but none had bothered to call about those dues. Rather, it seemed to me as if they jumped at the opportunity to tear at us as we went down. In the next few weeks and months, we learned not to be surprised at such behavior.

In moments of crisis, one's world tends to become simplified, and its people and events fall into distinct categories. They did so now. Predictably, a number of people who used to call on me for information, for contacts or favors, vanished from the scene. Meanwhile, quite a few of the people whom I tried to call about one matter or another were suddenly not available or "in conference." Others were carefully distant in their manner. Only my creditors were ever anxious for a chat, and the most eager and anxious of all was Henry Sears, an ex-partner from the old days at Webb & Knapp. It was Henry and I who, amidst the two-A.M. merriment at the Club Monte Carlo in 1946, signed the basic document turning over to the United Nations the seventeen acres that now house their headquarters. Henry, a well-to-do man in his own right, was made 1.5 million dollars richer when

I bought him out of Webb & Knapp in 1948. We had parted friends. Recently, in trying to save Webb & Knapp, I had signed a note for $250,000 to Sears' wife. Now, for this note, he pressed me with a harsh zeal that none of my professional loan sharks could match.

But others went out of their way to offer sympathy and regrets, and, in some cases even help. The great majority, however, stayed neutral, uninvolved, waiting to see what I might do. Moreover, there seemed to be more than a touch of old Japan in modern America: I learned that there was betting in certain quarters that I would choose to end the drama samurai-style, by committing suicide. At the same time, an extramarital liaison I had once formed was also making news. The pain and embarrassment that this brought to my wife was intense. She suffered deeply. Though in the end she loyally stayed with me, as I had always believed she would, there were moments when my depression was absolute. But killing myself was something I was not about to do.

What I did do was join my son and my son-in-law, Ronald Nicholson, in a new company, General Property Corp. Since my personal assets were subject to the claims of creditors, I could not be an owner. I became a consultant to the company. For financial backing we turned to the investment firm of Lazard Freres. We needed little over a quarter of a million dollars to start promoting various properties we had acquired. After much deliberation, Lazard Freres, which in times past had made more than seventy million dollars from various Webb & Knapp ventures, agreed to provide some capital, but there was a condition: Henceforth they would have the right of first refusal on all General Property Corp. projects. Such an arrangement would, in effect make us lifelong vassals of Lazard. We turned down this offer and set up the new company on a more modest scale with our own financing. To begin with, we took over our old Webb & Knapp offer and set up the new company on a more modest scale with our next move was to acquire control of our own building, 383 Madison Avenue, and it was this maneuver that led to my autobiography.

The underlying lease for our building was held by the Metropolitan Life Insurance Company (I had sold it to them in 1948). The lease had four years to go, but Met Life agreed to sell it to us, and Equitable Life agreed to buy it—if we could persuade the major tenants to sign new leases for twenty-one years.

We went to the building's three prime tenants. The advertising firm of Batten, Barton, Durstine & Osborn, whose lease was just expiring, were agreeable to a new lease, especially since we also offered them much of the space Webb & Knapp used to hold. The Carrier Corporation (whose lease had four years to go) took a bit more persuasion, but it was prime space at a prime rate, so they also extended their lease. Last came Holt, Rinehart and Winston, whose lease had another twelve years to run.

I stopped in to see a friend at Holt, Rinehart and Winston and told him we would like to renew their lease.

"But it runs to 1977 now," he said reasonably.

"I want you to extend it to 1986."

He laughed. "You're crazy; come back in twelve years."

"No, I'm serious," and I explained what we were doing.

My friend reached into his desk, pulled out a manuscript, and handed it to me. The front page was titled, "The Mad, Mad World of William Zeckendorf."

"What's that?" I asked.

"It's a book suggestion. How do you like it?"

"I don't."

"Well, we'll make a bargain. *You* write your autobiography for us, and *we'll* extend our lease for you."

I'll do almost anything to close a deal. We shook hands. General Property Corp. now had its first building, and I had my first book.

With a safe home base established at 383 Madison Avenue, General Property Corp. began to move out and around town. Having little capital of our own, we reverted to the tactics and style of the early 1940's and became packagers and promoters for other people. Our reward was in the form of fees or a piece of the profits. We tackled all kinds of assignments. For instance, it was my son who arranged the purchase of the *Queen Mary* by the town of Long Beach, California, and acquisition of the London Bridge by the McCullough people. It was General Property Corp. that assembled the land for the new Gimbels store at Eighty-sixth Street and Lexington Avenue in New York. We bought, held, and profitably sold an old Webb & Knapp property, the Manhattan Hotel. We also conceived and promoted the conversion of the old Bell Telephone labs, by the Lower West Side docks near Greenwich Village, into the Westbeth cooperative artists' colony. Rather early in the game, the word that William Zeckendorf and friends were alive and busy at 383 Madison Avenue began to spread. Once more, deals and propositions began to come to us.

Only my personal assets, not my brains, were in hock. I still knew how to make money for people. Moreover, with the fantastic pressures of Webb & Knapp's last few years off my back, I was beginning to feel like a man suddenly released from solitary confinement. True, the trustee for Webb & Knapp had filed a suit against me and the other directors of Webb & Knapp, but I had done my best to save the company, as I had in the past done my best to build it. My conscience was clear. For the present I was busy and relaxed. Marion and I saw more of each other. We went to plays and we traveled. We spent one summer in France, the following Christmas in Portugal. I had turned over our estate in Greenwich to creditors, but we had acquired a quiet place in Westchester County and were very happy. Marion had been completely cured of a facial skin cancer by a new and remarkable therapy developed at Memorial Hospital, and her morale was high. We were both enjoying a sense of renewed happiness and confidence. In the spring of 1968 Marion flew to South America for a month's tour. She planned to wind up her trip with a visit to the Inca ruins in Peru. From there she would fly to Guadeloupe in the Caribbean. She was to arrive at 8:30 P.M. I flew down to meet her plane. The next day we were to fly to Santa Lucia to board the *France* and sail back to New York.

I arrived in Guadeloupe two hours before Marion's plane was due. I had brought her miniature pinscher Mimi with me and held her as we waited. The scheduled arrival time came and went for the flight from Peru, but no plane landed. I walked over to the counter to make inquiries in my very poor French. The attendant made a Gallic face and a gesture with his hand, an up-and-down gesture. I thought he meant the plane was about to land. A few moments later the announcement came over the loudspeaker: the plane had crashed.

The sensation from then on was one of being in a dream from which I couldn't wake up. For a time I sat in the airport manager's office, then finally pulled myself together and tried to call New York to tell my children what had happened, but it was impossible to get through. I went back to the hotel where we had reservations for the night, bathed, shaved, and lay down. All this time Marion's dog, sensing the tragedy, had been whimpering. Now she insisted on creeping up to lie by my side.

The first plane out of town was at nine o'clock the next morning. I boarded it. At Antigua I took the dog off for a walk. Coming back aboard, I found, sitting on the aisle, my old friend Winthrop Aldrich and his wife. Glad to see familiar faces, I told them what had happened and cannot remember anyone ever being so solicitous and kind. Later, two other old friends, Dr. and Mrs. Howard Rusk, came aboard. They too were a solace, but there was no real consolation. Marion had been my friend and my confidante. She had given me insight into worlds I would never have known without her—the worlds of art, archaeology, music, and ballet. At the most dramatic moment in my career, when I was buying out my partners in Webb & Knapp, she urged me on and offered to put up every penny that she had in order to help me. She loved me, she forgave my transgressions, and now she was gone. In clear weather her plane had crashed into a mountain. There were no identifiable remains; the victims received a mass burial.

In New York, Dr. Norman Vincent Peale conducted a memorial service. Services were also conducted at the C. W. Post College of Long Island University, of which I was chairman of the board of trustees. Literally thousands of letters of condolence came in for me. I answered each and kept on with my work. Thank God for work! I was difficult to be with for a time, but dropping a curtain of work about myself was the best way to adjust to the situation.

After Marion's death I decided to declare personal bankruptcy. Making money is something I can always do. There are certain debts of honor I shall see are paid, but filing for bankruptcy was the only way to finally clear my entanglements with Webb & Knapp and start a new life.

As for the present and immediate future, I am busy. Continually and enjoyably busy, keeping up with just some of the opportunities that come my way to get things done. For just one example, quite early on my comeback trail, I met (I made it my business to meet) a young entrepreneur, a descendant of Vikings, a yachtsman, and a ship-owner—Jakob Isbrandtsen of American Export Isbrandtsen.

Jakob is a tough, energetic man with the handshake of a dock worker and the mind of a Yankee trader. He is an early riser, so am I, and over a series of six- and seven-o'clock breakfasts we worked out a continuing and convoluted and mutually beneficial series of business transactions. He had acquired control of Equity Corp., a holding company, that had properties which we were interested in. It turned out that he was also interested in acquiring new docking facilities around New York, resulting in our assembling two miles of waterfront property on Staten Island for the Isbrandtsen company. The modern containership port that will evolve on this site will do much to keep New York a major shipping center. Shooters Island presently blocks the channel to this site, but what we saw that nobody else could then see was the possibility of dredging up the sand and gravel that form Shooters Island. We will pipe this material over to stabilize and build up our low-lying Staten Island holdings into prime land. The end result will be a much safer ship channel and expanded ship facilities for New York.

Again, while in search for a profitable solution to the parking problem in New York, I conceived of a new building and space-use technique that has a phenomenal range of applications and implications. My joint partners in this new venture are the hard-headed engineers who run Morrison-Knudsen Co., Inc., the worldwide construction firm, and the U.S. Steel Corp. They joined with me after I had my new system carefully designed and engineered by Carlos J. Taveres, a brilliant California architect and engineer.

Basically, what we have is a new and inexpensive way of building in water. Take the new, twin-tower Trade Center presently under construction in New York. It is being built on fill land where the river once flowed. To create this land, first a bulkhead had to be built out into the river. Then fill was trucked in to create new land. Later this fill was dug out again so foundations could be laid for buildings. Then the buildings began to go up. This process is time-consuming and costly.

I thought to myself, Why not build concrete caissons or some kind of floating dock whose underside is sloped to the actual contour of the underlying land? These concrete units can be floated into place, sunk, tied to piles driven down to bedrock, then the water pumped out. Now the foundations are in place for the buildings, plus a huge area for parking or storage. What's more, instead of digging and carting off a lot of dirt, all that is needed is to pump out water, a cheap and quick operation—and the displaced water helps hold up the structure. In fact, the structure has to be anchored down, or it would float away.

The more I thought about it, the better it sounded. I voiced the idea to a number of architects, but they only smiled dubiously and tried to change the subject. I have been around architects and engineers long enough not to take them completely seriously and decided to go to Taveres, who is highly regarded in the construction field. He took to the idea, analyzed its possibilities, and came up with a series of designs and cost studies that would make an accountant weep for joy. Basically it works out as follows: Using our system, a builder would create a concrete plaza, upon which buildings would then be constructed, at a considerable saving in cost compared to present landfill methods. But, aside from his saving per square foot of land, the builder using our technique would, in effect, be getting hundreds of thousands of cubic feet of usable space below the plaza absolutely free.

After we had gone over these figures a number of times, I contacted U.S. Steel and Morrison-Knudsen. Accepting the logic of Taveres' figures, they immediately saw beyond them to the marketing implications. Think of an STOL (Short Takeoff and Landing) air building built out into the Hudson—planes on the roof, passenger terminals below that, aircraft-maintenance decks and auto parking even farther below in the space that could not otherwise be afforded. Envision a great ship dock handling massive container cargoes. Today such a dock needs acre upon acre of back land, called the "farm," to take care of storage and routing of cargo. With our system the "farm" would be right there in the form of layer after layer of storage area reaching down to the sea bed. Eventually, our new system is also going to be used to build a supersonic jet port at sea. There the owners of homes, naturalists, and conservationists won't join forces to prevent the building of an airport; there the sonic boom won't be a problem; there no clogged highways will force the air traveler to miss his flight.

While we nurse along this new development in the use of space, I work on half a dozen bread-and-butter projects at the same time. I am enjoying every day of my renaissance. As to my previous life, which is what this book is supposed to be all about, I say this: If I had it to do over again, I would—only bigger and better.

· 1 · Beginnings

WE NEW YORK ZECKENDORFS are actually misplaced Westerners. My grandfather, a frontier merchant, lived, traded, and sometimes fought with the Indians in the Arizona Territory. Zeckendorf wagon trains carried the mail and delivered supplies to the many mining camps ringing Tucson, and my cousins still own and run the department store, now called Steindorf's, which my grandfather William Zeckendorf opened in that town.

In September, 1867, when Grandfather rode into Tucson with thirty thousand dollars' worth of goods in twelve wagon trains, Tucson's established merchants were less than pleased. By the time Grandfather had managed to rent an old adobe building for his proposed store, the local storekeepers had had several private conferences among themselves. They approached Grandfather with an offer to buy him out, lock, stock, and miner's picks, for sixty-five thousand dollars. Grandfather accepted. He returned to New Mexico where he and his two brothers lived, with a fine profit in hand. That next year William went back to Tucson with an even larger wagon train of goods. This time the local impresarios were not buying. So Grandfather had to open a store, and he settled down to make his mark upon the country.

A while ago I was invited to Tucson for the centennial celebration marking the founding of the original Zeckendorf store. There were bands, a parade, the usual flow of goodwill, and long speeches. As a guest of honor, I sat in the front of the reviewing stand. I noticed that throughout the performance one man seated in the back of the platform kept staring at me. Every time I turned my head, I met his gaze, so when the ceremonies were over I turned to him and asked, "What can I do for you, sir?"

"I have an indiscreet question to ask," he said.

"There are only indiscreet answers. What's your question?"

He introduced himself as head of the anthropology department at the University of Arizona and said that he had been studying my face and wondered if I had any Apache blood.

I looked at him for a moment and answered, "No, but I have reason to believe the Apache may have some Zeckendorf blood." Before his marriage, Grandfather had lived with the Indians for a time, and I have no doubt that he partook of all hospitality offered.

Grandfather was an activist, a gregarious man with a zest for life and a flair for publicity. Soon after he arrived in this country from Germany, he moved to Tucson, and from then on the local paper regularly reported his announcements about new shipments of goods or his shooting at robbers trying to break into his store in the night. The safe arrival of a wagon train of goods, his brother's marriage, the coming of Christmas, and his own birthday were all occasions for treating the town to a public display of fireworks. As some dry wit remarked in the June 11 *Weekly Arizonan* of 1870:

On Sunday last, Mr. Zeckendorf called the attention of every man, woman, and child to the anniversary of his birth by a magnificent display of fireworks. The spectators generally enjoyed the sport and made Z. the recipient of sundry congratulations upon his extraordinary good luck in not having died while a little baby, and his subsequent fortunate career made manifest by his living presence, "whole and entire." The grandest pyrotechnic display of the evening, which marked the closing of the celebration, consisted of the burning of Don Fernandez' stable and hay ignited by the spark of a Roman candle in the hands of Z. or some other man.

By now Grandfather had become a deep-dyed frontiersman—he had even scalped an Indian caught rustling cattle. He was also leader of a posse that tracked down and hanged three robbers who had murdered a local Mexican-American merchant. In the war against Geronimo's Apaches, Grandfather served as aide-de-camp to General Nelson Miles. In 1886, after Geronimo's surrender, he was Tucson's parade marshal for a gala honoring the general. I still cherish an old photograph of him, a big, broad-shouldered man, once again in uniform for this occasion.

As the frontier quieted down, so did its citizens. Grandfather eventually became a member first of the territorial and then of the state legislature, but for all his many side ventures, his world centered around his store, where he sold everything from crowbars to diamond stickpins. The store was famous throughout the territory, and whenever the command of the local military establishment changed hands, it was a custom for the outgoing commander to bet the new commander a bottle of whiskey that he could not name any merchandise carried by an eastern department store which was not also on sale in grandfather's store. The outgoing officer invariably won, even, as happened one time, when the new man asked for a pair of ice skates.

Grandfather's Tucson store prospered and the year he had spent socializing in New York City, before he went West, had not been wasted. In 1872 he returned to the big city and married lovely eighteen-year-old Julia Frank. The young couple spent their honeymoon on the second transcontinental train trip of the Union Pacific across the plains and mountains to Oakland, then sailed across the bay to San Francisco and on to San Diego. On the morning of their departure from San Diego to Tucson by stagecoach, Grandmother for the first time saw her handsome, flamboyant new husband in his native habiliments. He arrived at breakfast with a pistol on each hip, crisscrossed bandoliers of ammunition across his chest, and a rifle in his hand.

From what we know of Grandfather, he was probably laying it on just a little bit for his young bride's benefit, but as they got along the trail that day, they were hailed by a posse of U.S. cavalry that had been sent to meet them. The preceding stagecoach—and also, as it turned out, the stagecoach that followed theirs—had been held up. Those were the bad good old days.

Grandfather was, for a time, owner of what later became the Copper Queen Mine. He probably grub-staked the finder and then bought him out. That mine became the basis of the Phelps-Dodge Company, one of America's leading corporations and principal copper producers. The story goes that Dr. James Douglas, a mining engineer from Canada, came down to the territory looking for mining properties. (He was the grandfather of Lou Douglas, who was on the board of Webb & Knapp and has been a good friend for many years.) Dr. Douglas dropped in on Grandfather and said, "Mr.

Zeckendorf, I have examined your mine and I think it's got great possibilities. I'm going to recommend it as an investment to two young clients of mine who are just graduating from college. They're Boston people with money."

In due course, Douglas returned to Tucson and reported his recommendation had been accepted. It was proposed that Grandfather sell his mine to the new company, keeping eighty percent of the stock. The Bostonians would take twenty percent and supply 200,000 dollars' working capital. Grandfather quickly agreed and asked the young men's names.

One was Phelps and the other was Dodge—the genesis of the great Phelps-Dodge Company, which eventually bought out my grandfather and operates the Copper Queen Mine to this very day.

Grandfather was also a charter member of the Pioneer Society of Arizona, but after his retirement, he spent the last ten years of his life in New York, where he died at age sixty-four in 1906. I was born in 1905 and never knew him, which has always been one of my greatest regrets.

As things turned out, we had much in common.

As an article in *Life* magazine said of me, "He led a thoroughly undistinguished childhood." This is quite accurate, but my childhood was also a very pleasant one. My father, Arthur Zeckendorf, had left Arizona as a young man. He married Bertha Rosenfield, who came of a family of early settlers in Detroit, and I was born in Paris, Illinois, where Father for a time ran a hardware business. Shortly after this, Father went into the shoe-manufacturing business on Long Island, where he eventually became a vice-president and part owner of Jacobs & Sons, one of the first mass producers of footwear for the new mail-order firms. We lived in the semirural town of Cedarhurst, where we children played at cowboys and Indians in fields where superhighways, supermarkets, and row after row of suburban houses now stand. My clearest memory is of long tramps through the fields in the company of my dog Mickey. I had many friends, but I was also a bit of a loner. By the time I was eight or nine I had discovered that if I acted up enough, I could get thrown out of Sunday school each weekend and spend the day fishing. Father, who had grown up in an adobe home in Tucson, was not much upset at this touch of Huck Finn in his son. He was a cultured, quiet, and kindly man who did not believe in strict authoritarian controls, and I was his only son. My sister Ann, five years younger than I, was even more willful (at least I seem to remember her winning most of the battles around the house). Neither of us was what could be referred to as a repressed child. Mother, who was one of fourteen children, might have scolded a bit more than Father, but she also let us grow our own way, while keeping us very much aware of being part not only of our own immediate family but also of the entire family.

We were still living on Long Island when America entered World War I, and for us children and most adults, all that the war meant was a new kind of excitement and glamour. We attended all the parades in the nearby Long Island training camps. Soldiers and officers, including dashing young aviators from Floyd Bennett Field, came to the house regularly for supper. This glamour in the home was short-lived, however, because Mother, who had always yearned to live in New York City, finally got her way. In 1917, when I was twelve, we moved into a spacious apartment in the Darrleton at Seventy-first Street and Broadway. This was a section of town to which many well-to-do Jewish families were then moving. The apartments were new, and there was a bake shop or candy store and a fancy delicatessen on every block. The population density was high, but, at least by present New York standards, an amazing number of people knew each other. On the Jewish New Year it was the custom for the gentlemen and their ladies, in their furs, to walk up and down that part of Broadway greeting their friends.

At that time New York still had one of the finest public-school systems in the country. I was enrolled in the local school, and on my first day there something happened that taught me a very important lesson. It was the classic new-boy situation; I was teased and taunted, and the hazing went on during most of the day. I finally turned to the biggest of my tormentors and said, "All right, meet me outside." Everybody knew there was going to be a fight. When school was dismissed, a gang of kids was milling around by the steps of the back yard, waiting. My opponent was waiting too. I was frightened, but there was nothing to do about it. I took off my coat and started running down the stairs at my enemy. My seeming eagerness must have startled him, for I noticed that he wilted just a bit. The fact is, I was expecting to get knocked down and was rushing in to get it over with, but when I saw him flinch, I gained new courage. He gave up after one or two punches. This minor incident was soon forgotten by almost everyone but me; it taught me a lesson that later applied in business every bit as much as it did in a high-school playground: If you show hesitancy or fear, you may already be half-defeated. If you put on a bold front, and fight with everything you have, you can win. Moreover, once you have won a few battles, you are usually left alone: in the jungle, no animal thoughtlessly attacks the lion.

I did not finish high school; most of the courses bored me completely. In order to enter college, I prepared at a cram school, Clark's School for Concentration, and completed sixteen regent's exams in one week, something of a record at the time. At age seventeen I entered New York University. It was 1922, I was in my teens, and America was in its Roaring Twenties. College meant football games, raccoon coats, parties, delightfully giddy flappers, and not much work. I majored in commerce, played football, joined a fraternity, became its president, and wrapped myself up in the life of "Joe College" for three years.

Though I now hold four honorary LL.D.s, I was a college dropout. The social life was pleasant, but classes were dull and a waste of time. Anxious to be in the real world of business, I quit college in my junior year to work for my uncle, Sam Borchard. I left a "thoroughly undistinguished childhood" to begin what seemed to be a thoroughly undistinguished career.

• 2 • Apprentice to the Trade

PRIOR TO the 1920's my uncle Sam Borchard had begun shifting his energies and capital from the shoe industry into real estate. By 1925, when I went to work for him, he was an important New York real-estate investor-builder worth quite a few millions. I was an untrained new employee, and Sam put me to work in the housekeeping end of the business. This consisted of collecting rents, placating those tenants with service complaints, and buying shades, awnings, soap, and fuel for Sam's various properties. Having neither interest nor patience with this end of the business, I kept popping into Sam's office with suggestions and ideas that might get me into the sales end of the operation. After many months, I finally got my chance. Sam had purchased 32 Broadway, an office structure next to the Standard Oil building in downtown New York. In spite of its strategic location, 32 Broadway was little more than half-occupied; poor management and an office-building boom had combined to strip it of key tenants. The building had cost Sam 1.2 million dollars. The yearly rent, he felt, should amount to at least $400,000, but it was only half that amount. Sam had called me into his office to explain all this, and said, "William, I am going to Europe with your aunt and the children for a few months. I want you to go down there and rent that building. You get that building rented, my boy, and you can be sure of a great future here with me."

So Sam went to Europe, and I went to work on his building. I tackled the job by taking the elevator to the top floor of each building on Wall Street. Then I worked my way down floor by floor, canvassing each office on each floor. On the theory that every third tenant's lease expired that year (three-year leases were then the norm), I would march in with the bold statement, "I understand your lease is expiring, and I'd like to show you space at 32 Broadway." My canvassing was very soon noted by the buildings' owners, who rightly suspected that I was stealing their tenants. They began asking, "Who do you want to see here?" before letting me onto the elevator. Only once was I caught short and escorted out of a building. After that I had someone photograph the directories of every building in advance and was always prepared with the name of a tenant in case I was questioned.

Of the prospective tenants I approached, perhaps one out of five would come over to 32 Broadway to have a look. Of every five that looked, perhaps one would take a lease, but that was enough. Bit by bit I began to fill our building. By early fall, when my uncle was due back from Europe, I had all but two small offices rented. When Sam's ship docked, I was at the pier waiting with the news. After the inevitable customs delay, Sam, in his dark suit and gray hat, came through the gate, dutifully trailed by my aunt Eva, my cousins Evelyn and Stewart, and a string of porters. Immediately after the first happy round of hellos, I gave Sam the story on 32 Broadway. I stood there waiting for the smiles and congratulations I thought were my due, but Sam merely turned solemn and nodded. Then, as we headed toward the taxi line, he shook his head, saying, "William, about those two offices—how long before you can get them rented?"

I walked off that pier like a dog whose master had given him a kick in the ribs, and then and there decided there could be no real future for me with Sam Borchard. The next day I walked into the office and announced my decision to quit. Sam was surprised. He said, "Why should you quit? I just raised your salary from twenty-five to forty dollars a week." That did it—the commissions to an outside broker on the leases I had made would have come close to $25,000. I told Sam what he could do with his forty dollars a week and left.

I decided to go to work for Leonard Gans, a personable young real-estate broker about town. Gans was about twelve years older than I and had already made an excellent reputation for himself. He had recently gained control of large sections of property in Manhattan's East Forties for the great real-estate developer Fred French. On this land French was building fashionable Tudor City, just across from where the UN now stands. Gans had taken over the land so discreetly that neighbors had not become alarmed and prices had not got out of hand. I had met Gans in the course of business, was intrigued by what he was doing, and went to him with a proposition. He had no property-management department. I still don't know why, but I talked Gans into creating a management department which I would head. I ran this business for a few months, but I became more and more restless. I was a late riser in those days, and I also went to bed very late, and it was a dark-of-winter's-morning call from a tenant complaining about plumbing that finally convinced me I was in the wrong field.

"I just wasn't cut out for this," I admitted to Gans, and gave up management to join him in general real-estate brokerage. For one year I lived on a drawing account of forty to fifty dollars a week against future earnings. I made not a single dollar. Through friends I had met and fallen in love with a young girl named Irma Levy, whose parents became very friendly with mine. Irma and I wanted to marry, but I had to earn some money first, and finally I found a good deal, the Pasadena Hotel at the southwest corner of Sixty-first Street and Broadway.

The hotel lease was held by a blowsy, tough-looking woman from California who must have weighed three hundred pounds. This elderly flapper was so heavily made up and so unkempt that she could have passed as a madam of a whorehouse. Certainly the hotel was little better. The smell of Lysol was heavy in the dingy rooms. The lady boarders gave visitors appraising looks, and furtive men were continually scurrying in and out the doors. Madam looked sixty. Her husband, a fine-drawn, nervous little fellow, who chain-smoked cigarettes, looked eighteen or twenty and never said much. It was always Madam who did the talking, and persuading that flower of the Golden West to agree to sell her lease for $75,000 took many visits over several weeks. When she finally did agree to a sale, she stipulated that she must be paid in cash. When I brought her a certified check for $75,000, she threw it back at me, saying, "I said cash, kid; that's not cash. I want my money in fives, tens, and twenties, and I want it delivered to *my* vault, in *my* bank, the Corn Exchange."

We cashed her check and sent two pistol-toting guards with two satchels of money to her place in an armored car. She and her husband sat down cross-legged on the floor, and the two of them counted the cash. Then they counted it again, and again, and a fourth time. When they were sure it was all there, we went to the bank. She put her money in the vault, and the deal was completed.

My commissions on sale of the fee and leasehold of that building came to eight thousand dollars. I could marry. I was twenty-three and had never before had so much money. It made me uncomfortable, and I thought we had better spend it quickly.

Irma and I were immediately married and sailed to Europe for our honeymoon on the *Paris*. On board we encountered a new world on the way to the old. We met a crowd of young boys and girls, some going over to school in England and France, others on the Grand Tour, and some "just along for the ride." This was 1928, and although America was immensely prosperous, this was long before the days when the average youngster traveled abroad. These were young society people and definitely out of our spending league. We put on as expensive a front as possible, however, and enjoyed every minute of the trip. There were bridge and poker games, dinner dances, and drinking bouts till the small hours of the morning. By the time of the Captain's Ball we were all one great, friendly group busy with plans to meet again on the Continent.

On arrival, Irma and I made straight for Paris and quickly learned that the "in" place was the Ritz bar; most of our shipmates were there. At that time the favorite pastime for most affluent Americans was playing the stock market. Americans in Paris would gather at the Ritz at three P.M. Paris time in order to place their "bets" just as the New York Stock Exchange opened at nine A.M. in New York. They followed the price quotations by means of the transatlantic cable. Our acquaintances all had money, plus a bad case of investor's fever, and they bought and sold stocks as if playing a casual game of roulette.

On our second afternoon in Paris, a couple of men came over to me and asked, "Do you want to do any trading?"

"Of course."

"What would you like to buy?"

Before I had left New York I had met Matthew C. Brush, president of American International, and that company was the first I thought of. Everyone was trading in thousand-share lots, so I said, "Buy me a thousand shares of American International." It was selling for about eighteen dollars.

A few drinks later they came around again saying, "Hey, Zeckendorf, that stock . . ."

"What happened to it?" I thought I had been wiped out.

"We need cash to meet the margin requirement for your stock. By the way, it's gone up four dollars."

"Sell it," I said after precisely one second's thought.

This was a "wash" sale, giving me profit on no actual cash investment. It is something not now permitted by the Stock Exchange, but at that time it was fairly common. Now I had a four-thousand-dollar profit, and with those winnings we left town. We traveled in high style in a chauffeur-driven car through France, across Switzerland, and down to Italy, sampling wines, museums, cathedrals, and vistas. Six happy weeks later, in Naples, we boarded the steamship *Roma* for home, and back in New York I concentrated on making a career.

New York real estate, like every other business in the country, was booming in the twenties. I was a young real-estate broker still learning my way around, but I had fine mentors such as Sam Brenner, a real-estate operator of unusual ability who was strictly a speculator. He never built anything and didn't want to, but he was a great man at buying and selling. He bought in the morning and sold in the afternoon. The greatest of all such traders, however, was Fred Brown, who treated real estate as other dealers treat commodities such as wheat. He knew how to handle the market, he was trusted by other brokers, and he took small profits on a large volume (ten or fifteen properties in a day). But it was such developers as Fred French and Henry Mandell who were New York's builders of vision. Mandell, for example, built office buildings at 1 and 2 Park Avenue and created London Terrace, the excellent block-long apartment complex on Twenty-third Street on New York's West Side at Ninth Avenue. Mandell improved any property he touched, and it was to Mandell that I made my next big sale, by contacting Otto Kahn.

Mr. Kahn, the railroad and financing magnate, patron of the arts and man-about-the-world, was an unusual and attractive personality. He was an elderly but imposing man. A lover of fine opera (and of lovely opera singers), Kahn had bought a great deal of property on Fifty-sixth and Fifty-seventh streets between Eighth and Ninth Avenues. He had offered the site, at cost, as a new home for the Metropolitan Opera Company, but his offer was rejected, and that fine property lay idle.

Though I was an insignificant New York broker to Kahn, I managed to arrange a meeting with him through one of my wife's cousins who worked for the investment house of Kuhn, Loeb. The old gentleman graciously granted me an audience in his paneled downtown offices, and I asked if he would permit me to sell his Fifty-seventh Street plot. He agreed, and I contacted Henry Mandell, who bought the site and built the Parc Vendome Apartments, which are a successful property to this day. I made some thirty-thousand dollars on that deal, but it was the last big money I would see for some time. It was now 1930. The Depression had arrived, and it was knocking us all galley-west.

The aftereffects of the 1929 crash were nationwide and cumulative, as industry after industry buckled and then folded. Real estate, even more of a credit operation than the stock market, was hit three times as hard in time, but it went its merry way for a good twelve to sixteen months before it began the great plunge. The delay was due partly to the fact that major real-estate borrowings are arranged months and even years before time. The real-estate business can thus ride out most recessions but tumbles farther and longer than most other businesses in a real depression. The Great Depression, for instance, was at its lowest ebb in 1937–38, but the low in real estate did not come until the early 1940's. Through the early 1930's, however, things were terrible enough.

Everywhere, jobless men, unable to maintain payments on their homes, saw those homes foreclosed. As the Depression took hold, more and more tenants moved out of apartments to cheaper quarters or moved in with relatives. Meanwhile, businesses either decreased their office space or, as they went broke, moved out. You could walk the empty corridors of some Manhattan office buildings to find floor after floor with only one or two tenants in occupancy, and often no tenants at all. As a result, building owners were unable to meet their mortgage payments. Thousands more automatic foreclosures followed.

Curiously, the laws of the land tended to abet and foster the spreading chaos. The inheritance laws and inheritance taxes were determined by what a building had cost to build rather than what it could be sold for. With prices dropping quickly, many elderly people were panicked into selling at distress prices. In order to save their property from being entirely wiped out by taxes based on their boom-time values, these owners rushed to unload their holdings as quickly as possible in a dropping market—thus helping depress prices even further.

It turned out that it could actually be a serious liability to own a free and clear asset. Generally, major pieces of property tend to be held and sold (or borrowed upon) in two forms. First, there is ownership of the ground or land, which is called the fee (a term which goes back to medieval days and the concept of fiefs). This fee might receive its income from the buildings upon it, an arrangement usually covered by a lease, giving the leaseholder the right to use that land, to put buildings on it, and to rent out all or part of the buildings through various subleases. One can own either the fee (the land) or the lease (the right to use the land or buildings on the land), or one can own both the fee and the lease to a property. If a ground, or fee, holder has permitted a building to be put up on his land under a long-term lease, he can and normally would dispossess a tenant who could no longer meet his payments. But during the Depression (and under the tax laws of the day), if the ground owner repossessed his building, he would have to pay income tax *at the ordinary rate* on the pre-Depression value of the building. Since taxes were based on what the building cost rather than on what it could be sold for in a depressed market, the taxes resulting from dispossessing tenants sometimes were five times the actual value of the building. This strange situation provided those who could ride out the storm with some special opportunities. The General Realty and Utilities Corp., a newly formed investment group underwritten by Lehman Bros., held the lease and picked up the fee of 444 Madison Avenue from the Gallatin estate for a song. They simply suggested turning back the building to the estate. This was, in a sense, a legalized form of blackmail; if the estate did take over the building, the government would send it a tax bill for the assessed value of the building. This bill would be many times the value of the land and could ruin the estate. There was a good bit of this cornering and squeezing going on. The Ritz Carlton Hotel, which cost at least twenty-five million dollars, sold for $725,000 with $100,000 worth of liquor in it. The Murray Hill Hotel went for something on the order of $683,000. The Pierre Hotel, whose fee was owned by the Gerry estate, was another prime example. The Gerrys owned the ground at Sixty-first Street and Fifth Avenue, which they leased for $450,000 a year net to the hotel owners. Considering this $450,000 income at a five-percent return, that ground was worth nine million dollars. The hotel building had cost in the range of twenty-five million to build. But the whole package, ground and building, was sold to Mr. Getty, the oilman, for 2.5 million dollars and in turn sold by him ten years later for almost ten times that amount.

The tax laws have since been changed. Buildings are now taxed at their market value, but this is no comfort to those who were wiped out during the Depression. Even those who, by quick action and adroit maneuvering, managed to preserve their fortunes on the business front could, if they owned a co-op apartment in New York, be completely overwhelmed on this flank. Co-op owners were mutually responsible for the property they jointly owned. If enough members of a co-op went broke, the load this imposed on the remaining solvent members could be enough to pull these people under as well. The regulations governing co-ops were eventually changed to permit limited liability to members, but for many years the antiquated laws and the lingering effects of the Depression made real estate a ripe field for those with the money and the stomach to take unfair advantage of the situation.

For all of their tragedy, however, these were also times of change and excitement, and there were moments of ironic humor. For instance, we had an elderly maid, Anna, who was a little hard of hearing. Anna had lost her savings when the Bank of Europe, a small East Side bank that was patronized mostly by people of Czechoslovakian background, had closed without notice. From then on Anna hoarded her small salary under her mattress. I called her in one day and said, "You mustn't do that anymore, Anna; it's not good for the country." I explained to her that the President had spoken out many times against hoarding. "Put your money in the Bowery Savings Bank," I said.

"Oh, no, no more banks for me."

"You put it in the Bowery Savings Bank, Anna, and I'll guarantee you against its loss." The irony of my guaranteeing the Bowery Savings Bank when I could hardly pay Anna's salary was delicious, but it shows the psychology of credit: she accepted my guarantee before she would accept the Bowery's, and did as I told her.

It happened that I had an interest in a second mortgage that was subordinate to a first mortgage the Bowery Savings Bank was in the process of foreclosing. Under the law, all parties of interest must be given notice in such a foreclosure. One night I overheard a conversation in the vestibule between Anna and a caller who said he wanted to see me.

Anna asked, "What do you want to see Mr. Zeckendorf about?"

"I am from the firm of Cadwalader, Wickersham and Taft. We represent the Bowery Savings Bank."

Hard of hearing though she was, Anna heard the words Bowery Savings Bank, and her ears were up as he continued, "They are foreclosing . . ."

She did not know what he meant, but she heard the dread word "closing." "Yes, yes."

"I came here to serve Mr. Zeckendorf."

Anna heard him say he came to *save* Mr. Zeckendorf.

I stepped into the vestibule and found a weeping Anna, her arms around the young lawyer, saying, "Oh, please, save me too!"

Sadly enough, it was often the sound, debt-abhorring investor who was most cruelly hit by the Depression. Generally there are three categories of real-estate investors—those who borrow nothing, those who borrow the maximum, and those who borrow conservatively. The nonborrowers, such as the Astors, who owned all their properties free and clear, could ride through almost any storm. Predictably, those speculators who borrowed the absolute maximum on their projects were among the very first to get wiped out. And yet, it was the conservative investors who ultimately suffered the most.

Speculative builders, who were mortgaged to the hilt and beyond it, were the first to cave in—and the first to have court-appointed receivers take over the mortgage or bond holders. When a receiver takes over a property for the mortgage holders, he is not faced with the costs that faced the previous owners; he is accountable only for real-estate taxes and payroll. This means his total costs are sharply cut and he can greatly reduce rents for the properties he runs in order to make them attractive to tenants. Furthermore, being in a sense a political appointee, he may (especially in a time of chaos) want to make a career of his appointment. If this was the case, the worst thing that could befall such a receiver would be to make such excellent profits that his property soon recovered and he was no longer needed. The best thing that could happen to him would be to receive just enough income to pay the minimum charges needed to keep his particular ship afloat, while maintaining his own and his lawyer's fees. When the new management cuts rents, it is in unfair competition with the building next door, which has to carry the weight of a conventional mortgage and rents. As a result, those buildings in receivership soon send their conservatively mortgaged neighbors to the cleaners as well, and that is exactly what occurred in the 1930's.

My admirable friend Henry Mandell lost the Parc Vendome and other fine properties through early foreclosure. The Uris brothers, though they came back to figure among New York's most active builders, were wiped out; they went through bankruptcy personally and corporately. The Tishmans, another family of builders whose structures are now all over New York, were practically washed out. Dave Tishman, by a tremendous personal effort, and by hanging on long enough—until the insurance companies finally realized there was no real profit in wiping people out—was able to save himself.

By the late 1930's, property-burdened banks and insurance companies were offering foreclosed holdings at truly phenomenal bargain prices. At the lowest ebb of the Depression, for instance, the Mutual Life Insurance Company of New York sold off forty-two East Side midtown dwellings for twelve thousand dollars apiece—and lent the buyers the money for the purchases. Today these buildings are worth $230,000 to $300,000. Mutual Life of New York, by ordinary accounting methods, was at that time probably insolvent. Their real-estate investments, mainly in New York City, had next to no market value and insufficient income to support the mortgages Mutual had put on them. To keep things from completely falling apart, Shields, the company vice-president in charge of mortgages, would readily make mortgage loans that virtually ignored the matter of adequate payments needed to pay back the principal. He would renew existing mortgages indefinitely on the theory that the rise in value of the land would eventually be great enough to recover any principal. In the meantime, the company would at least be earning interest on its loans. Shields was right, in the long run, but in the long run we are all dead, and he died before his point could be proved. The company's new administration altered course drastically. In the early 1940's Lou Douglas, whose grandfather was mining engineer for my grandfather's Copper Queen Mine, came in as president of Mutual Life. He did an excellent job, but with a policy radically different from Shields'. Heretofore, Mutual Life had invested largely in New York City real estate. Under Douglas an embargo was put on any New York purchases. Instead, to raise cash the company sold off a great many assets, including its railroad bonds, at bottom market prices and began seeking investments around the country. As a result of this investment policy, Mutual is now a very strong company, and the stop order on New York investment has long since been lifted, but for a time they were the softest insurance company in town.

As a New York City real-estate broker, I made my living on two fronts. On the one side I was a negotiator for property owners trying to salvage their estates by renegotiating mortgages with banks and insurance companies. Meanwhile, I also kept busy scouting out the increasingly scarce buyers for properties that the banks and insurance companies were doing their best to unload. Early in the Depression Irma and I had moved from our first apartment at Ninety-fourth Street and Lexington Avenue to occupy an entire floor at 44 Park Avenue. Under normal circumstances we could never have afforded such a place, but I was occupying it in return for help I had given to a friend. Though I didn't always earn it, I managed to spend close to twenty thousand dollars a year during the Depression. By the standards of the 1930's we were affluent—even if often broke.

My personal life, while at least as hectic, was not nearly so successful as my business career. Irma and I had had two children, William, Jr., and Susan, but over the years it was becoming increasingly obvious to both Irma and me that we were mismatched. From my earliest days I have loved football games, late-night bridge and poker sessions, and marathon parties. I thought of little else but working hard and then having a good time. Irma, on the other hand, was a woman of deep cultural interests and intellectual yearnings. She was disdainful of many of my cronies and their activities. She had many friends of her own, and in deference to our marriage, I abandoned much of my old life, entered into hers, and attended and enjoyed the opera, the theater, and dance performances. This was a life hitherto unfamiliar to me and something for which I am still grateful, but it seemed to me that Irma was too much in awe of or, perhaps, too enthralled by some of her more pretentious friends. These people by their near-worship of "culture" robbed culture and themselves of real meaning or relevance. Irma and I were both willful, and the differences between us in outlook and needs eventually led to a complete breach. We drifted apart. I began to find other women increasingly interesting, and a divorce seemed the only reasonable conclusion. This took place in 1934. Immediately after the divorce she married the noted music critic Irving Kolodin. We have remained friends, and Irma's delightfully chipper mother is still very much a favorite of mine.

As a combination bachelor and family man, I took a small apartment in the Hotel Lombardy on East Fifty-sixth Street. My parents had an apartment there as well, and until the time of my father's death in 1938, I regularly breakfasted with them. My father and I went to his whist club at least once a week, and I made it a point to try to see my children at least once a day. The children stayed with me during the summers, and one year, thanks to Depression prices, I picked up a thirty-foot, gaff-rigged sloop for one thousand dollars. It was a beamy, comfortable boat, with hospitable below-deck space, which we moored at a club on Long Island Sound. One summer we lived in the clubhouse, the next we rented a nearby apartment. I kept the children in good private schools, but my road to affluence was erratic. I was often in debt, sometimes little more than two jumps ahead of the sheriff, and forever scrambling for some way to turn an extra dollar.

Whenever I did get a little money ahead, I tried to put it to work. One such project, with my friend Sam Silver, was the conversion of the old Chatham-Phoenix Bank on Fifty-seventh Street near Third

Avenue into the Sutton Theatre. We had put all the money we had into that theater, but at the first faltering, a Manufacturers Trust bureaucrat named Harry Frey closed us down and turned the refurbished property over to someone else.

Another project, one that did work, was the conversion of three coldwater tenements on Eighty-fourth Street between Lexington and Third avenues into a single apartment house, which, though long since sold off by us, is still making money for its owners.

As a young, sometimes affluent divorcé, I led an active social life. I was especially fond of fine restaurants, and a favorite dining spot was the fabulous Ritz Carlton Hotel. If it still stood today, that hotel would be declared a national landmark, but Harvard sold it to the Uris brothers, who replaced it with one of their wedding-cake office structures. Outside New York there were a number of excellent restaurants, such as the Round Hill and the Beaux Sejours on Long Island, which served the finest duck in America. However, the finest place was the Bird and Bottle in Garrison, New York. This was an eighteenth-century mansion owned by a wealthy drug manufacturer who kept a nearby cattle and dairy farm. The mansion was beautifully preserved, for it still had its original broad-beam and hand-pegged floors, and was furnished with period furniture. There were numerous open fireplaces and liveried serving men at table. There, at a private dinner by a fireplace, one could get delicately seasoned black-bean soup or shrimp bisque, black-angus steaks, the like of which I have not seen to this day, plus fruit pies in season with thick natural cream one could cut with a knife. Everything was served in pewterware. Walnuts and port followed the dinner, and the port was served in a decanter that played a song as it poured. As the Depression wore on the Bird and Bottle degenerated into a tearoom, but at its peak it was the most wonderful restaurant around. The only place that could compare with it was the old Stage Coach Inn in Locust Valley, Long Island, which flourished during the late twenties and early thirties and served such a massive stirrup-cup cocktail that a man could drink only two, or possibly three, and still walk around.

During the racing season groups of us would drive to Saratoga for weekends. There, after the day's races, discreetly operated gambling casinos took care of your evening time and money. The old

United States Hotel, with its grand porch and fine rooms, luxuriously accommodated us, some with wives and others with dear friends. A bachelor once more, I frequented these places as often as I could, and often when I shouldn't.

One pastime I had virtually given up by the late 1930's, however, was bridge. Through Dr. Maurice Louis, a friend of my father's, I had become a familiar at the New York Bridge Club. I was good enough to occasionally find myself playing with such bridge notables as Mike Gottlieb, Lee Langdon, and Oswald Jacoby. The stakes at these games ran a dollar a point, which I could not afford, but a number of club members used to syndicate my bridge game (the way some investment bankers later syndicated my real-estate projects). I enjoyed the company and the minor glamour of these tournaments, but when I found myself waking up at night and replaying a hand, I decided I would either have to take up bridge full time or drop it. The same was true of gambling, which similarly fascinated me. Henceforth, I reserved my main energies for real-estate transactions, where I substituted speculation for gambling.

Meanwhile, the many dozens of business projects, schemes, and coups with which I struggled, although they ate up time and energy, did not seem to be getting me anywhere. During the Depression, I remember once looking at the $200,000 worth of life insurance I carried, wondering if I might not be worth more to my family dead than alive. But such thoughts were rare and brief.

By 1938 I felt that all I was doing in the brokerage business was scrambling up straight walls. When the reputable if not very profitable firm of Webb & Knapp offered me a partnership, I accepted.

· 3 · From Journeyman to Master

WHEN I WAS still a boy in knee pants, the City of New York passed a major new pollution-control measure. Steam engines were banned from the city; electric engines must be used in their place. The New York Central was ordered to cover up the railroad tracks (from Ninety-sixth Street to Forty-fifth Street) that led into Grand Central Station. The ensuing resurfacing and cosmetic job created Park Avenue and a land boom. As soon as Park Avenue was created, smart developers began lining up to acquire leases in order to build luxury apartments over what had once been railroad yards and right-of-way land. The owners and managers of the Central, though they had at first fought this redevelopment vigorously, now found themselves the pleased owners of a fabulous realty empire. The railroad did little development as such, but leased its land to builders and developers.

In 1922, when I was entering college, four gentlemen organized a new company to, in part, help the New York Central handle some of its leases. One of these men was W. Seward Webb, a descendant, on his mother's side, of Commodore Vanderbilt. Another was Robert C. Knapp, a vice-president of Douglas L. Elliman & Co., a well-known realty company. The other two partners were John and Eliot Cross of the architectural firm of Cross & Cross. The new company was called 385 Madison Avenue Inc., after the location of its offices. The building stood on railroad land, and the Crosses had designed it. The new company took over the management of New York Central's ground leases in such locations as the Barclay Hotel, the Park Lane, the Yale Club, and other choice sites.

In 1933 the company changed its name to Webb & Knapp. Knapp died, however, and in 1936 both John Cross and Seward Webb decided to retire. Eliot Cross, no longer much involved in architecture, was left in charge of Webb & Knapp, and that year he took in two new partners, a young lawyer named John Gould, and James Landauer of Douglas L. Elliman & Co.

Eliot Cross was an urbane gentleman, a graduate of Groton and Harvard. With his brother John, he had designed many of Long Island's finest houses. They also designed New York Hospital and the Tiffany Building on Fifth Avenue. The Crosses designed excellent buildings but were traditional architects. The only modern structure they ever put up was the General Electric Building at Fifty-first Street and Lexington Avenue. Legend has it that while they were visiting in Europe a younger associate carried the project so far forward along modern lines that it was impossible for the Crosses to change it back.

In any event, in 1936 Eliot Cross was trying to revitalize Webb & Knapp by bringing in new blood. In 1937 I had been the broker in the sale of an office building at 369 Lexington Avenue to Webb & Knapp. The next year, when several major tenants moved out, the building began to lose money. Webb & Knapp asked me to bring in some new tenants. I was able to repopulate the empty floors rather quickly. John Gould, who was company president, invited me to join the firm, and I accepted.

My association with Webb & Knapp brought me a perceptible increase in general esteem among my fellows, a degree of economic stability (I would be sure of a paycheck), but I also took a cut in salary. Even as a partner I drew only nine thousand dollars a year. The solution to this situation was to get the firm making more money, but except for a few side ventures, I did very little at first. From 1938 to 1940 Webb & Knapp devoted its primary energies to consulting and to the management of buildings in which we or our clients held an interest. It was not till 1940, when Henry Sears, a well-to-do young cousin of Cross's, joined the company and contributed $400,000 in working capital, that we began actively to acquire new properties on our own account.

Of the five partners now in the company, one was an architect, one a lawyer, and one a capitalist; Landauer and I were the only real-estate men, but Landauer was essentially a manager-consultant. What I brought with me to the company were thirteen journeyman years of experience in the buying, selling, financing, and renting of New York real estate. I was familiar with almost every block of property in town, knew or was known to most important brokers and a great many bankers, as well as numbers of insurance men. I also brought ebullience and personal drive. If some of my partners were rich, I was ambitious. Thus, through a combination of background and personality I became the chief enthusiast, contact, and idea man for the organization. Inevitably, I began to draw the firm in new directions and into new developments, with some results which proved as much of a surprise to me as to my partners. For example, there was the matter of Webb & Knapp and its first fling at high life, via the acquisition of a nightclub.

One of the first properties we bought after Harry Sears joined us was a two-story building on the corner of Fifty-fourth and Madison. The building, which cost $400,000, subject to a $250,000 mortgage, contained a series of stores on the avenue side and the Monte Carlo nightclub on the Fifty-fourth Street side. The club was operated by Gene Cavallero of the Colony Restaurant and Felix Ferry, who was known as Fefe. Fefe, a Romanian, had made a name for himself as a showman in Europe. His most famous enterprise was importing long-legged, good-looking American showgirls to Monte Carlo for his "Monte Carlo Follies." He had a fine thing going until he made the tactical error of taking the show to London. There, to the delighted horror of the tabloids, a sizable number of his long-stemmed American beauties ran off to marry smitten young English noblemen. Those of the girls who stayed married eventually became highly respected ladies of the realm, but the abandoned Fefe, his chorus line sadly depleted, decided to recoup his fortunes via a new Club Monte Carlo in New York. Fefe's new club was the plushest combination of snobbery and effrontery New Yorkers had ever seen. Even in black tie a man felt out of place; white tie and tails was the style. Of course, the nightclub was a great success.

The Monte Carlo attracted many distinguished society people plus a crowd of hangers-on, but a number of these fashionable people, as I later learned, were buying on the cuff. To an outsider the place seemed a gold mine. The inner entrance was always crowded with standees waiting to be seated. The cash registers tinkled comfortingly, and since I found it difficult to get past the inner entrance, I was impressed. This just had to be the most successful and profitable nightclub in America.

Lulled by the obvious security of the income from a lease held by such a successful nightclub, we bought the building that housed it. And, as one of the landlords, I could now hope for a decent table. We had owned the property only a few weeks, however, when Gene and Fefe came to pay me their respects.

"Boys, what can we do for you?" I asked.

"We're broke," they announced.

"You are what?"

"We're broke. We owe money to contractors, to trade creditors, we . . . just ran out of working capital." But, they said, the nightclub was in process of turning the corner. Fifty thousand dollars was all they needed to get out of their bind.

Naturally, I was shocked; our double-hulled, unsinkable investment was beginning to look like a miniature *Titanic* foundering in ice cubes. Here was a nightclub so popular you couldn't get into the place, yet its operators could not pay their rent. Webb & Knapp didn't want to go into the nightclub business, so we agreed to refloat the boys with $50,000. After all, there were all those customers at the door. A few months went by, and Gene and Fefe were back at my office. They needed another $50,000. Again we reluctantly handed out the cash. That must have seemed to them like the beginning of a beautiful friendship, because six months later I looked up, and there they were again. By now I was getting the best of service at this haughtiest of places, but I was about to prove there is no gratitude in this world.

As our tenants walked in, I said, "Before you talk, boys, I want to ask you a question. Are you here for another fifty thousand?"

"How did you guess?"

"Well, I just invoked divine guidance and got the message. But I have news. At the prices you are charging us, we can't afford to eat there anymore. That means you are out and Webb & Knapp is in the nightclub business."

The situation was grim, but we immediately changed the club's policies, dropped the white-tie routine, cut off the socialite spongers, and encouraged the cash-paying middle class. I put in as manager a Runyonesque character I knew named Dick Flanagan. Later I hired Sam Salvin, a famous restaurateur, to handle food and beverages.

Within six months the club was making money. At its peak, it did a greater volume than all the rooms and restaurants of the St. Regis Hotel put together, and had netted a half-million dollars before we sold it in 1948.

Part ownership of a nightclub turned out to be great fun. I had my own corner table, with phone, plus the solicitous attention of the waiters and chef. For five years I dined at the club several evenings a week entertaining friends, business acquaintances, and occasional passersby. I did as much business there as from my Madison Avenue office. There was a certain comfort in knowing that at least part of the money we spent went back to Webb & Knapp, but what gave the entire period its greatest flavor was that my second wife, Marion, was my constant companion and hostess at these sessions.

My first meeting with Marion could have come from a romantic movie writer's opening scene for a film about the Big City. I was walking through the Upper East Side one spring evening and had stopped for the light when I heard a commotion behind me. I turned and saw a pretty woman with a poodle on a leash. Her dog was being mauled by a very angry bulldog who was not on a leash. I grabbed the bulldog and threw him to one side, at which point the owner ran up and took the animal in tow. This kind of attack was unusual, as the poodle was a female and the bulldog a male, so I wrote down the bulldog's license tag and rabies numbers. The poodle's left ear had been slashed, and we took her into a nearby drugstore for a touch of mercurochrome and a Band-Aid. Throughout all this I noticed that the poodle's owner was extremely attractive, and though obviously upset, very gracious. While she was thanking me for the second or third time, I introduced myself and suggested that we could use some first aid ourselves. Would she join me for a cocktail?

As Marion later said, "After all he had done, it seemed a little silly to say, 'How dare you!' "

I found her very intelligent and utterly charming. More adventurous than her sisters and friends in Waycross, Georgia, she had come to New York some years previously. By the time we met she was a devoted New Yorker. We were married in Palm Beach, Florida, in December, 1940. After our honeymoon we drove up to Georgia to visit Marion's family, then headed home. On the return trip, driving through Pennsylvania at night, we were caught in a small-town speed trap. A local justice of the peace cheerfully took the last twenty-five dollars I had in my pockets and a few hours later, with the gas gauge nearing empty, we approached the George Washington Bridge. The toll ate up the last of my silver, and we wheeled into town flat broke, very happy, and with nowhere to go but up.

Later that year Frank Russell, of Brown, Wheelock, Harris, Stevens, Inc., old and reputable New York real-estate brokers, came to my office to find out if Webb & Knapp were interested in buying the fashionable building at 1 East Sixty-second Street.

I told him we were basically brokers and managers of properties, rather than dealers, and that we didn't have enough capital for that sort of transaction.

But word must have been out that we did have a little venture capital, because Russell kept feeding out more information. "Old George Blumenthal, the investment banker who married the widow of Henry Clews, moved her out of the Clews mansion up to his property at Seventieth Street and Park Avenue. It's really more of a merger than a marriage, they've both got so much money. . . .

"Anyway," he continued, "the old Clews home has been converted to an apartment building by an architect who bought it from them, but you know how architects are; he went overboard on his construction costs and was caught short. Blumenthal has foreclosed a $148,000 mortgage on the property. That $148,000 is lots less than the cost of the alterations, but that's all Blumenthal wants. Bill, it's a good deal."

I answered that we might pay $148,000 if Blumenthal would take a small amount of cash, such as five or ten thousand dollars, and extend us a mortgage for the remainder. That kind of money, we could raise. A day or two later, on a Friday, Russell called. He said, "Mr. Blumenthal wants to meet you. Be at our office at three o'clock."

I showed up as asked. After a bit of chit-chat, Blumenthal said, "Well, young man, I understand you want to buy this building for $148,000 with a mortgage. . . . But we in the investment business aren't accustomed to buying and selling that way; we deal in cash."

It seemed incongruous for an investment banker to shy away

from a simple mortgage. I said, "We brokers are poor, and you bankers are supposed to be rich. Why don't you lend us the money? We'll work it out for you." He held off, however, and we talked and finally brought down the sales price to $125,000 plus another $5,000 in cash from us, but he was still unhappy. Finally he said, "Give me a cash offer."

"All right sir, I offer you $72,000—all cash."

"That's ridiculous."

"Well, you wanted a cash offer. There it is. Why don't you take the weekend to think about it?"

On Monday morning Frank Russell called. "Bill, now you've got puppies." Blumenthal had accepted our cash offer.

Stalling for time, I said we would need to search the title.

Russell gave us thirty days, which meant that we had thirty days in which to raise $72,000. I took a deep breath, signed the contract, put up five thousand of our own cash, and started looking. I had heard that the Troy Savings Bank was in the market for New York City mortgages. When I showed them the certified $148,000 balance sheet of the company that owned the building, the Troy people said they were sorry, but the very most they would lend was $105,000 at four-percent interest. Even my simple arithmetic told me that the $105,000 loan was $33,000 more than I needed, so I agreed to the offer. The Troy bank, however, would give us a mortgage only after we had acquired the property. I still needed cash to pay off Blumenthal. So next I went to see the New York Trust Company and my friend Charlie Stewart, later president but then a vice-president in charge of the branch at Fortieth Street and Madison. He lent us the $105,000 so we could give Mr. Blumenthal the $72,000 in cash. Stewart was per-fectly safe in doing so, because he had a commitment to get his cash back in the $105,000 mortgage from the Troy Savings Bank.

That gave us the title to the property and a sweet little profit of $33,000, but then I went through the rent rolls and found that the penthouse duplex apartment was occupied by Mrs. Vivian Clews Spencer, a niece of the deceased Mr. Henry Clews. I called on Mrs. Spencer and suggested that she buy the house.

"Mrs. Spencer, your rent is five hundred dollars a month. Even at the top interest rate of four percent, six thousand per year of rent represents the equivalent of $150,000 of capital tied up just to pay this rent. But, madame, if you buy this building, you'll get enough income from rental of the other apartments to carry the building—and your own rent will be free! This will free $150,000 of your own capital, and that is like finding money on the street." She was intrigued. After further talks with her lawyer, we had a deal—on one condition: she wanted to unload her two houses, one in Tuxedo Park and the other in Southampton, at fifteen thousand dollars each. We agreed to this second-hand-house rider. She turned over to us $20,000 in cash plus the two houses, and took over the $105,000 Troy Savings Bank mortgage. This gave us another $20,000 of cash in hand, for a total of $53,000. We eventually sold her two houses at close to $15,000 each and wound up (on a $5,000 investment) with a profit of $83,000.

On this one operation, which took a little over a month to arrange, we had made twenty times the profit that would have come to us as mere agents. But the Blumenthal-Clews transaction not only highlighted the advantages of being solely in charge of an operation, it brought into focus a number of other factors. Specifically, I became aware of the existence of a Depression market of sellers, such as Blumenthal, who would sell property at tremendous discounts if they could get cash. At the same time, partly because Depression-caused retrenchments had left various institutions with idle cash, one could get some quite extraordinary low-cost, long-term loans and mortgages from banks and insurance companies—if these lenders saw a "safe" investment. Moreover, if you could provide them with a "market rationale," the value these mortgagers put on a property could be quite high. By providing a *cash market* for Blumenthal, by doing this through the device of providing a "safe, high value" *mortgage market* for the Troy Bank, and *then* by providing Mrs. Clews Spencer with a self-liquidating income property, I had provided a needed service to three quite separate principals, to everyone's immediate advantage and at a handsome profit to us.

This made me keenly aware that it paid to look at the real-estate business not as an end in itself but as a device for bridging gaps between the needs of disparate groups. The greater the number of separate groups (or their needs) that one could interconnect (or satisfy), the greater the profit to the innovator-entrepreneur.

These insights on "service" and the uses of "complexity" were to become elements in the majority of my most successful real-estate ventures. There was a gap, however, between my newly developed insights and the opportunity to apply them on any scale. Webb & Knapp didn't have the capital or credit to make a proper, profitable impact in the field of real estate. And that is the way things remained —all of us working hard, doing well, but not accomplishing anything truly spectacular.

Drawing on our own modest capital, with additional loans from some of the partners and their families, we began to do a bit of buying and selling. We picked up income properties in the Middle West, Pennsylvania, and, of course, New York. These purchases ranged from as low as $5,000 to as high as $500,000 in price. Where Webb & Knapp didn't have the financial weight to swing a deal alone, we syndicated our projects with other investors. By the end of fiscal 1942, we owed $740,000 on various loans, but controlled assets of some two million dollars. Webb & Knapp was on the move. My salary was back to twenty thousand dollars a year, but my personal financial situation was unchanged. The check for my son's first term at Lawrenceville was returned with the notation "insufficient funds," and my tailor was waiting payment for my last two suits. By now he knew that I would always pay, but he also knew that he might have to wait.

• 4 • Astor Risks

By EARLY 1942, Webb & Knapp was making money from investments, but as major investors we were barely off the ground. What we desperately needed was some outside impetus, and we received that boost, courtesy of Vincent Astor.

In 1784, Vincent Astor's great-grandfather, John Jacob Astor, a dry and rather solemn man, arrived in the United States from Germany. He made his first fortune in the fur business, then a second in the China trade, and yet a third by investing his previous gains in New York real estate. When he died in 1848, he was the richest man in America. The family split into two main branches. Some of John Jacob's heirs moved to England, where they became very British and, in the case of Lady Astor, notoriously and flippantly anti-American. The British Astor-family fortune, however, which remained largely American-based, escaped the onerous, special British taxes during the two world wars, and thus provided the British Astors with the best of both worlds. Meanwhile, the American branch of Astors also flourished, and this fortune was also New York-based. As New York continued to change and grow, the diversified Astor holdings changed character accordingly. By 1942, Vincent Astor, of the American Astors, held as his share of the estate a $50-million spectrum of New York real estate, including the St. Regis Hotel at Fifth Avenue and Fifty-fifth Street, a number of midtown apartments and brownstones, various downtown lofts and office buildings, as well as Bowery tenements, meat markets, and a few rundown houses on the West Side. Approximately one-third of those properties was unprofitable, and the net revenues of the whole were roughly one-half million dollars per year.

In 1942 Vincent Astor, a naval-reserve officer, was called to active duty. He decided to put the management of his properties in the hands of an outside, disinterested group. To this end, he interviewed a number of management companies. However, it turned out that

Astor's attorney, Roland Redmond, was a close friend of Eliot Cross. Astor was socially acquainted with both Crosses (they went to school together) and Henry Sears. Therefore, when Webb & Knapp were invited to make a proposal on handling the properties, we had an edge on the competition, but the edge was very slight.

At this point, three of my partners, Gould, Landauer, and Sears, had been called into the armed services, and the fourth, Cross, was playing a relatively inactive role in the business. I had agreed to stay on and run the show until I was drafted, and therefore I was the only active partner left in Webb & Knapp. As it turned out, I was never drafted, being too old at each successive draft call.

The first I knew of a possible Astor arrangement was when I got a rather enigmatic phone call from Roland Redmond. His firm had been requested, he said, to find a management company to handle Astor's affairs while the commander was in the service. Would we care to enter the competition for this role?

I was so taken aback that I had to stall for time, and I simply answered, "I'll call you back."

The only reason for this delaying tactic was that I thought somebody might be pulling my leg. After fifteen minutes or so, I telephoned Mr. Redmond at his law firm, Carter, Ledyard & Milburn. When he answered, I knew that the voice I had heard before was the same and that I was talking to headquarters. I let Redmond know we were indeed ready and willing to be of service and asked what we might do.

"Come down to my office and I'll give you a list of the properties. You can study them and give us your views."

When I arrived, Redmond showed me a long booklet with blue backing, each page identifying a property, its cost, its depreciated book value and profitability. In all, the properties came to fifty million dollars, debt free, but with consolidated profit-and-loss tables showing a slight deficit.

I studied those tables diligently and had soon prepared a written proposal. Cross, however, also arranged for the two of us and Redmond to meet informally with Astor in his 120 East End Avenue suite. The American version of the old-school-tie system had now come into play, but it would still be my job to cinch the deal.

At the time, the Vincent Astor estate was being handled by John Carrington Yates, a tall, slender man, and John Coulter, a diminutive, very pleasant fellow with a florid complexion. Their respective sizes made them look like a very odd couple: something like the ascender and dot of an exclamation point. They were charming gentlemen, but really little more than caretakers and rent collectors for Astor. Yates had been an actor and was an active member of the Lambs' Club. He was among Astor's favorite drinking companions.

Astor, an avid yachtsman and an intimate friend of Franklin Roosevelt, held the naval rank of commander. He fancied himself chief of U.S. antisubmarine operations off the Atlantic Coast. The Navy people with whom he worked had other ideas, but the millionaire socialite's post did give him and his naval friends a certain amount of convivial shore time in New York, and it was on such a visit that we met him. He was then in his early fifties, had a reputation as something of a ladies' man and also as an earnest drinker. I once saw him in later years put a lump of ice in a nearly full water glass and swig it down in almost one gulp. It wasn't till he mixed a second drink that I realized those were martinis he was swallowing by the tumblerful.

That afternoon, in the spring of 1942, he drank Scotch until, after an hour or so, he said, "Well, it's time for cocktails now," and started on dry martinis. As the hours went by, he became slightly less comprehensible, but he had a terrific capacity, and the business aspects of our meeting were over relatively early. His first question was what I thought of the idea of various firms submitting written proposals on how his estate should be managed. My response was that it was a fine way to conduct a letter-writing contest but no way to select a real-estate man.

"What are you talking about?" he growled.

"Each of these companies is going to submit the best letter they've ever composed, but a letter-writer is not necessarily a real-estate man. What you should do is ask these men to demonstrate their ingenuity and wisdom by showing you what they've already accomplished. Find out what they have been able to prove about the evaluation and the growth and development of values in real estate. You don't have to know how clean they're going to keep the doorstep and or how they're going to fire the superintendent if his shirt is dirty." Astor, seated in his chair, gave a grunt and paused. He nodded a bit over his drink and finally asked, "Well, what do you think of my properties?"

"For the most part, Commander, they stink; they are outmoded."

No one said a word. The creak of someone stirring in his chair crackled like gunfire in the silent room. I knew I was the only bona-fide real-estate man in the room. I had been doing some keen trading for Webb & Knapp on a modest scale (where it is most difficult to do). We were sitting there drinking Astor's liquor courtesy of the "old-boy" network. As Webb & Knapp's "new boy" I was pretty sure of myself, but obviously I had to approach Astor from a strictly professional standpoint rather than a social one. And I saw that as a distinct advantage, since this was a business talk and not a class reunion. Cross and the others had the social weight, but I was the only cutting edge that could make this weight count, and I sensed rather quickly that straight talk appealed to Astor and that he probably found it a welcome relief.

When given the chance, I told him which properties he should get rid of, how to get rid of them, and what he should acquire in their place. None of this took very long, but we stayed for a few extra rounds of drinks. When we left in the early evening we were in a mild glow composed of three parts alcohol and one part feeling we had won our case. We had.

On a June afternoon in 1942, we were engaged as exclusive consultants for the reorganization of Astor's holdings. The next morning I went to our apartment door to pick up *The New York Times*, and there on the front page was the story. This front-page coverage made us overnight the most important real-estate firm in America. I began to get congratulatory phone calls and offers of doing business from dozens of people I had never heard from before, and we immediately, and with a purpose, began moving and dealing in a dozen directions at once.

The business of selling off Astor's less desirable properties was even less difficult than I had expected and taught me anew that there are a great many nonrational though quite real factors in real-estate values. Some, for instance, have to do with whom or what a piece of land or property is associated. The inn where George Washington slept, the house where Washington Irving lived, the sword General

Sheridan waggled at his countrymen—all these properties take on a certain associational virtue and value. I soon learned there was an invisible but tangible aura about the Astor properties that made them attractive: if the great Astor estate had owned them, they must have extra virtues, because Old Astor had been so shrewd. But this was only one incidental part of the attraction of these properties.

At this time a number of refugees who had come to the United States from Hitler-controlled Europe were becoming modestly prominent in the dormant New York real-estate market. These new buyers were far less interested in the total price of a property than what the actual down payment would be. A low down payment gave them maximum leverage for the inflationary rise in values that they were anticipating. Taking a reverse lesson from the Clews-mansion deal, and the opposite tack from my cash-hungry friend Mr. Blumenthal, I sold for very low cash down payments but at steep prices. In this way I got a sales price of, say, a million dollars on a property that would have sold on the cash market for $400,000. Of the million dollars, I might take $50,000 or less as a down payment, in addition to a piece of paper in the form of a mortgage. Then I would turn to the mortgage companies to sell off my paper. They would ask, "What is the price of the property?" and I would say, "One million dollars," and when they asked what we wanted from them in cash, I would suggest a peak of, say, $666,000. I would immediately follow this with the announcement that Astor would accept a second mortgage for the remaining $284,000 of the million-dollar price. The fact that Astor would take a subordinate mortgage served as a psychological guarantee, making the mortgage buyers courageous enough to take our paper.

Having converted our paper mortgages into usable cash, we then went forth and bought blue-chip properties; we would mortgage them at a good rate (their good income and the Astor name again helped), and with this second wave of cash I would again go out and buy up more choice properties at cash discounts in order to repeat the process. We bought property in Texas, California, in Georgia, Long Island—across the whole of the continent. In this way we not only made some shifts in Astor's New York City holdings but also put twenty-five percent of the profits of the new Astor empire into growth areas about the country.

When we made our initial proposal regarding the management of the Astor estate, I had refused to state a flat fee. I explained that when we delivered he could pay us what we were worth: if we didn't deliver, he didn't have to pay anything. At the end of the first year we had added enormously to Astor's assets and tripled his earnings. Through his lawyers, Astor kept prodding us to present him with a bill, and finally I did so, for the amount of $350,000. At the same time, I commented that he did not have to pay us a thing if he thought the bill out of line. I held my breath. Astor's lawyers blanched when they saw the fee, for the commander was known to be tight with a dollar, but when they presented my bill Astor said, "Pay him, and send him a bunch of flowers from me."

We turned Astor's properties back to him in September of 1945, some 152 transactions after our first sale for the estate. The estate had increased by $15 million and Astor was now taking in $2.5 million in yearly profits.

My relationship with Astor gave me my first close look at and contact with a world which, because of its wealth and exclusiveness, fascinated and attracted me. However, this world did not always capture my respect. I found Vincent Astor quite amiable, sometimes humorous, but not very bright. He had inherited a native shrewdness from his forefathers. Nevertheless, if he had not also inherited his great fortune, he probably could not have done much on his own. Although he ruled his employees and dependents with a willfulness and sometimes a harshness that brooked no independence, our own relationship was always cordial, for I was not his subordinate but his consultant, and I was making him a lot of money.

Astor was very consciously social and outspokenly snobbish. He lived in a very narrow, self-satisfied, but not particularly brilliant or generous circle. He had, I remember, a particular dislike of his half-brother John Jacob Astor, a great hulking man whom Astor and his friends referred to as Jack Ass. As scion of a famous American family, Astor felt an occasional urge to flamboyance and noblesse oblige. He wanted to be a noted philanthropist but was too engaged with the social aspects of being an Astor to do very much about it. He had a series of very nice wives, three in all, but he left no heirs except his foundation. Astor's fortune is one more that will gradually filter back to the community. There was a certain low-key tragedy in all this. Like the last of a long line of kings, he was the last of a long line of Astors, cast in the shadow by some of his forebears, but was too much a prisoner and lover of his own background to break out into his own.

After Astor took back control of his properties, we tried a number of times to interest him in various propositions. He turned down the great majority of these suggestions and kept his own counsel. Soon we drifted apart, each having served the other well. We left him a much richer man than he had been. And his fees to us created the capital base from which Webb & Knapp's real-estate empire grew.

• 5 • The Mechanics of Progress (1942–1945)

BETWEEN 1942 and 1945 Webb & Knapp earned $835,000 in fees and commissions, plus $872,000 in profits from operating various properties. During this same time, our total assets grew from two to seven million dollars while our tangible net worth of assets over liabilities had climbed from minus $127,000 to over two million dollars. This was just the beginning of our great growth period.

How did we do it? It was really very easy. It was also great fun, and as some have suspected, we did it with mirrors. The formula also calls for contacts in proper places, lots of travel as well as travail, a pinch of ingenuity, careful study of the tax laws—and a crystal ball.

The crystal ball we used was the simple, built-in type. The only trick was not to be so awed and frightened by the present that you were not able to see the future that lay within it. In an America that had been traumatized by the Depression, I was one of those who recognized that the Depression was past and then acted on this recognition. A great many others, thinking the Depression was still with us, did in fact keep it here for themselves, out of sheer habit of thought.

The reasons for this mental freeze were as varied as the individuals I met. All over the country I found a great many men who had been so humiliated, so jolted by the Depression that they never regained anything close to their pre-1929 trust and confidence in the world or in themselves. I discovered others who for various reasons had grown accustomed to the status quo determined by the Depression. They did not look for and did not see the implications of the new jobs, the new growth, and the resultant changes underway around them. Both groups, conditioned by disaster, were prepared for nothing else.

Given a different perspective, it took only a modicum of imagination to spot properties which were highly undervalued and which it would be wise to buy. The problem was not in understanding what was going on but in convincing others that it was indeed going on—and might continue for a few years. That is why, in order to get some major retail companies to move into properties we held, I took to offering them low, depression-proof rents with a percentage-of-profits clause in the contract. We had more faith in their eventual success than they did, and this faith paid off in handsome profits for them and for us.

Excepting barter, which I have sometimes resorted to, the acquisition of sizable amounts of property calls for sizable amounts of money. While learning the virtues of buying for cash and selling for credit, I was discovering that there are multiple sources and uses for money in real estate. In addition to our Astor earnings, we used, as I have previously indicated, bank money, first-mortgage money, second-mortgage money, and sectional mortgages (regular first and second mortgages divided into two or more sections and sold to small investors). Another way of garnering quantities of ready cash is to make money for others, and we had done this by syndicating special projects with both individuals and groups. We organized twenty-two such projects from 1942 to 1945.

One company we did syndication work with was the Interstate Realty Corp. of Boston, of which Benjamin Swig, the hotel man, was a principal. With them we entered into at least a dozen purchases and sales of retail properties all over the country. We sold property in Texas which had cost $141,000 for $165,000 after leasing it to F. W. Woolworth Co. In Syracuse we bought a $357,000 department store and sold it five months later to Bond Stores, Inc., for $425,000. Usually we handled the details of the transaction, although Interstate handled the purchase of Hotel Edison in New York.

Franciska Bator was another partner of record with us in a number of ventures, but she was acting for her husband, Victor Bator, a Hungarian émigré, lawyer, and unofficial investment scout for a group of his fellow nationals. Another continual investor was Irving Geist, a vice-president of Consolidated Retail Stores, but our cast of backers, like our business, was constantly changing. In 1944 Webb & Knapp, Interstate Realty, and four individuals bought a small mill in York, Pennsylvania, from the Southern Kraft Paper Co. for $25,000, which we then sold to a manufacturer, who needed new manufacturing capacity, for $65,000. Again, with Louis Kramer, a long-time New

York real-estate investor, we worked out a variety of transactions, including the purchase, for half a million dollars and resale, for $650,000, of Best & Co. on Fifth Avenue. As word of our activities got around, we had less and less trouble finding backing and partners. Who turns away a man who could make money for you?

What had first opened many doors for us was that I was buyer for a fifty-million-dollar empire, the Astor estate. I suspect that even without the Astor background I would have pulled Webb & Knapp to the forefront of the industry, because the opportunities for growth were readily available, but the Astor connection saved us time and made the path more pleasant. In Houston, Texas, for example, I discovered a most genial and abiding Texan affection and respect for money, especially if there was a possibility of their getting some of it. Since I was offering top prices for town real estate, I found I was readily granted the status of honorary ambassador. My first contact there was with a man named Hester who turned out to be the finest real-estate man in Texas, and a charmer until he had a few too many drinks; then he would turn surly, insulting to women, even his own wife, and nasty to his best friends. When sober, however, Hester was the kindest of humans, and although I'm not sure which is the real Hester, I presume it is the sober one. Hester was real-estate man for Houston's tycoons. It was through him that they put their syndicates together, and it was through him that I met various oil, cattle, and banking people such as Jim Abercrombie, Bob Henderson, Bill Smith, and their unofficial chieftain, Jesse Jones, the multimillionaire, lumberman, oil man, U.S. Secretary of Commerce, federal-loan administrator, and, as such, dispenser of billions of dollars in U.S. peacetime and wartime investment loans.

Texas' inordinate share of wealthy individuals, like Saudi Arabia's excess of Cadillacs in its automobile population, is not necessarily a sign of extraordinary diligence and perspicacity among its peoples, but of happy accident—in the form of great oil deposits. Plus, in the United States, the passage and continued political defense in Congress of the 27½-percent tax-depletion allowance. This 27½-percent tax allowance on oil revenues has, for over a generation, had an effect not unlike that of daily funneling of hundreds of millions of dollars in foreign aid into an area. Not only have the citizenry in general benefited, but, as happens with all massive aid projects, many individuals both within and outside of the area acquired extensive fortunes plus the confident self-esteem which an excess of money in the bank gives to us all.

Among the many fine people I met out there, Jesse Jones and his Houston associates formed a particularly shrewd and far-sighted fraternity, for, as I shall point out later, they did great things for their city and region. Though I sought major investments in Houston, I was never able to bid successfully against the deep pockets of these local satraps. These gentlemen tried to keep not only their investing and lending close to home but also their spending. It was courtesy of this group that a few years later I was to witness a most wry and utterly deadpan display of rich men's gamesmanship.

I was a guest of Billy Reynolds of Reynolds Metal on Derby Day in Louisville, Kentucky. Early that morning we were gathered with a selection of local notables, a great many of them track stewards. In order to prime us for the strenuous day ahead, mint juleps had been served at nine o'clock. At 9:30 Jesse Jones called from Houston. He and a few friends wanted to come up for the Derby but did not have a box; could anyone help him out? Of course, every single box had been taken months before, but the race stewards' throats turned dry at the thought of all that Texas money lying idle in Houston when it could just as well be flowing into the coffers of the Louisville track. So, after a few thoughtful sips at their mint juleps, a group of stewards matched straws, and the loser gave up his box to Mr. Jones. A properly thankful Jones promised to arrive at the head of a party of twelve.

The Houston crowd got up there in time for the Derby. Thirteen men filed in instead of the twelve that had been expected, but for the kind of money they represented, no Kentuckians were about to feel either offended or superstitious. All through the race the track stewards kept eyeing Jones' box waiting for the big spenders from Texas to file out and place their bets, but not a man moved. And it wasn't until after the race was over that the Kentuckians found out why: the thirteenth man in the Houston box had been a Houston bookie.

Because Webb & Knapp was buying all over the country, I found myself stitching a crisscross pattern of trips across wartime America. Airplanes were smaller, fewer, and often preempted by military or government officials. Gasoline was rationed, so travel was by train. And World War II was the railroad industry's last great moment.

Streaming smoke and soot, trains rolled between one city and another with passengers sharing their seats in shifts. There were waits of two or three hours for a seat in the dining car, and the club car, a stand-up cocktail party for strangers, invariably ran out of liquor. And yet, for all the uncertainties and delays of wartime travel, I enjoyed those trips, especially the longer ones. Those crowded trains taught me many things about the country, other people, and myself.

They also introduced me to the "courtesy" networks, where, for example, a banker in San Diego would help me out with a hotel reservation, and when he came to New York, I, in return, could supply him with tickets to a hit play.

I was often able to get theater tickets through my friends Lee and J. J. Shubert. We met when, as agent for Astor, I sold the Shuberts a number of midtown theater properties. Lee Shubert was a keen-witted and jolly man with the face of a Sioux Indian. Although twenty years my senior, Lee had become a close friend whom I enjoyed sharing confidences with. Marion and I had dinner with him and Marcella Swanson regularly. Lee's relationship with Marcella was a novella in itself. He met her when she was a fifteen-year old member of a skating team known as "The Swanson Sisters." Their romance blossomed as she matured, and that romance lasted throughout their lives. They maintained separate households, but we all thought of and accepted Marcella as Lee Shubert's mistress. We assumed their relationship was not bound by any legality, until, in 1948, the papers announced that she was suing for divorce. For all their separate homes, they had been secretly married for many years.

Some three months after this scandal in reverse and their divorce, I stopped by to see Lee in his office. He explained to me that they had been married since 1936 but he was used to an unbridled existence and could not stand the pinch of the marriage harness, hence the separate homes. He looked rather glum, so I asked, why they didn't get together again.

"No . . . we're through."

"Well, why don't you let me give a small dinner just for the four of us at home?"

"No, no," he answered. "I wouldn't want to do that. Besides, she wouldn't . . . care for that. She would never come."

"Suppose we find out?"

Contrary to Lee's expectation, Marcella jumped at the idea. They arrived separately, Lee late as usual, and although they were a bit uncomfortable and strained with each other, we had a pleasant enough dinner, and Lee escorted Marcella home.

Two weeks later Shubert called me from Miami. "Marcella and I are down here having a second honeymoon. We're married again and we're going to try living together as well."

One reason for Lee's long-time skittishness of formal marriage ties was his proclivity for extracurricular activity. In his time, he had struck up warm, if brief, friendships with numbers of aspiring young actresses, and he kept an old straight-backed chair in his office which he would not part with and which, with a wistful shake of the head, he would, from time to time, give a reminiscent pat. The young ladies he had interviewed for parts had sat across from him in that chair.

In a valiant effort to defy time, Lee underwent countless sun-bathing and masseur sessions, dyed his hair, and avoided his true contemporaries, whom he thought ossified. His career, however, dated back to the turn of the century, and he had a wealth of anecdotes about people in and about the theater. One of his best was about John Jacob Astor, Vincent Astor's father. In New York, as in London and Paris, from the 1890's through the 1920's it was fashionable for wealthy stage-door Johnnies to besiege their lady loves with flowers, affectionate notes, and invitations to wine and dine away the hours until dawn. One particularly lovely young thing, after a protracted siege, had accepted the attentions of John Jacob Astor. My friend Lee, who sometimes had an avuncular interest in his charges, as well as a personal one, was aware, in those days before Actors Equity, that diamonds are a girl's best friend. He asked this not-quite-innocent miss whether she was acquiring any insurance against either the disaffection or demise of her elderly protector. The young beauty replied, "Oh, yes, he's very kind to me. I get $1,727 every time I see him." Why exactly $1,727, puzzled Lee? It seems that the first time she had granted her favors to her admirer this was the sum total the grateful man had on him. Since he was a gentleman and multimillionaire, he could never henceforth offer less to his young protégée. But that was in another era. After a severe Depression, stage-door waiting had not only lost its panache, but was bad public relations. Styles had changed.

My own style of life had also changed. I was now a transcontinental traveler and an active trader. In time, as I became more familiar with various cities and regions, I found I could do a good deal of my buying from my New York office. My memory of a city or a quick look at a map and photographs, together with a quiz of a local broker or banker, would enable me to determine accurately what a property was worth and what kind of mortgage we could get.

Throughout this period, my work for Astor took up only half of my efforts. The properties we bought for ourselves we might hold on to for a number of years (their income was always welcome), but trading was our greatest interest. Once we had "proven" a property by signing a high-grade tenant to a good lease and by refinancing the mortgage, we were happy to sell it off at its newly established value to local investors and then move on. I also learned the needs of buyers or tenants, such as Woolworth's or Allied Stores, and when we spotted something they *should* like, I would buy it and then turn it over to the most likely tenant. Even in these relatively simple deals the transaction often became complicated.

All in all, from 1942 through 1945 Webb & Knapp handled some ninety purchases and seventy-five sales. The profit margin of any one of these transactions ranged from zero to several hundred thousand dollars. The average range was from thirty thousand to fifty thousand dollars. As fast as we made money, we put it back to work (with leverage), but we grew as quickly as we did only because we were also able to make good use of the existing tax laws.

As I pointed out earlier, one of the tragedies of the Depression was that various tax laws, which had seemed sensible and equitable enough in normal times, turned out to work special hardships on owners and investors during the Depression. Ironically, once the real-estate situation began to improve in the 1940's, other tax laws similarly conceived and intended for normal times readily served as tax shelters to those who could see and take advantage of them. One such device, the tax-loss carry-forward (with some modifications) is still much in use. The tax-loss carry-forward gives a company that has suffered losses during a certain period a tax allowance in order to help it recover and remain, over the long run, a healthy, taxpaying entity. Any profits it may make for a certain number of years are declared to be tax-free until such time as its total profits equal its previous losses. Therefore, by properly merging a winner (a money-making company that would normally pay taxes) with a loser (a company that had racked up capital losses and therefore had a tax credit), the resultant combined company would utilize the tax credits of the "losing" company to save the profits of the "winning" concern.

In 1943, for instance, we bought a number of New York commercial properties which formed part of the Havermeyer estate from the trustee, the Bankers Trust Co., for $440,000. In a few years' time we were able to sell the properties with a profit to us of approximately $530,000. If the property alone had been all that we bought, it would have been simply just one more profitable deal, but what we acquired was more than the properties. We had purchased all the stock as well, and therefore the actual companies that owned the properties. On the company books these properties had an aggregate, pre-Depression book value of 3.6 million dollars. When, after a complex series of paperwork exchanges, we sold off the properties at more than we paid for them, but at less than their book value, the residual companies wound up with a capital loss of more than two million dollars showing on the books. As a result, this two million-dollar book loss became a two-million-dollar tax credit. This meant that the next two million dollars in profits, which we were able to make through the residual companies, would be tax-free. Through a number of such carefully chosen purchases of stock and sales of property, I kept Webb & Knapp a tax-sheltered concern throughout the war and for part of the postwar period.

I was neither the first nor the only businessman to recognize and make use of this and similar opportunities in the tax structure. Later, Royal Little, a shrewd Yankee entrepreneur-industrialist, through his imaginative use of tax-free foundations and tax-loss carry-forwards, would so effectively and notably shelter his Textron empire from taxes that great portions of the law were rewritten.

We bought property largely outside of New York City because real estate in New York was moribund. From 1939 on, throughout the rest of the country factories were being built or reopened to supply the Allies and our own rapidly expanding armed forces. Soon most were on double shifts. But this resurgence was industrial rather than financial, which is to say that the money did not come from Wall Street. New York, the financial and office capital of the nation, hopefully watched and waited for its own resurgence, but, as regards real estate, there was almost a ten-year lag. As a result, New York overbuilt in the 1920's, remained underoccupied through the late 1940's. Whole floors in modern office buildings were used as employee recreation areas. Even prestigious Rockefeller Center was, as late as 1946, forty-percent unoccupied.

When we bought outside New York City, we were merely putting our money where America's growth was strongest. From time to time we took some flyers in foreign real estate, as in the case of Mexico City, but only because in my enjoyable new role of transcontinental bon vivant, Mexico was where I sometimes happened to be.

Marion and I first went to Mexico in 1943. At that time Mexico was not the well-traveled tourist center it has since become. Mexico City was a great capital and sophisticated urban center, but it was still almost purely Mexican. The floating gardens of Xochimilco, which the fast-declining lake has since left mostly stranded, were then floating paradises. Farther south, in Tampico, I hunted on the Tampico River and its nearby lakes, where after a gun was fired, the drumming wings and loud calls of brilliantly colored birds taking to the air made it impossible to hear anything else. And at that time, Acapulco, though a famous resort, was still a relatively small town with a character of its own rather than the high-rise, hotel-and-tourist-dominated place it has now become.

On our first day in Mexico City, Marion and I visited the ruins at Teotihuacán, in the middle of the great valley of Mexico. We visited the enormous Temple of the Sun and Temple of the Moon, with their flanking structures, gathering places, outdoor theaters, and temples. The Toltecs had a way of life quite different from ours. We think of them as primitive, but the design of the buildings and site is bold, balanced, and beautiful and surpasses much of what has been created since.

That first experience of Teotihuacán has left me with a sense of how the proper combination of mass, space, and setting can complement each other. It was to enormously influence what I consider to be the most important work of my life.

Marion scampered with her camera to the top of every pyramid she could get to. It was not till late afternoon that, elated and pleasantly tired by places and thoughts new to us, we returned to the Hotel Reforma. There, after washing up, we stopped in the lounge for a before-dinner cocktail. The bartender sent over two tequila martinis for our inspection. They were something new, but quite tasty. We downed them. A friend called over to me. I turned away from the table to speak a few words to him, turned back to Marion, and she was gone! She had collapsed and slipped soundlessly out of her chair. Mexico City's notorious high altitude and the excitement of the afternoon had combined with the tequila to hit Marion's bloodstream with all the power of a dozen sister martinis from north of the border. While various old-timers nodded knowingly at this latest tribute to altitude and the national drink, we beat a smiling if slightly shaky retreat to our rooms. Marion almost immediately recovered, but we had supper (mourning dove with wild rice) sent up to our rooms. Later, now fully warned and fully fortified, we sallied forth again to pay our homage to the local Bacchus.

In our hotel was Mexico City's finest nightclub, Ciro's, which was operated by A. C. Blumenthal, an expatriate New Yorker. We made Ciro's our night headquarters, and sooner or later anybody of consequence among local or visiting revelers would make an appearance there. Wartime Mexico City, like Geneva, Zurich, and Lisbon, was one of the world's key espionage centers. The city boasted a full quota of spies, covert and not so covert, as well as counterspies, would-be spies, and volunteer counterspies of all shades and price tags. Since in Latin America it is as difficult to keep a secret as it is to learn the full truth about anything, the town buzzed with rumors and details of plots which, sooner or later, we all heard about.

All through the forties we often vacationed in Mexico. Since I can no more resist a real-estate deal than a smile at a pretty girl, each trip to Mexico saw me toying with a venture there. Although I began some preliminary negotiations, the business mores, local rules of the road, and diversity of the under-the-table dealings made those negotiations different enough so that it meant I had to keep a constant eye on my projects, or else things all too easily went awry. For instance, one spot where I did see desirable properties was in a tiny little place just a few miles south of Acapulco called Puerta Marquesa. It was then a tiny Indian fishing village, but I could tell it would flourish as a second Acapulco. It was eventually developed by some wealthy local politician and has become one of the most valuable pieces of real estate in the country, but I did not buy there because of restrictive local laws, which prohibit foreign ownership of coastal land and of large land holdings of all types. Often local citizens are used as front men to get around this law, but I decided against this gambit, for it would have been too vulnerable to permit a massive and truly forceful development of the area.

Some years later I did acquire the site of the British American Hospital in the center of Mexico City. Marion and I were on our way to Acapulco and had stopped in Mexico City for a few days. Sam Katz, a leader of the American community in Mexico, gave a dinner party for us, and before dinner he and I took a stroll near his home. We walked past the nearby British American Hospital, which consisted of some ten beautifully landscaped acres in the heart of town, just one block north of the Avenida de la Reforma. Katz asked me why I didn't buy the property.

"Why, is it for sale?"

"As a matter of fact, it is. The association is planning to build a new hospital. If you want to buy the property, I think you can, maybe even tonight. Three of the trustees of the hospital are going to be at dinner." These trustees were the most influential on the board and could persuade the other members. Sam thought they might be willing to accept $750,000.

The price seemed quite low to me, and I told him I'd buy it for that price.

After dinner Sam mentioned my interest in the property. The trustees said they would sell for $750,000. That was fine with me. I didn't try to bargain. I hate to bargain. If, in my judgment, a property is worth the asking price, I see no reason to try for less. A lot of shrewd dealers think this foolish, but I notice that others tend to lose more business, and to poison relationships, by trying to refine an already good bargain beyond a reasonable point. There is a much better flavor left in everybody's mouth when such haggling is avoided. I wanted the property, their price seemed reasonable to me, and so we were in business.

Rather than be a lone, vulnerable gringo, it seemed like a good idea to have reliable native partners in the deal, and my Mexico City lawyer, Rafael Oriomuno, recommended Sacristán, a prominent Mexico City banker, who agreed to join me as equal partner. Later, Sacristán offered to buy us out. I agreed to sell our half for almost $750,000 profit, which gain made a handsome return on expenses for any and all of my previous trips to Mexico.

A common Wall street myth had it that I wandered into Webb & Knapp one day during the early war years to use the phone. The partners of the firm then went off to war, and when they returned, found I was in charge and that they had become millionaires. This is not precisely accurate. It is true that during the war years Eliot Cross, then an elderly man, was not well, and had assumed a relatively passive role in the firm. My three other partners, whom I kept on full salary throughout, were called to active duty in the armed forces. But on return they were not quite millionaires.

Jim Landauer received only one-half million dollars as his share in the partnership when he resigned from the firm in late 1945. When Eliot Cross resigned in 1946, he received $800,000. Because the one hundred or more transactions which multiplied Webb & Knapp's fortunes were of my devising, my partners of course returned to a situation in which I was in charge. Naturally, the other partners were free to generate as many separate transactions as they wished when they returned, but I had an enormous head start. Once having established a base, I continued to work under the impetus of increasingly exciting projects.

I was beginning to be caught up with the idea of moving the United Nations headquarters to New York City.

· 6 · "X City" Becomes the United Nations

Since I now live on Beekman Place overlooking the East River, I occasionally pass the United Nations headquarters. Every time I do, I feel a certain pride, as well as the sharp bite of frustration. The pride is for having the United Nations in New York, because if it were not for Webb & Knapp the UN would not grace New York City at all. The frustration is over the unmistakable fact that the UN's setting and approach vis-à-vis midtown New York are totally inadequate. The UN is separated from the rest of town by a Chinese wall of old and second-rate buildings.

The city now has plans for creating a new UN approachway, but twenty years have passed since our first efforts to do something in this area, and it is difficult to guess how much longer it will take to actually get something done. I fought a major battle with the City of New York over this issue. I had hoped to give both the UN and the city vital breathing space and added luster—but I lost. Nevertheless, the basic UN transaction remains one of my proudest achievements, for we are not all granted the opportunity and thrill of moving the capital of the world on a few days' notice. In addition, the development of the UN site gave me ideas that paid off handsomely for other cities. And yet, every time I go by the so-called approachway the city gave to the UN, I feel the old and righteous anger start to stir.

Originally the present site of the UN was a wooded, riverside hollow commanded on the north and west by abrupt, low-lying hills. As the city grew, trolley lines, then a series of wharves and tightly packed warehouses, were built by the river's edge. Sometime after the Civil War this nest of buildings was turned into a string of slaughterhouses. Time froze, and that's what remained there through 1946. One result was that New York's famous midtown area, "with everything for the tourist," could even boast it had an 1890 Chicago-in-miniature complete with cattle pens, packing plants, and an all-pervasive, stomach-turning stench! Theatergoers thronging out of Wednesday matinees on Forty-sixth Street had to scuttle out of the way of open trucks hauling cattle from the West Side docks to the East River charnel houses. On days when the wind blew from the east, the smells from the slaughterhouses reached to Third Avenue and beyond. This is why the section of Tudor City backing on First Avenue has no windows. Luckily, the prevailing winds in New York are westerly, but in 1946, when land prices in midtown Manhattan ran at $100 to $150 per square foot, prices in the immediate odor zone around the slaughterhouses ranged from two to five dollars per square foot—with few buyers in sight.

The slaughterhouses had been there for so long that they seemed untouchable. Since the Swift and Wilson meat packing companies, who owned the slaughterhouses, held an irrevocable and presumably profitable franchise to operate in Manhattan, there seemed little hope of ever getting them out.

Brokers often "offer" a property for which they have no franchise. If they find a willing buyer at a good price, they then go to the property owner with a proposition and the hope of making a bargain. Previously, the slaughterhouses had been peddled on just this basis, so I was skeptical when, late in 1945, John Dunbar, a real-estate broker with Cushman & Wakefield, Inc., offered to sell us this choice property, especially when he offered the property at a steep seventeen dollars per square foot. Considering the two- and five-dollar-per-square-foot values in the area, his price seemed preposterous. I challenged whether he could make delivery at any price. He informed me that his wife was a Swift and that the Swifts and Wilsons had agreed to sell the land jointly, through him.

Dunbar had approached us first. (Thanks to Webb & Knapp's growing reputation as an active firm, we were getting more and more such first offers.) I asked, "What would you say to an offer of five dollars per square foot? That's well above the going price over there." Under those terms, he answered, he would have no choice but to try elsewhere. He was authorized to sell only at seventeen dollars per square foot. Though I argued and bargained, and eventually suggested a possible twelve-dollar price, he remained adamant. While we discussed a solution, I thought to myself that at seventeen dollars per square foot the property would cost some 6.5 million dollars. But with the slaughterhouses gone, I was sure the price could jump to fifty, possibly to seventy-five, and maybe even as high as one hundred dollars. For a 6.5-million-dollar investment (much of this in the form of mortgages) we might make a gross profit of sixteen million dollars, thirty-two million dollars, or more. Then, there were the value-depressed properties around the slaughterhouses, which would also rise in value from a two- and five-dollar base. So I said, "Well, I'd like to keep this off the market for a while. Let me talk it over with my partners." I left him sitting there while I met with Gould and Sears. They immediately agreed we should accept the seventeen-dollar offer, and I returned to Dunbar and told him he had a deal.

We arranged that Webb & Knapp would put up one million dollars for a one-year option against the total 6.5-million-dollar price. At the end of the year we were to pay the remaining 5.5 million dollars. In the meantime, the packing companies would quietly make arrangements to relocate, and the agreement between us would be kept secret so as not to precipitate a price-rise land rush in the area.

The next problem was where to find one million dollars in cash. I solved that by forming a syndicate consisting of ourselves, a Chicago financier, and two New York real-estate speculators.

With the slaughterhouse option in hand, we now needed as much of the two- and five-dollar-per-square-foot land surrounding them as possible to bring down our average cost. I hired some three or four brokers to buy different properties in the area as quietly as possible. During the summer, Marion and I took a three-week trip to South America to throw the hounds off the scent, but the rumors of our activity began to spread. In one case a canny fruit peddler and his wife, who had just acquired two five-story buildings on a key corner lot on First Avenue for ten thousand dollars held out against my buyers for months. Everytime we agreed to a price, they would change their minds and raise the ante, till they finally got $100,000, but generally we were able to get the properties we wanted. We bought what we could north of the slaughterhouses to Forty-ninth Street and also acquired a number of lots to the west, between First and Second avenues. In all, we picked up about seventy-five properties totaling eight acres at an average price of nine dollars per square foot. These individual purchases were financed by local banks and insurance companies.

The next thing to be determined was what to do with the parcel of land we had assembled. Marion and I took to walking over to the edge of Beekman Place after dinner. There we would stare south toward the slaughterhouses, outlined by First Avenue and the welter of east-west cross streets, to the rising bulk of Tudor City. During the fifth or sixth of these visits, an idea came to me. I visualized a great, flat, rectangular platform stretching from the elevation of Tudor City east to the river and then north to where we stood on Beekman Place. This raised platform would stretch over the local streets, where service and parking facilities could easily nestle, and where city traffic would continue to flow as it did now. On the platform itself would rise great modern buildings, with cleanly designed plazas between them.

The prototype of such a platform had been constructed in 1913 when the city forced the New York Central Railroad to cover the ugly network of open railroad tracks lying to the south and north of Grand Central Station. This roofing created Park Avenue, and a fortune in real-estate values, but what I was proposing was a greater and more unified development.

That night I could hardly sleep as I chased my own ideas, tied them down with facts and figures, altered them, made compromises, returned to original notions, and finally realized that I was no longer dealing with fantasy but with genuine possibility. Now I needed a top architect to help work these concepts out in concrete form, and I turned to Wallace Harrison, whose work on Rockefeller Center had brought him a deserved and estimable reputation. Harrison agreed to work on the East River, and his completed plan was designated "X City."

"X City" was to be a city within a city whose design adapted to the New York areas around it. At the south end of the immense seven-block-long, two-block-wide platform, we planned to build four office buildings which could fit comfortably between Forty-second and Forty-fifth streets. At Forty-fifth Street we allowed room for a combination airlines terminal and office building, a single facility large enough to allow for the growth in air travel: at that time there was nothing supplying that need, and there still isn't. That area of Manhattan also lacked a major modern hotel, and we planned one across from the terminal. This hotel would permit a shift in emphasis away from the office structures and toward the residential section. The north end of the property would be devoted to a series of apartment buildings which would blend in nicely with the expensive residential character of Beekman Place. In the space between the curves of the airline and hotel buildings, I planned a possible new home for the Metropolitan Opera. Adventuring even further, we proposed an adjacent floating nightclub, a marina, and a variety of other attractions in the East River itself.

Looking back at what has happened since in New York, one can see that "X City" was an economically practical as well as aesthetically pleasing conception. I set up the architects' renderings and a scale model of the project in a side room at the Club Monte Carlo, where at lunch I could display it to prospective clients. My plan was that the four southern office buildings were to be occupied by four large corporations, and that each building bear the name of its tenant. For a starter, we began serious negotiations with the Mutual Benefit Life Insurance Company of New York, with Time Inc., and with the Aluminum Company of America. Arthur Vining Davies, who, as chairman, ran Alcoa as a personal fief, was intrigued by "X City" and promised to take a building if we could call the whole project "Aluminum City." Foolishly, I demurred. At that time, most aluminum building materials were as yet untried, or yet to be conceived. Also, I was afraid the name "Aluminum City" might drive away other potential clients.

This was a major undertaking for everyone involved, and the project by its nature could not be moved quickly. By December, 1946, I was still lining up clients and backers. The Wilson and Swift people were beginning to wonder where the remaining 5.5 million dollars due to them was to come from. So was I. I was not worried, but I was wondering—and we did have a deadline. Even as raw land, however, the properties we had assembled were so massive and potentially so choice that backers and buyers would always be available. The challenge was not in selling land but in creating value by using it judiciously. Not since Columbia University turned over its midtown properties for the construction of Rockefeller Center had such a great land parcel as ours become available in New York. What we were proposing in "X City" would rival Rockefeller Center. In fact, by overriding New York's nineteenth-century grid pattern of streets, yet not disturbing it, we would have surpassed Rockefeller Center. Here was a chance for inventive, original, and eminently sensible use of a city's core. All my energies from the time of conception had been directed to the achievement of that specific goal. Suddenly a new, totally unexpected possibility developed.

During all of 1946, the United Nations had been plagued and perplexed by the problems of finding a permanent home. Robert Moses, New York's commissioner of parks, tried to sell the UN on a permanent location at the site of the World's Fair in Flushing Meadows. Another proposed solution had been a great campuslike development in Westchester County near the town of Greenwich on the periphery of New York. The UN, rejecting Moses' plan, received a rebuff in return from the Westchester-Greenwich area, where the staid property owners, rising up like the minutemen at Concord, organized to keep the foreigners off the sacred soil of exurbia. However, practically every other major city in the United States eagerly offered sites. The most likely contenders were San Francisco and Philadelphia. The Russians objected to San Francisco on the grounds that it was too far from any major diplomatic center. It seemed that, by a matter of elimination, Philadelphia would be selected, and so certain did the choice seem, that in December, 1946, Philadelphia was in process of condemning property for its proposed UN location.

At breakfast on Friday, December 6, just one day before the special General Assembly meeting called for the approval of Philadelphia as the UN site, I read the report of the debates on the UN site in *The New York Times*. At that moment it occurred to me that we at Webb & Knapp had an ideal site for the UN right here in Manhattan! Turning to Marion, I said, "I'm going to put those bastards on the platform!"

"Which bastards on what platform?"

"The UN—I'm going to put them on the platform over the slaughterhouses."

"Oh, my God, how are you going to do that?" Marion asked.

I wasn't sure just how we would pull it off, but as soon as I got into the office I spoke to Gould and Sears. We had a chance, I said, to stop the UN move to Philadelphia: we could offer our East Side property as a headquarters site. Somebody would have to see the mayor. I suggested that Gould go, since he was president of the firm. He thought the whole thing a wild idea and declined, saying that in any event he did not know the mayor. When I said I did know the mayor, Gould said, "All right, you go. But," he added wryly, "don't use our names."

When I called Mayor William O'Dwyer and asked him if he would like to keep the United Nations in New York, he fervently said that he'd give an arm, a leg, and various other parts of his body for the chance, but that none of them was particularly salable. I then asked him to put Miss Holly, his secretary, on the extension phone. I was going to dictate a statement he could take to the United Nations: "We hereby offer to the United Nations approximately seventeen acres on the East River from Forty-second Street and First Avenue north to Forty-ninth Street for any price they wish to pay."

O'Dwyer, taken aback, interrupted to ask how we could possibly say that.

I told him that the matter of the UN site was now so close to the deadline there was no time for trading. Unless I said price was no object, they would think this was a trick by a real-estate operator to stop their Philadelphia negotiations, and then hold them up for millions. It had to be a carte blanche. We would either capture their imagination and start them rethinking, or we would not, and one of the critical elements would be the price. Then, with a laugh, I said, "Besides, I hardly think that the United Nations' first move would be to take a man's property away from him and offer nothing. I'll take my chances on that."

He said, "O.K., but don't laugh. I'm taking my life in my hands going down there to do this."

The next day, Saturday, I received a call at home. "This is Pollock of the United Press, out at Lake Success. I want to verify something. Is it true that you've offered seventeen acres of Manhattan property to the United Nations?"

I said it was true and asked if there was much interest.

"Interest! There is a revolution! They are going wild down there in the assembly. Philadelphia is dead. In my opinion, they're going to accept." This was almost precisely twenty-four hours after I had first called Mayor O'Dwyer.

The UN-site offer was front-page news the next morning, and the UN was in turmoil as it tried to encompass this new development. I was in no way involved in the discussions. The mayor and his associates, the State Department, and the UN now had the ball. As it turned out, the key person in this mixed group was a superactive young man named Nelson Rockefeller, a member of the mayor's UN-site committee.

On Tuesday, December 10, Marion and I and Henry Sears and his wife were celebrating our anniversary and Henry's birthday at the Monte Carlo. Wallace Harrison walked in carrying a map of the East Side property. He was accompanied by Frank Jameson, the Rockefeller public-relations counsel, and a man from the State Department. Harrison announced, "The United Nations wants an option on the property."

"I gave it to them."

"But they want a price."

"I gave them that—anything they want to pay."

"Stop kidding around."

"This isn't kidding. Sit down, have a drink."

"What about the price?" Harrison asked.

"What do you want to know that for?"

"What did you pay for it?"

I said, "Six and a half million for the slaughterhouses, but the property now goes much farther north than that, right up to Forty-ninth Street."

"Slow down," he said. "Would you sell it for eight and a half million?"

I told him I would sell for two million or whatever they were willing to pay. Harrison asked me to give them an option for 8.5 million dollars, so I drew a line around the property on the map and said, "By the way, I'll throw in a present—fifteen thousand square feet on the north side of Forty-seventh Street, so it will force you to go at least as far north as Forty-eighth Street." I presented them with this extra land to persuade them to expand their lot northward as they should.

I'd had a lot of champagne by that time, but I had drawn the property line clearly, and I then wrote, "All the property within the boundary of this line is under option for thirty days to the United Nations." And I listed the blocks involved. I called Harry Sears over. "Is this O.K. with you, Harry?" He agreed, and I said, "Put your fist down."

Sears signed, I signed, and that's the only contract we ever had with the United Nations.

The next morning at 10:30, my head throbbing from the previous night's champagne, I was in my office but wishing I wasn't when the phone rang. The girl said Nelson Rockefeller was on the line. When I picked up the phone, Rockefeller's brisk voice crackled, "Is this Bill Zeckendorf?"

"Yes."

"We've been up all night patching up the details, but it's going to work. The old man is going to give that 8.5 million dollars to the UN, and they're going to take your property. See you soon. . . . Good-bye."

The property was being purchased! I couldn't believe it. I signaled our switchboard operator and told her to find out who it was that had called. She buzzed back to say it had indeed been Rockefeller. I gingerly put on my hat and carried my hangover home. As I came into the apartment, I told Marion, "We have just moved the capital of the world."

On Saturday, December 14, eight days after my first call to O'Dwyer, the General Assembly formally approved New York City as the site for United Nations headquarters.

Some of the basic ideas and details of the "X City" project came into being in the UN complex. In part this was because Wallace Harrison, in view of his connection with the Rockefellers and his excellent work on Rockefeller Center, was named a member of the international committee of architects that designed the UN. It was Harrison's opposite number Le Corbusier who, in my opinion, made the major contribution to the topside portion of the complex. In fact, sitting in my apartment and explaining what he felt was needed, Corbusier drew a prototype design of the UN on the back of an old envelope, which I kept.

However, my conception of an imposing, high-level platform running above First Avenue from Forty-first Street to Fiftieth Street ended up as a quite modest widening of First Avenue, with an underpass below this level. Similarly, the limitation of the northern property line at Forty-eighth Street robbed the UN of the grandeur it might have had—and of the additional space it would need later for expansion. Considering the many political, financial, and personal elements that were involved in arriving at the final designs, this meanness of purse and shortness of vision in the design of the UN can be understood and even forgiven. What ultimately evolved was attractive and workable. What is regrettable is the faulting of a proper approach to the UN, as well as a proper setting for its buildings. For this, as for so many other failures of civic vision, only we New Yorkers and our feud-happy politicians and administrators are to blame.

In order to get the UN to settle permanently in New York, the city administration, eager as a would-be lover, was at first willing to promise anything asked of it. The actual compact was arranged so hurriedly, however, that many items, such as the details of site planning, were left unspecified. Then, once the project was consummated, once the nuptial knot was tied, as it were, the city's ardor and willingness to please waned to near-indifference.

The first signs of this cooling on the part of the city were evident as early as March, 1947, when a UN spokesman chided the city for lack of boldness and vision in its share of the site planning. The city, in the person of Commissioner Moses, gave a soft reply, but paid no attention to these murmurs. And the true indicator of New York's valuation of the UN was the travesty of an approachway it eventually built on Forty-seventh Street. On the south side of Forty-seventh Street between First and Second avenues, the city carved out a half-block-deep slice of land. Forty-seventh Street was then "widened." South of Forty-seventh Street the city built a dark, narrow mall with dull, gray stones, lining its floor and walls. This drab vest-pocket park and bit of road were designated as the official approachway to the UN. The main vista for most of this "approachway" consisted of the backsides of a series of tenements and factories on Forty-sixth Street. Today, if one does not entirely overlook the "approach," it is all too easy to recognize it for what it really is—a dreary drying-out place for the drunks scattered among the few benches, and a parking site for fume-spouting buses. An entranceway to the putative capital of the world it is not.

Distressed by the city's poor excuse of a plan, the local chapter of the American Institute of Architects proposed an approach plan, which was ignored. In July, 1947, with the blessing and backing of the AIA and of the UN, we at Webb & Knapp proposed a unified approach plan that did justice to, and in fact enhanced, the UN situation. What we proposed was the razing and redevelopment into one superblock of the land ranging north from Forty-sixth to Forty-ninth Street and west from the UN site to Third Avenue. North-south traffic on First and Second avenues would be overpassed, to create a giant mall that connected the UN to midtown New York. The buildings fronting on this mall would accommodate theaters, shops, offices, and apartments. In conjunction with the UN buildings, this approachway would have been one of the architectural jewels of the world. We know from Webb & Knapp's experience in Denver, Montreal, and Washington, D.C., that this approachway would have generated a great amount of business and tourist traffic. It would not only have been profitable in itself, but would have bought great revenues to the city. Most important, it would have upgraded and set new standards for the whole of what was then a seedy and uninspired east-midtown area.

But this great and exciting project was never to be. It collided and broke against the personality of one powerful man, Robert Moses, New York's Commissioner of Parks, City Construction Coordinator, Chairman of the Triborough Bridge Tunnel Authority, and wielder of vast funds and great influence in New York. Moses is the greatest public servant New York City has ever had, for he has been a builder of scope and imagination. I later worked with him on a number of projects. We became friends, and Moses is the kind of friend who stands by when lesser men have fled. However, Moses, like all men, has certain weaknesses. One blindspot, for instance, is his seemingly inherent inability, or great reluctance, to step beyond the design and building restrictions that were imposed upon the city by the previous generation's intoxication with grid-patterned streets. Another weakness centers on his natural but extensive pride of authorship. Our plan clashed with his on both these counts. I had a furious public and private battle with Moses over this approachway. He was then at the very peak of his power. As many a politician and errant businessman has sadly discovered, Moses is a past master at the art of civic war. I found myself and my motives distorted by Moses in his reports to the Board of Estimate, and was subject to consequent suspicious inquiries in the press. To the editors of *The New York Times* (which kept its reporting objectively biased in his favor), Moses was in those days sacrosanct, a demigod who could do no wrong, while I was branded as a suspect witness. Try though we might, my allies and I could never effectively get our message across to enough key citizens to change an essentially political decision.

Moses won the battle between us by sheer, brute force. I say brute force because he twisted the mayor's arm, but the mayor's arm was available for the twisting, and that is where I was caught by surprise. I was sophisticated enough to know that you don't often get things done by fighting in the newspapers. Like many a businessman about town, I was aware that presentations and arguments before the Board of Estimate or meeting of councilmen are often only the decorative topping to decisions and understandings that have been previously worked out. But I stepped willingly into this particular power play because I thought the situation was still fluid and because I thought we had Mayor O'Dwyer's backing. In fact, we did have such backing right down to the end. Then the mayor turned on us.

The mayor had agreed to my coming down to City Hall with a three-dimensional model of our approach plan to make a presentation at a special hearing of the Board of Estimate. After great difficulties in getting the model, which covered several tables, through the crowded corridors and past various official guards to the doors of the main chamber, we found we would not be allowed to display it. Then, when I stepped into the chamber to testify, O'Dwyer looked over at me and snapped, "What do you want?" From his tone I realized that this was not an ally; this was someone who was against me, and I thought, "What the devil has happened to O'Dwyer?"

O'Dwyer, a handsome, genial man with the drive and skill to work his way up from police patrolman to a seat of high power in the city, was a product of Tammany politics. He represented the best and worst of that organization. Shrewd, charming on most occasions, he could be as harsh and hard as a Seventh Avenue creditor when it pleased him. He had flair and a good deal of imagination, but, as I was learning, he could seldom rise for long above the fascinations and machinations of clubhouse politics. Later I heard from various political contacts that O'Dwyer's original encouragement of my plan vis-à-vis Moses' approachway had been a convenient maneuver, a ploy used to get another project okayed which he wanted and Moses did not. Moses fell for this ploy of the mayor's, and as these two came to final agreement, I and any hopes for an effective approach to the United Nations were sacrificed to Tammany politics. All I knew at the time, however, was that we were before the board and that O'Dwyer was suddenly unfriendly. I said, "Your Honor, I am here to present my plan for the approach to the United Nations."

"Before you do any presenting, I want to ask you a question. Do you have any property in the area that's going to require condemnation under your plan?"

"Yes, your Honor, I have. Every member of the Board of Estimate and yourself knows every piece of property we own, and we are willing to have that property condemned along with the rest in order to be sure that this plan goes through. We recognize that the value of the property is much higher than any condemnation award that we could possibly receive."

"We'll draw our own conclusions as to whether your motives are so holy—or whether your motives aren't to sell the city your property at condemnation."

As the talk went on in this vein, with others joining in, I was flabbergasted. I noted that these comments were impugning the honor of my firm and myself and added that we did not own more than six percent of the total landmass of the plan. Then, as the mayor or some other member of the board continued to harass me, I knew our cause was lost. By now I was so angered that I decided to go down with all guns blazing. Standing up in front of the board, I challenged Moses to make his comments without the mantle of immunity, and invited him to sue me for mine. I also accused the board, elected officials all, of having abdicated their powers to Moses, a nonelected official, and this, of course, was like spraying oil on a red-hot griddle. The politicos' sputtering rose to a roar. I was ordered out of the room, but I yelled back that I was an American citizen with a right to speak and be heard, then stalked out of the chamber on my own.

The next day *The New York Times* described the meeting as the bitterest debate in recent City Hall history, but in fact it was no debate, it was a cry in the wilderness. All I got for my trouble was a public black eye. Nonetheless, I spoke up for the record, and I'm glad I did, because I was one-hundred-percent right and have been so proven. This was one case where my friend Moses was one-hundred-percent wrong.

After this encounter, in order to clear away any possible question about Webb & Knapp's alleged special interest in holding property for condemnation, we sold off our holdings in the proposed approachway area and continued our fight for a decent plan, but it was a quixotic campaign. By now the design for a minuscule approachway was, in effect, unassailable. The citizenry, poorly organized or apathetic, could bring little pressure to bear.

One good thing that did come of the encounter is that John Price Bell, a reporter from the *Telegram*, came to get my side of the story. I was so impressed by his questioning that I later offered him a position at Webb & Knapp that obviously needed filling, that of director of public relations. For many years Bell did a very effective job in this position, and I never forgot the harsh lesson Moses had taught us. Henceforth Webb & Knapp undertook no major project in a city without recruiting support from two key sectors—financially important local groups and the general populace.

Another constructive and important result of my involvement with the United Nations is that it led to my first meeting with the Rockefellers, whose vision and magnanimity made the UN settlement in New York possible. This estimable and talented family deserves great credit for the UN and for a great many other visionary projects, such as Fort Tryon Park, the Cloisters, and the Museum of Modern Art. It is true, as some have pointed out, that had Webb & Knapp developed "X City," Rockefeller Center, then only sixty-percent occupied, would have faced serious competition. The alternative creation of the UN headquarters on Webb & Knapp land tended to help bring new businesses to New York—and to Rockefeller Center.

I became for a time a special consultant to the Rockefellers on real-estate matters, and as such persuaded them to combine their personal holdings into their real-estate company. The gross rentals from this real estate then would sufficiently overshadow income from other investments so the owners could escape the quite heavy personal-holding-company taxes.

As to Webb & Knapp's role in the UN operation, we admittedly made a good profit selling the properties surrounding the original slaughterhouse site, but we sold the slaughterhouses at a very modest price, and gave up many millions in future profits on a very valuable property. I had a bit of a struggle getting my syndicate partners to go along with the UN deal, and had, in effect, to buy one out by giving him full title to his share of our total acreage.

When, as the UN's champion, I was so gauche as to lose the battle for a decent approachway, an embarrassed UN Secretariat pretended they hardly knew me. At the dedication ceremonies for the new buildings, my wife and I were seated well to the back of the area, while a great many others, who had had far less to do with the realization of the project, were at the front and center of activities. Sometime after these ceremonies, I was called upon by Andrew Cordier, then the undersecretary at the UN and now the president of Columbia University. He told me he was going to ask a favor of me. Louis Orr, the well-known artist, had agreed to do an official etching of the United Nations buildings for five thousand dollars. Cordier wondered if I would donate the money. I was feeling a bit battered by this time and countered by asking why he didn't go to some of the people who made money on the UN project, the architects, the engineers, the builders. We had only sold the property to the UN, and that at a sacrifice. Why at this stage of the game, I asked him, did he come to me for five thousand dollars? I hadn't been treated very cordially.

He said, "I know you haven't, but I also know you are good-hearted, and I hope you'll do it for us."

I thought for a while and then said that I might donate the five thousand, but only under certain conditions. These conditions were that I get the number-one etching, the original print, plus the exclusive right to use the design as an emblem on the securities of my company, on my silver, china, glassware, in fact, anywhere that it pleased me. Cordier said the UN would be delighted to grant me this exclusive privilege. Having made a number of sacrifices for the UN which were now completely taken for granted, I was amused that for only five thousand dollars I was being treated in the manner royal. Somewhere here there was a moral to be drawn, but I was too busy on too many other projects to concern myself about it.

· 7 · End of an Era,
Start of a Reign

DURING THE WAR period Webb & Knapp had been closing as many as three or four transactions a week. Since an acquisition or sale might take anywhere from a few days to several months to close, we always had two dozen or more active transactions in hand. After the war the number and especially the size of our operations increased. Our old range of $30,000–$150,000 a project jumped to $100,000–$1,000,000, with many transactions well above that amount.

For example, even before the UN operation got under way I had made a purchase, in conjunction with Messrs. Eisner and Lubin, two real-estate speculators who later were part of the UN syndicate with me, that in terms of acreage and total profit far exceeded our more famous East Side project. We had acquired six waterfront miles, practically the entire Hoboken waterfront, from the Stevens family, who had held it since 1784. The price was $7,250,000. Our syndicate put down 1.25 million dollars in cash. By pledging one hundred percent of the stock of the eighteen different corporations involved, including a small nine-mile switching railroad, we secured the additional six million dollars from Bankers Trust.

With the UN site the problem had been acquiring sufficient land to make it possible to bring about a change in midtown New York; with Hoboken, it was the reverse. We had to break the acreage into marketable units. We sold two of the piers to the Holland-American Line for something over two million dollars. We sold another segment to J. W. Galbreath, the realtor, for almost four million. Another couple of piers went to the East Asiatic Co. for 1.8 million dollars, and General Foods bought a building and property for $900,000. These sales put our investment group 1.4 million dollars ahead. Next we arranged a number of shifts and exchanges of stock and of real estate between our two partners and Webb & Knapp. The net result was that Webb &

Knapp bought out Eisner and Lubin and took over the remaining waterfront. We sold various of these properties, to wind up in 1949 with 2.3 million dollars' profit to Webb & Knapp, plus properties with a market value of 1.6 million dollars.

Finding new buyers or new uses for old properties had become a Webb & Knapp specialty. In 1947, when we acquired the Wright Aeronautical plant in Paterson, New Jersey, at a public auction, we paid 3.2 million dollars and then profitably resold parcels of the property. Also in 1947 I bought the Terminal Warehouse Corp., a square-block cluster of old buildings in New York running from Twenty-seventh to Twenty-eighth Street between Eleventh and Twelfth avenues. The price was 1.8 million dollars. We tore down walls, put in new elevators and new handling equipment. With the old property now geared to volume operations, top accounts such as Macy's came in to lease valuable space. We eventually sold the business for nearly five million dollars' profit.

These new and larger transactions tended to take longer to consummate than many of our previous ventures. One transaction, for instance, that I particularly enjoyed was our West Side television-studio venture: it took three years.

In the fall of 1946 a broker offered to sell us the New York Riding Academy and a number of other buildings between Sixty-sixth and Sixty-seventh streets at Central Park West. The properties were owned by Metropolitan Life Insurance, and the price was a little over $700,000. I turned him down because this was essentially a residential area, and the West Side was déclassé. We would rather buy land at higher prices and get a better long-term deal on Park Avenue.

A few weeks later, however, I happened to be going across town on the Sixty-sixth Street transverse through Central Park. A traffic tie-up had me stalled in front of the riding academy, and on impulse I parked the car and walked into the place. There were a number of costumed riders about, some taking the jumps, others doing flat riding. When I stepped through the door, however, my eyes were drawn to the beautiful high-vaulted ceiling, and I said to myself, "This is no residential site, and it's no riding academy. It is a television studio."

I went over to a telephone booth near the entrance, put in my nickel, and called the broker. "What price did you say you wanted for the riding academy?"

"Seven hundred and twenty thousand, twenty percent in cash."

"I'll take it."

As soon as the contract for the "studios" was signed, we wrote letters offering the property to CBS, NBC, and every other possible user of a TV studio. We promptly received return letters graciously acknowledging our kind offer, but nobody had any use for a television studio. That put Webb & Knapp in the hay-burner business. We bought 150 horses for rental purposes. We bought a lot of oats, we sold a lot of manure, but we did not sell very many rides, and at the end of each month we showed a net loss for our efforts. After a few years of this, and a certain amount of unhappiness on the part of the other members of the syndicate we had set up to buy the property, I was ready to admit that it was a mistake. We were too far ahead of the times.

I was ready to give up and call Fred Ecker of Metropolitan Life who had the mortgage, and say, "When do you want the deed delivered?" when the phone rang.

A twangy, upstate Yankee voice said, "This is E. J. Noble, radio man." I thought it was a radio repairman calling until he went on, "That barn of yours . . ."

"What barn?"

"You know, that thing on the West Side."

"Do you mean our riding academy?"

"I guess that's it. If you will take a big enough loss, we'll take it off your hands."

I then realized that the Noble who was speaking, and whom I later got to know pretty well, was the owner of Life Savers Corp. and of the radio network that became ABC. Noble was a brilliant man with a great sense of humor, but he was also one of the chintziest men I have ever known. If he had been just a little more astute, he would have sent some broker with his heels worn down and the cuffs off his pants in shreds, and they would have gotten the property at a bargain rate. But when Noble came on the line himself talking like a second-hand rug dealer, I knew that my hour had come: television was upon us. After due dickering I sold him the riding academy for $1,160,-000. Three weeks later I sold one of the now equally valuable adjoining buildings for $120,000. That riding academy and adjacent buildings became the cornerstone of ABC's television arm and an important factor in their early success, because it gave them an excellent production capacity.

All around us the promise and opportunity Webb & Knapp had seen in the country before and during the war was now coming to fruition. Realizing this, we kept stocking up on new properties the way a retailer stocks up for Christmas. We became known as an outfit that had money or could find it and was not afraid to buy big. More and more brokers and principals took to bringing their best projects to us first, and I encouraged all comers. I never refused a phone call from a caller with a deal in hand. It was a policy that paid off.

For example, in 1947, Smitty Davis, a well-known Western broker, a highly successful buyer and seller of newspapers, magazines, and radio and television stations, walked into my office. Davis was a shrewd but jovial man who liked to make a splash and live it up. Eventually a prime occupational hazard, liquor, got the best of him, and he went all the way down the drain with it. His wife, whom he had taught to live on a rather grand scale, became a telephone operator, and he lost his beautiful homes throughout the country. But at his prime he was a freewheeling go-getter, and he had a fascinating proposition. He could deliver twelve thousand acres in the Santa Monica Mountains. This was the largest tract of undeveloped land within the extensive limits of the city of Los Angeles. With the fantastic building boom under way there, this property was bound to zoom in value. He invited me out to meet his friends Robert L. Smith, the publisher, and Manchester Bodie, the editor, of *The Los Angeles Daily News;* they controlled the property. Some years later Bob Smith also fell upon hard times, when he lost his paper through financial difficulties. There were no jobs open to him until I made him head of Roosevelt Field, where he worked for the last ten years of his life.

I flew out to the coast, and we drove out to the site, which extended all the way from Sunset Boulevard to the San Fernando Valley. Rising from sea level to a 1,900-foot elevation, the property encompassed several major canyons and part of Mulholland Drive. Standing on top of the highest peak, I could look one way and see downtown Los Angeles, as there was no smog that day. Looking out to sea, I could see Catalina Island, and to the other side lay the San Fernando Valley. My hosts said they could put this tract together for two hundred dollars an acre or 2.4 million dollars. I bought it, reserving a spot on the highest peak for myself.

Five years after our purchase of Mountain Park, we would buy an even greater tract of land, Indian Trail Ranch, in Florida. This great holding, lying eight miles west of the Palm Beach airport, covered sixty-three thousand acres. We bought control of the property at twenty-two dollars an acre. Not too long after, United Aircraft built a plant nearby. This raised the value of the land dramatically. We sold out at ninety dollars an acre. By the mid-1950's we had also sold out Mountain Park to Lazard Freres for eight million dollars.

Both the above properties have since greatly increased in value. Lazard Freres, in time, will gain four or five times what they paid us for Mountain Park. The Indian Trail properties may now be worth three hundred dollars an acre, but what we sold the properties for were good prices at the time and followed the Webb & Knapp pattern. We could not hold all our properties, because we would need the money to meet our tremendous commitments in yet another new field.

This new field was construction, which I moved into gradually and with no inkling of what a grand and passionate obsession it would eventually become.

Our first major construction project, 1407 Broadway, in spite of a first and most disturbing crisis, was phenomenally successful. At the time we bought into it, 1407 Broadway was a vacant, partly excavated lot. The original property and building became available when the two spinster, eccentric old Wendel sisters died. The property was sold to Louis W. Abrons, a successful builder and real-estate dealer who, back in the old days, when I was an associate of Leonard Gans, had offices in the same building as we did at 285 Madison Avenue. Abrons later sold his firm at the peak of both real-estate and stock markets to head a company publicly underwritten by Lehman Brothers called General Realty and Utilities Corporation. They raised some thirty-five or forty million dollars of paid-in capital and went about the business of acquiring, developing, and financing real estate and were in the second-mortgage market. Abrons in the early 1940's bought the Wendel property on behalf of a private syndicate. By the time the war came, this group had demolished the building and partially excavated the lot, but wartime shortages and controls put a stop to any further work. There the hole stayed until a shrewd broker named Sam Hirsch put his imagination and energy to work on it.

To explain what happened next, I must describe something about two major and related industries, the textile and garment industries in New York. The sales and administrative offices of most of the textile industry then located at Worth Street, which is just north of the Wall Street financial district but south of Greenwich Village and of Canal Street. The garment industry, centered between Thirty-fifth and Fortieth streets near Seventh Avenue, were the principal customers of the textile manufacturers. A continual seller's market could be maintained, because the industry was dominated by a small group of family-owned mills down South. Those mills that weren't family-owned were controlled by managers who were their friends. It was a close-knit social setup, both Yankee and southern. The members of these concerns had their offices and their own private club and dining rooms down at Worth Street. Some of those buildings, with their iron fronts and beautiful grillwork, are still there. On the inside they have some of the finest of paneling, wood-joiner work, fireplaces, traditional paintings, and period furnishings to be found in the whole city. These old-line textile people, long settled in a social and economic milieu pleasantly reminiscent of the 1800's, understandably were unwilling to move uptown and become modern. Notwithstanding this reluctance, a new movement had been getting under way in the industry. Many technically antiquated companies were backed to the wall and new groups of investors were taking control of them. Other investors were starting up completely new concerns. The old order, under assault, would obviously have to adapt by moving closer and becoming more responsive to its market—the garment industry. That is why Hirsch and others felt that the textile industry might be ripe for a mass move uptown.

The project remained in limbo, however, until 1948, when Hirsch called and said he'd like to see me. He showed up with the plans for a new building at 1407 Broadway and a list of tenants who had indicated by letters of intent or otherwise that they would be interested in coming in. Burlington Mills, United Merchants & Manufacturers, Springs Mills, and a great many others had tentatively signed. Abrons, who owned the site, wanted to get out, and was asking for 4.5 million dollars, or roughly one hundred dollars a square foot, which I thought was very inexpensive. Hirsch was only a broker, however, and what he needed was firm evidence of financial backing in order to convince possible tenants and long-term lenders that the project would go ahead. If he could get equity financing, it would in turn produce the primary mortgage financing. There seemed very little doubt that the project could be brought off—if we primed it with equity money. I asked him what he needed.

"I need a million dollars."

"Will a letter agreeing to put a million dollars on presentation of the papers do the trick?"

"It will."

I called in my secretary, and I wrote Hirsch a letter of commitment for a million dollars. In exchange he would do the work, take commissions, and get a twenty-five-percent piece of the deal. Of course, I didn't have one million in cash; Webb & Knapp's cash balance was under $400,000, but money was something I could always raise.

Later Hirsch asked if I'd mind whether somebody else came in on the deal. I asked who. "Bill Rosenwald wants to come in. He is one of the Rosenwalds of the Sears Roebuck fortune. His attorneys and some others would join, too."

I said that would be all right, and we had cut ourselves back to fifty percent. Later a second group, including Charles Meyer, the building contractor, one of the outstanding steel engineers in the country, joined us. Meyer's contracting firm, J. H. Taylor Construction, would do the building. The group headed by the Meyer family included some members of the Kuhn, Loeb firm and other relatives. By the time we got through with these additions, Webb & Knapp was down to twenty-five-percent participation, and the project went ahead. However, as the building came closer and closer to completion and final renting, I found that my relationship with some of the others was becoming unworkable. They were contentious and kept trying to block or alter my own leasing and selling arrangements. I decided the best thing to do was sell my share of the property or buy my way out of the arrangement, and I so informed my syndicate partners. Since it was an obviously sound project, I expected them to buy me out. I could use the funds elsewhere.

They made an absurd proposal: they offered to buy Webb &

Knapp's quarter interest for $500,000, but said if we wanted to buy them out, it would cost us two million dollars for each one of their quarter-shares. Since there were three groups involved, this meant they wanted six million dollars for their quarter-shares but they would buy us out at only $500,000—twenty-five percent of what they'd sell to us for.

I asked "Are you sure you mean that?"

"That's exactly what we mean."

Then I said, "I'd like to have a meeting of the entire partnership so that we can resolve this."

Obviously, some of my more predatory Syndicate partners reasoned I was in a squeeze with other projects and needed the money badly. They thought they could take us. They were very prompt about holding that meeting. Our gathering of the clan took place at the law offices of Stroock & Stroock & Lavan on lower Broadway. At this conference I found my friends and their legal brains sitting around looking expectant but not saying much. With their eyes agleam, they looked like wolves waiting for the lamb to trot in and lie down so they could gobble him up. I was the officially designated lamb, and to get the meeting under way I asked them to repeat their proposal.

"Well," they said, "we'll pay you $500,000 for your quarter-share. We will sell our quarter-shares to you at two million dollars a quarter-share."

I sat back in my chair, looked around the group for a while, and waited. They sat watching. I gave the top of the table a slap and said, "O.K., you've sold out. I'll take it."

For a moment there you could have heard the carpet beetles munching on Stroock & Stroock & Lavan's rugs; my taking up their challenge was the last thing my "partners" expected. While they were still stunned, I pointed a hand at the lawyers and said, "Go ahead, draw the papers now."

They said, "We want a deposit of a million dollars."

"Make it $500,000." They agreed to that because they figured I couldn't raise the money. This way they would get $500,000, or my stock in the venture, as collateral security for my guarantee—and they would be getting this for nothing. They were almost right, too, but I signed up.

Now I had the property but I just didn't know how to handle it, because all other Webb & Knapp projects had already been syndicated and resyndicated, so there just was no further cash on tap. A few weeks later, the day set for the closing, I still didn't have the money. I went to the meeting at ten o'clock, and my friends were there, waiting. I asked for an extension of time, which is a courtesy one normally gets automatically, but they refused it to me, so I put on my hat, saying, "I have all day to close; rest easily boys," and walked out the door.

The gun was at my head, and the timer to set it off had started ticking. I had already tried every conventional and a number of quite unconventional methods of finding capital, all with no success. Now it was time for the most direct approach conceivable. I went over to the Chase Bank, without an appointment, and walked into David Rockefeller's office. Partly because I had been of service to the Rockefellers as a consultant, but largely because he is a gentleman, David Rockefeller immediately saw me. I said, "David, I want to borrow six million dollars, and here's what I want to do with it and why it's a good deal. . . ." I explained 1407 Broadway.

Rockefeller thought the idea sounded fine. He asked me to take it up with John Scully, and if he thought it was a good safe thing for the bank, Chase would go along with us.

I went over to John Scully, Vice-president in charge of real estate, and Scully looked and listened and said, "I think this is O.K., Bill." He picked up the phone and called Rockefeller to give the loan his blessing. I had explained to Rockefeller that I needed the money that day. From my side of the table I heard Scully say, "All right I'll do that," and he ordered me a check for six million dollars. It takes a little while, even for the Chase, to handcraft a six-million-dollar check, but now the ticking that had been sounding in my head since ten o'clock had stilled. As for the men waiting in a Broadway back room for my money, they could sit. I made a few phone calls on other business, then at five o'clock in the afternoon went over to that closing. Stepping into the room, I walked silently up to the table. I reached into my coat pocket, let my check for six million dollars waft softly down to the table top, and said, "Gentlemen, drop your stock on the table."

The men who had been trying to pulverize us, men who didn't need to make their money that way but could not resist the temptation to do so, received an excellent return for their efforts: I met their price; they more than quadrupled their original investment. But they and my other syndicate partners who had gone along with this one-sided bargaining session now had to sit back and watch us turn 1407 Broadway into the most lucrative real-estate venture in New York. My first job was to pay off the Chase, and we did this, but over a period of many months we brought in so many tenants and we so fractionalized and sold off the various aspects of 1407 that we ended up, depending on how you count these things, with up to thirteen million over and above the six million dollars paid back to the Chase. We sold the lease and later leased it back. We sold the fee and later leased it back. Then there were an outer lease, an inner lease, and various sandwich leases which I shall explain elsewhere. Meanwhile, the building kept filling with tenants. This is what happens with a bold project, where, in the first instance, you make some sacrifices to get your first key tenants. Then, because you have a fine building, and because it catches on, rents go from a discount to a premium in value. The early leases, as they mature or as tenants decide to expand in a successful building, later take on yet another increment in value, and 1407 today may be worth thirty million dollars. Inflation, like a rising tide, comes to all ships, but 1407's value rise was based on concept and execution. Our success at 1407 later led us to another fine venture, 112 West Thirty-fourth Street, but by that time Webb & Knapp would be a quite different kind of company.

In 1948, when the 1407 Broadway project started, we were a partnership, albeit a fatter partnership, than my partners had returned to after the war. Our total assets in 1945 were 6.6 million dollars; by 1948 they were twenty-five million. Our net worth was 5.6 million dollars, and gross income from operating properties was 3.2 million. Almost everything we owned, with the exception of the Club Monte Carlo, was making money, and the Monte Carlo situation was about to change.

The Monte Carlo was one of the finest nightclubs in town. I had a policy of changing the decor every season, at great expense. Both the food and service were excellent. We had two orchestras and a regular clientele, but costs were high and nightclubbing as a way of life was beginning to fade, not only for many New Yorkers, but for me. I still had my corner table but was finding it more of a blight than a pleasure. At every visit a continuous procession not only of friends and acquaintances but also of total strangers (and occasional diners, complaining that their steak was too rare or too well done) was in perpetual parade around our table. Marion got so she hated the place because it was impossible to have a quiet, uninterrupted meal. I was coming to a juncture in life where a part-time office and unofficial court in a nightclub was neither so much fun nor fitting. Yet, though it had begun to lose money, I would not think of closing the club down because of pride in the place and also because of a sense of loyalty to our employees. Then, in June, 1948, we were threatened with a strike by the bartenders' union. At first I didn't believe our people would strike; our relations were excellent. And because of their pay and their tips, ours were probably the richest bartenders in town. I decided that if our men did strike, I could only answer by striking our colors—in a very special way.

At five o'clock on a Wednesday afternoon, when we got word that the bartenders were indeed going out, I went down to the club. From there I called the union leadership and asked permission to talk to the men. Under the law I could not address my employees without the union's approval, and they asked what I wanted to say. I replied that I wanted to praise the union and its leaders.

"You want to tell them about us?"

Since they were a little incredulous, though inclined to be pleased, I said, "That's right," feeling very much like Marc Antony. They agreed to an oration, and the union leaders and our bartenders and all our other employees on the premises came into the side dining room, where I had once signed over the East Side slaughterhouses to the UN. I gave a short speech:

"The first thing I want to tell you is, we are believers in unions, in organized labor, and in the right to strike. Everything you are doing is right, and your leaders are right. They have told you to strike because we don't pay you enough. All of this is a product of American society, all of this is part of democracy. It is also a matter of democratic privilege that the employer has the right to try to run in the face of the strike. He also has the right to lock out the strikers, which is the opposite from the right to strike, but we wouldn't do a thing like that.

Now, with all deference to your union leaders, who figure you men can get more money by striking for it, we are not going to pay—because we can't afford to. If we can't afford to pay, under the democratic capitalistic system, we have to go out of business. We said we wouldn't lock you out, but we won't stand for a strike, and we won't run any scabs. So you don't have to worry about the strike anymore or parading around outside. This place is now closed and will never open again.

"But let's all have a glorious finish. Tonight is yours. You waiters, busboys, chefs, bartenders, everybody. We will let no outsiders in. You can invite your wives, your girl friends. The hat-check girls can ask their boyfriends. The music will play until four in the morning. Anything you want to eat or drink is on the house."

They had the wildest night that's ever been had in any nightclub. None of the public was allowed, and we closed at five or six the next morning. We closed for good, in a blaze of glory, and we got publicity all over the world for that, so much so that when Marion and I took our first long trip to Europe that summer, when we went to the great nightclubs on the Continent we were greeted like royalty at a restoration. The European nightclub owners, captains, and waiters alike thought it the greatest thing in the world for a man to close a place as I did. When we had left for Europe, our own captains and waiters had come down to the boat begging us to reopen the club, but I said no. I'm glad I experienced running the Monte Carlo, but I feel about it the way a man does with eight daughters: he wouldn't take a million for one of them or give two cents for an additional one.

We had a vacation of at least six weeks. It was my first real break from business since the start of the war. We went to Paris, naturally, and then traveled about the countryside sampling three-star restaurants, tasting the air, and testing the wines of the Loire and other districts. I had developed an interest in wines, which this trip served to increase. Eventually I became a Chevalier de Tastevin as well as master of what is possibly the best wine cellar (for burgundies) in America. My personal attitude on wining is to let the future generations worry about their own top vintages. We owe it to ourselves to drink our fair share of the best available to us. I enjoy the best vintage possible at every meal now, as I did on that special trip in 1948.

After weeks of luxurious lazing by the sea and a weight gain of ten pounds, I came back to New York, sated with rest and full of ideas. I was eager for new challenges—and found them waiting.

My partners met with me and said they had decided to liquidate the business. They wished to sell off our assets, pocket our cash, and go our separate, coupon-clipping ways.

• 8 • Good-bye, Partners; Hello, World (1948–1952)

AT FIRST I was upset by my partners' decision to liquidate Webb & Knapp. For one thing, I liked my partners and enjoyed working with them. Also, we had a team of experienced employees who were used to my ways and worked at my pace. Outright liquidation of the firm would both dissipate its momentum in the marketplace and break up our work force. Besides, since the appreciation in value of many of our properties was just becoming evident, their forced sale would be like sending green peaches to market; we would have to sell at a discount.

Gould, however, had become ill with tuberculosis and wanted to get out of business altogether. Sears, who was independently wealthy, had no great ambitions or desires in real estate; he was more corporate-oriented. Then, too, both men, though equal partners with me, must at times have felt all the frustrations of passengers in a fast-moving vehicle they could not control. Like the rear men on a bobsled, they were appreciated for the extra weight and lean they provided, but since ninety percent of Webb & Knapp's business was interconnected projects of mine, they were discouraged from fiddling with the controls. Finally, by temperament my partners were investment managers (Webb & Knapp's original business had been the management of properties) rather than investor-speculators. Though highly appreciative of our gains, they felt Webb & Knapp should assume a more conservative and more comfortable role. I, on the other hand, was bent on a new program of speculative growth. We all knew that eventually I would win out, which, in part, is why they decided to get out. But once all this was clear, I began to see in their departure not so much potential trouble as a fantastic opportunity. I would buy them out and go on from there!

I bought my partners out for over five million dollars. To raise this money, Webb & Knapp went on a selling spree, and I went one million dollars into debt. The whole thing took little more than a year, and the company kept growing throughout.

Many of our activities during this period, such as the sale of the riding academy to the ABC network for television studios, were propositions whose time happened to have come. Others, such as our sale of the Club Monte Carlo property to Astor for 1.26 million dollars and the sale of 383 Madison Avenue, which housed Webb & Knapp headquarters, to Metropolitan Life for seven million, were part and parcel of the liquidation effort needed to pay off my partners.

From the very moment I decided to buy out my partners, I determined not to allow this situation to create a hiatus in Webb & Knapp activity. I kept the company moving at an even faster pace in order to pay off the partners and also to recoup the costs of this purchase through a series of bigger and better ventures. Thus, between September, 1948, and November, 1949, at which point my partners were out of the business, Webb & Knapp sold 22.5 million dollars of real estate, plus 2.7 million dollars of joint-venture properties and over 3 million dollars in securities for a total of more than 28 million dollars. Most of this money went to pay off mortgages. The bulk of the remainder was immediately reinvested. For instance, in order to sell our headquarters building to Metropolitan Life, I had to put 3 million dollars into modernizing and air-conditioning the property. The continuous demands on Webb & Knapp for cash for such investments and for new purchases sometimes led to difficulties. At a critical moment in the maneuvers necessary to arrange buying out of my partners, it was Marion who helped me keep the deal viable. With time running out on our original arrangement, I had not yet been able to raise the agreed-on cash. After consultation, my partners informed me that for $250,000 beyond the sales price they would give me a thirty-day extension. If I could wrap things up in that time, they would not go ahead with a liquidation. If I could not raise the necessary cash, they would liquidate, and I would be penalized the $250,000. Marion urged me to go ahead with the deal and offered $250,000 of her own money.

As it turned out, I did not need Marion's offering. The Wall Street firm of Lazard Freres had offered to provide me with three

million dollars in cash in exchange for two-thirds of the shares of
Webb & Knapp, with my buying back these shares in six months'
time at a one million-dollar profit to Lazard Freres. I decided to
accept this high-cost arrangement, and while visiting Charlie Stewart
at Bankers Trust, told him of the agreement. He said, "That seems
a little steep. . . . Maybe we can manage something a little more
reasonable." From Stewart, Fred Ecker of Metropolitan Life, and
Jim Lee of the Central Savings Bank I was able to arrange a great
series of sales, leasebacks, and loans by which my partners received
their respective monies, as well as the liquor left over from the Club
Monte Carlo, and bowed out of the real-estate business.

Webb & Knapp's next major project was the creation of 112
West Thirty-fourth Street, which stands midway in a long and busy
block between Sixth and Seventh avenues. More important, it lies
between Macy's on Thirty-fourth Street and Gimbels on Thirty-
third. I began assembling this property lot by lot in 1942. It was one
key property which I was careful not to discard during the sell-offs
I made to raise the cash to buy out my partners. One particularly
difficult maneuver in our getting the property together involved takeover of a city-owned firehouse on Thirty-third Street. The city was
magnificently indifferent to a sale of the property until, through
extensive persuasion among local politicos and functionaries, and at
a cost of $375,000, I arranged a swap. For $375,000 we built a new,
much larger, more efficient, and better located firehouse on West
Thirty-first Street. Into this new station the city moved the men and
equipment from their old station and from another station on Twenty-
ninth Street. As a result of the swap, we got what we wanted—a
key property. The city got a better firehouse (with a recreation
room and solarium for the fire fighters), as well as the possibility of
income from the sale of the Twenty-ninth Street firehouse. Everyone
ended up better off than they started.

We eventually acquired 74,270 square feet of property between
Thirty-fourth and Thirty-third streets, 36,340 square feet of this land
now being in one piece. I always expected we would sell the property
to some department-store group, but a series of discussions with
Sam Hirsch persuaded me to try something else.

To understand what we did, one has to realize that New York City, where you can buy anything, is really a giant, Oriental bazaar in concrete disguise. It is the greatest such bazaar in the history of man, and, true to the type, it is a marketplace where birds of a feather and merchants of a type flock together—the money lenders and speculators in one section downtown; publishing, TV, and advertising men in midtown; and the cloth merchants in between. Nowhere is this segregation more evident than in the garment district. Textiles, for example, are at 1407 Broadway. Men's clothing, women's coats, and women's dresses are nearby. If buyers from department stores in Iowa, Georgia, or Colorado wish to buy $14.95 dresses, they can find ninety percent of the industry that makes such dresses in or near one building. The $25–$30 dresses will be similarly located near each other. The garment district, to a store buyer, is the equivalent of a blocks-long counter display, with the goods spread out in regular, if overlapping, categories.

At that time, the children's-wear industry, though concentrated near one or two buildings, was somewhat scattered. Hirsch felt it might be susceptible to a mass relocation, and I decided to make this new location 112 West Thirty-fourth Street. We began lining up clients, and met with almost instant success. In fact, every time we turned around, we had to redesign the building to make it bigger. We eventually changed the plans five times, to wind up with the biggest and tallest building that city regulations would permit.

At a time when retail space on West Thirty-fourth Street was worth two thousand dollars per running front-foot in annual rent, I took a tremendous amount of this space off the market to give our building a luxurious, seventy-five-foot-wide lobby. Then we cut into the second floor to permit this lobby a fine, flared ceiling, and lined the walls with matched Siena marble. This imposing entrance-way set us back at least $150,000 per year in rents we might otherwise have received. Local realtors and retailers walking by the building shook their heads in disbelief at this waste of salable space, but only because they would not raise their eyes above ground level. I recognized that we could afford to lose ground income if, by giving tenants a prestige building, we could ask for rents fifty percent greater than those in the immediate vicinity. This is what we did, and by losing $150,000 in ground rent we gained at least $400,000 a year in office rentals—and had a fine building. Based on its current leases, that building is now worth some fifty million dollars.

Since retailing is so important on Thirty-fourth Street, we did devote the remainder of our ground area to store space, but with a very special kind of store. We designed a passageway for pedestrians between Thirty-third and Thirty-fourth streets, which in that area means between Macy's and Gimbels. Pedestrian traffic tends to be drawn to, and generated by, two or more well-placed major stores in much the way electricity is generated and made to flow between the opposing poles of a dynamo. Once we opened up a passageway between Macy's and Gimbels, pedestrians immediately flowed to and through it by the hundreds per hour. In due course, in Roosevelt Field, the prototype of the American shopping center, in Denver and in Montreal, as well as in other cities, we would make use of this principle of human physics, but Thirty-fourth Street was the first application.

The tenant we sought for this ground-floor property was F. W. Woolworth Co., who, when I pointed out that getting a store between Macy's and Gimbels was like getting a license to print money, were immediately interested. The Woolworth negotiators, however, balked at the minimum guarantee I was asking for the lease.

I said, "We seem to have more confidence in the neighborhood and in you than you do yourselves. . . . I'll tell you what: the way to make sure you pay a fair rent is to let you have the space rent-free for five years. Whatever volume of business you do in that period will establish what you can afford to pay."

Their eyes lit up at this until I added, "However, since you don't want to do any gambling and it is we who will carry all the risk, we're entitled to have a share of your profit." When they asked what I meant, I replied that, whereas in most percentage-of-volume deals Woolworth's gave five percent, in this case we would want eight percent, and whatever this averaged out to over five years would be minimum rent. They demurred at first, but what I offered was really a no-risk arrangement. They knew business would be good in that store and finally agreed. As a result, we wound up with almost twice as much profit as we would have had from the original guarantee, which is as it should be. Perhaps it's only appropriate that Woolworth's was penny-wise and pound-foolish.

What I had long needed at Webb & Knapp was an architect who could help me put into concrete form some of the many ideas I was developing. It was in 1948 that I found my man, thanks to some help from Nelson Rockefeller.

At that time the second Rockefeller son handled many of the Rockefeller brothers' affairs. As a consultant, I was seeing him regularly, sometimes as often as three times a week. He was then, among other things, revitalizing the Museum of Modern Art, and in his office one day I said, "Nelson, don't you think it is about time that the modern Medicis began hiring the modern Michelangelos and Da Vincis? I plan to go into a great building program on a national scale, and I'd like to put together an architectural staff that could provide new thinking." I told Rockefeller about the kinds of construction and projects we had in mind, then said, "You are interested in modern art and in architecture; can you help?"

Rockefeller said that he could. He mentioned a man on the museum staff named Dick Abbott who had suffered some debilities from tuberculosis. Because of his health, it would be wise for him to ease out of museum work. Rockefeller stressed how knowledgeable Abbott was and how useful he could be in finding my architectural staff.

So Abbott came to us for a year as a talent scout to interview architects. I specified that the man was not to be the scion of a wealthy family, because in architecture they too often turn out to be dilettantes. Neither did I want him to be a long-time hack in the back of somebody's office, with his spirit already broken. Therefore I wanted a young man over twenty-five but under thirty-five years old, and of course he must show signs of talent and creativity. Abbott interviewed a dozen or more young men, some of whom were very fine, but none of them was the man I wanted, until he brought along Ieo Ming Pei, a professor at the Graduate School of Design at Harvard. (The architect Philip Johnson says he is the man who found Pei for us. It may be. Perhaps Johnson did recommend Pei to Abbott, but the first time I met Pei was through Abbott in 1948.)

Pei comes from a fine Chinese family. His father, a brilliant financier, had been a minister in the Chinese Nationalist government and had at times been associated with C. V. Starr, a millionaire insurance man in the Orient. Pei had never built anything, but when he and his charming wife, Elaine, came down for a visit, I could see from his sketches that he was truly talented. I also found him obviously intelligent and very imaginative, as well as a bon vivant and knowledgeable gourmet. It was a case of instant recognition and liking. I wanted him to join with us. Pei was apprehensive about becoming a captive architect, which might lose him a certain degree of professional freedom. He was also torn between returning to China and remaining here as a teacher, but I set to work and soon persuaded him that the kinds of things we were going to do would be so different and so much better than anyone else in the country was doing that as an architect he would not resist the challenge. Helping me, though I did not know it then, was some advice Pei's father had once given him: that the essence of good architecture was the ability not only to conceive of great buildings but also to tie them effectively to finances and economics. Part of Pei's interest in us was the opportunity we afforded to weld design to marketing factors. Through the extensive site planning and design for which he has since become famous, Pei and I made some notable architectural breakthroughs.

Pei's first job for us was to re-design our office headquarters at 383 Madison Avenue. I had taken Pei to see Ecker's office at Metropolitan Life, and getting there was half the fun; we had to pass acres of lesser offices to find Fred's, and I explained, "This is what I *don't* want. I don't want to be buried away in some inaccessible corner."

Pei had already noted that the great majority of visitors to Webb & Knapp came to see me and then went on to see someone else. His solution, therefore, was to start visitors off directly beside the place most of them wanted to go to—my office. Within the great open lobby and display area of the top floor of our building, he built a twenty-foot-diameter, wood-paneled, vertical cylinder, a headquarters within a headquarters—my office. On the roof above this self-encompassing cylinder we built a small penthouse dining room, which, in

view of the transactions closed there, proved possibly the most remunerative investment I ever made. Down below, alongside my office,
we laid out some open-air terraces with matched marble side walls
and shrubbery and statuary. We ended up with a unique headquarters
to which many prominent magazines devoted pages of pictures, all
very useful publicity for Webb & Knapp. Essentially, however, our
rebuilt headquarters was an office that worked for me, and that office
turret today dominates the whole of the twelfth floor at 383 Madison
Avenue as effectively as the lone turret of that famous Civil War
ironclad, the *Monitor*, once dominated its own deck and the water
for miles around.

Pei first came to us as an idea man, someone to put into visual
form the ideas I was generating, much in the same manner as Harrison had helped me to conceptualize "X City." Then we added a
staff and went beyond this phase. The first important outside job
that Pei did for us was a Gulf Oil office building in Atlanta, where,
learning fast, he persuaded Georgia marble producers to supply facing
material at very low cost as a form of advertisement for their product. This move was a prelude to some of the things we would do
for the aluminum and other industries.

Pei's next big job was Denver, which was a prizewinner too, and
from there we went from one architectural first to another. We
were a great team, each one teaching the other. One of the finest
things I ever did was to draw my friend Pei away from the halls
of academe and into the world of building.

Through ownership of the 333 outstanding shares of Webb &
Knapp stock, I was sole owner of the company. I was also deeply
in debt. But never, except for rare moments, have I ever had my
head very far above the financial water, and never have I let this
trouble me. We kept the company acquiring property and making
profits.

Our office force was still small enough so that after a quick
flight to Europe or a visit to Cuba with Fred Ecker and his wife,
Edith, I could bring back special gifts for everyone in the shop.
Because we worked long hours, everyone was aware and at least
partially familiar with most of the projects under way and their
actual or possible interconnections. We had a fine, tight ship that

was making excellent headway, but I was still dissatisfied. I wanted to do more, and decided to acquire superpower—American Superpower. American Superpower was an American Stock Exchange-registered company with which we merged and took over. That takeover provided the basis for some grand adventures.

If it hadn't been Superpower, it undoubtedly would have been some other company. We were ready for the move. Walter Mack, president of the Pepsi-Cola Co. and an investor with us in various ventures, brought Superpower to my attention as a potential corporate shell to shelter Webb & Knapp from taxes.

American Superpower, formed in 1923, was one of the fabulous and tenuous public-utilities holding companies (à la Insull) of the speculative twenties. Soon after it was organized it controlled a great number of utilities, such as Appalachian Power, Brazilian Power, Consolidated Ohio Edison, and Italian Superpower. The crash of 1929 had tumbled this empire. The Holding Company Act of 1933 forced the company to dispose of many of its assets at a loss, and in 1935 Bankers Trust Co. was brought in as consultant and trustee. Henceforth Superpower limped along with various bankers, lawyers, and a federal commissioner on its board. World War II gave it a boost by which it was able to clear up some of its back debts, but this was only a temporary palliative. By 1951 the company was still in trouble, and owed $114.50 on each of its sixty-three thousand preferred shares. The directors were looking for some way to liquidate the whole business to the satisfaction (or equal dissatisfaction) of the various owners and debtors. I showed up as a suitor, and soon thereafter we had a merger under way.

What we came up with was a reverse merger, American Superpower first changing its name to Webb & Knapp, Inc., a Delaware corporation, then absorbing my Webb & Knapp, Inc., a New York corporation. In exchange for my stock in the New York Webb & Knapp, with a net worth of forty-two million dollars, I received one million shares of junior preferred stock plus eleven and three-quarter million shares of common stock in the new Delaware Webb & Knapp.

The old Superpower's sixty-three thousand shares of senior preferred (now Webb & Knapp, Delaware, preferred) had a claim on 13.2 million dollars on the merged company's assets. Superpower's common shareholders, whose assets had previously had a negative value, now held stock in Webb & Knapp, Delaware, with an asset value of sixty cents per share. As a result of this transaction, I lost (on paper) ten million dollars, because, whereas previously I had as sole owner of Webb & Knapp a claim on forty-two-million dollars of net worth, I now had, as a result of dilution by merger, a claim on only thirty-two million. Nonetheless, I now had a publicly listed company. By sale of some of my stock I could clear my personal debts. The new company had a useful tax credit by which we could conserve and reinvest a greater share of our earnings. Then too, Superpower also provided ten million dollars in new working capital when we sold off its various stockholdings.

The merger was one more deal where all involved ended up better off than when they started. I now had a vehicle for my ambitions and started on phase two of my career.

Two

▪ Prologue

ON JOINING Webb & Knapp, I had, through some of my partners, been introduced to a segment of one of New York's many interlocking social and business circles. Drawing on these connections, plus others of my own, and greatly extending both, I became a national rather than a local business figure. In the process I also became aware of parts of the fabulous and shifting topography of American society.

Just as a man living in a mountain valley sees and is closely aware of only a few of the nearest great peaks above him, so, too, is it with a man comfortably settled at some modest elevation in our own society. If he begins to climb, however, he will soon notice from his new perspective that there are actually a great many peaks on all sides around him. What's more, once he has reached a high enough altitude, he will discover something else. He will see that many of the greatest peaks—interconnected by high ridges or narrow plateaus—are, at this new level, readily accessible each one to the other. The temptation to keep moving on this high ground can be irresistible.

Part Two of this book is an account of my travels and dealings among some of the denizens inhabiting the elevations and peaks of American society.

The importance to me of being on the heights was that in an hour I could achieve what previously would have taken a year or more of effort to perform. Otherwise I found the dwellers on the heights little different from their less advantageously placed brethren. There is a selection process which sees to it that a significant number of upper-level people are smarter, more aggressive, and in some ways more self-assured than the average, but a good many dwellers on the heights got there entirely by accident. They were born there. Others, like lowland birds blown far up a mountain by a sudden storm, found themselves at heights they never expected to reach but which they managed to adapt to. I did find numbers of tough, strong men who had worked their way up from the very bottom, but most had started out from a place within hailing distance of the height they reached.

Since it is generally pleasant to be rich, famous, powerful and influential, the great majority of people, who achieve some prominence have a profound interest in maintaining, if not improving, their position. To these ends they sometimes join with and at other times ruthlessly undercut their fellows. Since there are some quite precipitous slopes and occasional ice slides on the various routes to and about the heights, most people there are at core conservative and very much against anyone in any way disturbing their perch or their surroundings. I found it possible to join their ranks without discommoding or unsettling them, for one way to succeed is by aiding and supporting the position of others through new or ingenious ideas or projects. This usefulness to others is in large part the reason for my own success, though there were times when we quite consciously upset other groups for our own and quite often for their own good.

After taking over American Superpower, I launched Webb & Knapp across a grand range of great projects: from privately financed urban redevelopment to federally financed urban redevelopment and a whole spectrum of special opportunities. Because of the opportunistic nature of many of our ventures, it is difficult to say that at any given time Webb & Knapp went in such and such a direction. It was more a matter of my own urge to build, and the fact that one project led to another. Our first step toward private urban redevelopment, for instance, began in Denver in 1945 when we were still, even in our own eyes, almost purely buyers and sellers of property.

· 9 · The Town that Time Forgot

WITH TONGUE but partly in my cheek, I can say that I found Denver brick and left it soaring steel, concrete, and glass—with here and there a touch of marble.

When I first arrived there, Denver had no major building more than twelve stories high. Too spread out to be quaint and too ugly to be pleasant, the center of town was a relic of pre- and post-Civil War construction of the most depressing type. The various key business areas and the encroaching tenderloin district (the same people often owned sections of both) were difficult to distinguish one from the other. Most structures were fading five- and six-story brick affairs, often with cheap storefront façades built over the first story or two. Boosters told you Denver was a growing city, but the growth was in the suburbs. Denver, like so many other cities, was decentralizing so rapidly that its dry-rotted core had begun to fall in on itself.

We at Webb & Knapp reversed this centrifugal trend by creating some well-planned and badly needed building masses and open spaces in the core, which served to draw people and businesses once again to the center of town. As a result, Denver, which today boasts at least nine genuine skyscrapers, has a healthy city core that is much in use.

Very strictly speaking, the metamorphosis of Denver from a Cinderella city of brick and cinders into a genuine princess of the plains was not all our doing: others also built in Denver. But it was Webb & Knapp who saw the possibilities and led the way. We got there first to set the pace, and we set the standards for others to try to follow. In effect, we provided the first dose of intellectual and financial adrenalin to stir Denver out of its somewhat uneasy nineteenth-century slumbers into the present. Shaking this sleepy, self-satisfied town into reaching toward its potential as a city took many more years and many more millions of dollars than we first expected. There were times while we were in Denver when it seemed wise to take a quick profit and get out, but we never did this. I had made certain public promises to the city of Denver, and in the face of great difficulties, despite much public doubt and a good bit of pillorying by newspapers, we kept these promises—even though the majority of the well-established economic leaders in Denver did little or nothing to help this local development, in spite of the fact that their families had been living in and off the area for generations and, therefore, had most to gain from a renaissance of the town. In fact, it was the very hostility and resentment we met with that helped persuade me to see the job through. So, in a rather negative way, the local "leaders" did help the town and their townspeople to get ahead, by their active desire not to do so.

Locally, in terms of urban redevelopment, and regionally, in terms of the effects of well-placed seed money, our Denver project proved to be one of Webb & Knapp's most significant undertakings. Directly through our investments and construction and indirectly through the increased land values that drew other investors and new businesses to Denver, we created many thousands of new jobs. By putting millions into the area, we made some men rich. And as is the nature of things, we made even more people who were already rich even richer. Most important of all, however, at a crucial time we caught and quickened the pulse of an American city. For me *this* is the story of Denver, and for me that story began one day in March, 1945, when a wraith of a man in a wide-brimmed Western hat ghosted into my office to suggest a deal.

The man was B. B. Harding, a gaunt-faced Denver real-estate broker of sardonic humor and a likable if feisty disposition. A distant cousin of President Harding, B. B. originally hailed from Indiana. One of the Bs in his name was for a famous progenitor, Aaron Burr, and B. B. evidently took after his ancestor, for he was at least as prickly as Burr and sometimes behaved with the strange combination of desperation and indifference of a man living on borrowed time. In B. B.'s case the borrowed time, though on a favorable long-term lease, was real. As a young man he had contracted tuberculosis and had moved out to Denver in 1910 expecting to die, but proved either too mean or too curious about the world to die young. Aided by the good climate, he recovered, to go into insurance and real estate. With his independent, go-to-hell ways, Yankee humor, and acerbic personality, B. B. never entered into the fold of the local Denver satraps and the lowerarchy of their dependents and hangers-on. Instead, he ranged out at the edges of the herd, swinging in once in a while on a likely target, and over the years doing moderately well. He was involved in the land assemblage for the present-day Denver airport, for instance, and was active in Colorado Springs.

I had met B. B. casually once or twice before. He was in his sixties, with deep-sunken eyes and dark, mottled skin that clung to the bone. B. B. was a sight to frighten children and unready men; he looked like a messenger from some more desolate part of the afterworld, but if he was as lean as a mummy and twice as dry in the throat, he had imagination and aggressiveness, which I liked, and now he was here to propose a deal. Putting a map and various photographs of Denver on my desk, he pointed out a small city-block park called Court House Square. It was the site of the old Denver Court House, which, during the 1920's, had been torn down and rebuilt elsewhere. The plot had been on the market for years, with no active bidders since a California group offering $650,000 had been turned down sometime before World War II. B. B. had been talking with Denver's mayor, Benjamin Stapleton, and said we could probably get the property for $750,000.

From what B. B. could tell me and from what showed on the map and photographs, I could see that Court House Square was in the line of progress, possibly rapid progress. Changes in Denver, in my judgment, would inevitably move toward the square. The property was no longer in a prime location, but it had potential (depending upon what the town did) for the future. What the town did, of course, was the crux of the matter, and unfortunately Denver was so static that the center had not moved for forty years, nor had there been one significant new building in central Denver in at least thirty years. Nonetheless, I knew what was going on around the country, and more important, I also knew what would be going on in future. If local realtors couldn't or wouldn't see the growth getting under way around them, we could. From as far away as New York I could envision Court House Square as a choice property. Even the fact that nothing vital had happened to Denver real estate in forty years had its positive side: holding down the lid for such a long time meant that there was a demand waiting to be tapped. All we had to do was get into that town and *make* something happen. That afternoon I authorized B. B. Harding to make a $750,000 bid. This he went home to do, and shortly thereafter the fun began.

By the first part of May, with the Denver papers carrying banner headlines of Von Rundstedt's capture and of German surrenders in Italy, word that an "eastern" group had bid on Court House Square began to filter through from the back pages to the front. By May 5, 1945, with Allied forces taking Rangoon and U.S. troops fighting in Okinawa, an ordinance calling for sale of the square went before the city council, and word was out that the buyer was Webb & Knapp. The Denver garden clubs, I think, were among the first publicly to denounce the proposed sale, but similar groups of righteous citizens soon banded together in opposition to any and all intrusions by foreigners from the east.

In spite of these preliminary protests, the council on May 22 passed the necessary legislation for a sale. On May 23 Webb & Knapp announced a survey to determine what kind of top retail stores might be interested in building in the area. We soon had to stop this sort of thing. The issue of Court House Square was beginning to affect some of the local citizens in much the way General Custer's golden locks and famous promenade to the Big Horn had once affected the Indians to the north. New and apparently well-organized and financed protest groups kept popping out to decry the impending "sellout." A self-proclaimed protective taxpayers' association sprang forward to ask for an injunction against the sale, and at the same time a syndicate of local realtors, who had managed to ignore Court House Square for twenty years, suddenly offered a counterbid of $765,000. At about this point, like the beleaguered General Custer at the Big Horn, I was beginning to wonder where all the Indians were coming from, and my ally, Mayor Stapleton, at whom most of the arrows were directed, probably felt the same. In any event, the mayor had to back away from our previously agreed-on sale and to call for separate, sealed bids. I then made a second offer, and on June 7, when the bids were opened, we were top contenders, with a bid of $792,500 as opposed to the local offer of $777,700. As someone started to congratulate my representative, B. B. Harding, on our winning, one of the opposition lawyers jumped in to challenge our bid on a technicality. After a certain amount of bickering back and forth, our bid and a second on-the-spot bid of $805,000 by one of the leaders of a local group were rejected, and yet another series of sealed bids was called for. This next time we bid $818,600, as against the local group's $808,000; and so, once again, we won the contest—but not the prize, which continued to elude us.

The battle for Court House Square was to occupy us for four more years. Several separate local suits were filed to block our taking possession of the site. We had an excellent lawyer in Allen Hicks, a Denver man, and chain-smoking, bourbon-sipping B. B. Harding knew the inner workings of the town and state far better than he was generally given credit for. So we dug in and held on through these multiple assaults. What with appeals, recalls, and parades of witnesses and experts before the judges, we had to fight sixteen separate court actions. We lost some of these cases on the way up, but we always won the last appeal. It was not until December, 1948, that we cleared the list of all our court contenders. And it was not till close to the end of 1949, well over four years and $150,000 in court costs after our first bid, that we could take over our property.

In retrospect, I suspect that if certain people had let me know that they did not wish that property sold, and least of all sold to a Zeckendorf from New York, I just might have taken my marbles elsewhere. Instead, as we moved into the deal, I ran into back-door insinuations as well as accusations that we were crooked and that I was trying to buy the mayor, who was one of the most high-principled and honest men you could find in public office. This is what decided me then and there to make a fight of it. As early as August, 1945, partly on the reasoning that if Court House Square was a good buy, other properties near it were worth having, and partly to let the local boys know that we were in town for keeps, I bought two adjoining properties, the Kitteredge and Paramount Theatre buildings, on Glenarm Place near Sixteenth Street for $600,000. With control of these two buildings, I might be able to make a major assembly on that block. In 1946 we bought property on Welton Street, and I kept shopping around. Early in 1948, for instance, we picked up seven lots on Court Place across the street from Court House Square. With these purchases and our continuous search and testing out of the market, it soon became clear to everyone that we were in Denver in earnest and in a big way. It was we who were establishing the prices of the local real estate; and things were actually beginning to stir in that sleepy town.

Usually, since our activities moved real-estate prices well above their previously low levels, the stirrings about town were happy ones, but there were some disgruntled remarks about the change, and occasionally a sense of outrage. During these early days, B. B. Harding was "our man in Denver." He broke all stories of purchases and of possible purchases. He released all information about our evolving hopes and plans for setting up retail stores, hotels, offices, or some combination of these on our properties. B. B., now a news source, enjoyed this role immensely but did not let it in any way change his ways. If anything, he grew even more "independent," and this led to the Chamber of Commerce incident. By way of preface, I should note that Denver, up to this writing, has been able to maintain something that is increasingly rare in American cities: it is a two-newspaper city with quite avid competition between the morning *Rocky Mountain News* and the afternoon *Denver Post*. Either by the accidents of timing or of B. B. Harding's not always predictable caprice, the *Post* had been picking up a number of stories ahead of *The Rocky Mountain News*. One of the *News* editors therefore sent a reporter down to B. B. Harding's office to lodge an informal complaint and ask for a better break on news leads.

As I understand it, B. B., having enjoyed a good lunch and a couple of cocktails, sat with his feet on his desk as the reporter made his comments and request. Then, carried away by his own sense of drama, B. B., leaning far back in his seat, pointed a bony, cigarette-stained hand at the door and announced, "Why, if your editor was to crawl across that threshold . . . on his hands and knees . I still wouldn't give him a news break."

The reporter, unaccustomed in this age of public relations and concern with "image" to the histrionics of the old frontier, was taken aback. Searching for some proper rebuttal, he darkly mentioned that the Denver Chamber of Commerce would certainly be interested to learn that one of its businessmen felt that way. But this was like spurting gasoline at an already sputtering lighter. An inflamed B. B. Harding, feet on floor now, and leaning far forward on his desk, began to roar out his highly personal and colorful opinions of the Denver Chamber of Commerce as a whole and of its more august members in particular. He wound up with a brief phrase, beloved of presidents and mule skinners alike, to describe the pedigree of these gentlemen. The reporter, who had come in for a story, was smart enough to know when he had one. The next day *The Rocky Mountain News* carried a special feature bearing an only partially edited selection of B. B.'s comments and opinions of the Chamber.

Naturally there was an uproar in certain circles. I decided I had better fly out to Denver to soothe those hurt feelings with soft words. I assured the honorable members of the Chamber that B. B.'s opinions were strictly his own and that I personally had no information about any of them and therefore had no basis for such unfriendly comments. Moreover, I told them, it was pretty obvious I felt Denver was a wonderful place with a great future, as witness our investments in the city and our great plans for its future.

It was during this and a great many subsequent trips to Denver that I got to know something of the town and its inner workings, which were much influenced by its location and early history.

Denver is situated on a mile-high plain at the edge of the Rockies. With the main mountain passes and railroad routes well to the north and south of it, the town flourished after building its own railroad and linking it to other areas and systems. Because of its geographically central location in sparsely settled country, it came to exercise a modest sovereignty over its own state and nearby segments of adjoining states. Gold, silver, and mineral wealth from the Rockies were important, especially in the early days. Like Tucson, Denver became a supply point for a ring of satellite mining camps and towns during the hyperactive days of the 1870's and 1880's. It was to Denver that silver-rich Horace Tabor went to build his famous opera house. By then the handsomely furnished Windsor Hotel, financed by English money, was already delighting local and visiting nabobs and their ladies, with refreshments at its famous Silver Dollar Bar for the men, and gala affairs for ladies in its fabulous ballroom, with a dance floor suspended from the ceiling by cables to permit gracefully floating waltzes. Farther uptown, the Palace Hotel, with its grand, open lobby, also catered to the new-rich carriage trade. Denver, though still a raw town, even by Western standards, was acquiring patina with all the speed and fervor of a modern-day suburbanite antiquing her furniture. When the manager of the Brown Palace Hotel came up to complain about a party that the newly rich Pegleg Stratton was throwing, Pegleg did buy the hotel for one million dollars in order to fire the manager—but Pegleg was never "accepted" in Denver. Neither were Leadville Johnny, the silver-rich original owner of the hotel, nor his wife, the wonderful Unsinkable Molly Brown. Molly Brown might delight European and some portions of Eastern U.S. society, but she was much too yeasty for Denver's newly risen provincial society.

The Brown Palace Hotel is still in operation. In fact, till I put up the Denver Hilton, Brown's Hotel was the top hostelry in that town.

But Denver's days of flash and fame were brief. The era of gold and silver and guts and brass lasted only a few short decades, after which Denver, slipping fast into respectability, became famous mostly as a salubrious town for those stricken by tuberculosis.

The town was ever further quieted by the Depression of the 1930's, and it was not until World War II that it began to bloom again. With oil discoveries continuing in the continental United States, and with the development of the Williston basin to the north, Denver's central location and the spread of air travel made it a natural candidate to become one of the secondary oil capitals of the country. Tourism had also grown, and almost by seepage, as it were, Denver began to enjoy an invisible boom. I say "invisible" because for so many years, at least in the center of town, nothing showed. With general population rising and with various service industries moving into town and seeking space, the downtown properties were renting nicely, with little or no further investment needed by the owners. The return on investment on these properties, in terms of the original investments of many years ago, were excellent. Why, therefore, rock the boat? Better a tight and assuredly profitable real-estate market than an open and uncertain one. The logic was admirably conservative. It was also utterly unrealistic, for these gentlemen were overlooking some key points. For instance, they were consistently overlooking the even greater return on investment that imaginative new building efforts in Denver might develop. And with their eyes fixed on individual properties in Denver rather than on overall possibilities of the Denver area, they ignored all the many opportunities they were offered. If met imaginatively, these regional opportunities could propel Denver to a new position in the mainstream of American cities. If nothing were done, this growth and vitality would be transferred elsewhere. Only Denver's major property holders in conjunction with the local banks (which they controlled), could generate the capital and momentum to get Denver moving purposefully with the times, but this group was not about to act. This resistance to change could be easily ticked off to the Denver elite's liking of things as they were. But beneath this comfortable inertia there were ramifications, some of which were disquieting and bear unveiling.

Over the years we at Webb & Knapp have dealt with the official as well as non-official civic leaders of a great many cities. In almost every instance our presence has involved close dealings with the political and economic heart of a town, attracting support from those interested in what we could do for their city as well as what we could do for them. There was always resistance from those who might be upset by our plans. Denver was merely the first of such ventures for us, but a closer look at parts of the very special background of Denver will, I think, help later to explain something of other cities and perhaps about America as a whole, because as cities go, Denver, like a cartoonist's sketch, is a simplified and exaggerated but recognizable caricature of a type.

Some twenty local families in effect owned and sometimes directly, though more often indirectly, ran the town. Their management of the city's affairs was essentially passive and unobtrusive and kept most potentially rebellious voters, like the town itself, quiescent.

Welded together by time and social contact, where not knitted together by intermarriage, Denver's top families generally felt, thought, and acted (or more usually chose not to act) as a group.

What was most striking to an outsider about Denver's inner circle was its determined shunning of much of the outside world. Denver's local elite, socially inbred and (with individual exceptions) largely inward-looking, tended to share a highly self-conscious illusion of class and pretensions of place that in much of the East and parts of the West would seem ludicrous but which in segments of Denver were taken quite seriously.

A degree of small-town snobbishness and country-club-thinking is ever with us, but in an important capital city, where it reigned supreme, it was deleterious, for the underlying values evolved by the small group that controlled the town had a flavor of class-consciousness and restriction which was highly undemocratic.

In the light of all the above, it was inevitable, too, that a forceful move into the area by a Zeckendorf, a Jewish realtor from New York, would create even greater resentment and unease. The irony that my ancestors had been pioneering on the Western frontier before theirs had even got out there could only further aggravate some of these politely bigoted people. I did, however, win my battle for Court House Square. And, inadvertently, I did for a time split the ranks of Denver's ruling circles. This drew me even further into Denver operations than I had intended, and it happened as the court battles came to an end, when Claude Boettcher, one of Denver's elite, called me by phone.

I was in my New York office when I received the call that started me on an unexpected phase of our Denver operations. A very hoarse, very powerful voice said, "This is Claude Boettcher."

I said, "Yes, Mr. Boettcher."

"I'm in town at my apartment." (An enormously wealthy man with widespread interests, including an investment company with a seat on the New York Stock Exchange, Boettcher kept a duplex suite in the Sherry-Netherland Hotel.) "I'd like to come down and see you," he said.

"Mr. Boettcher, if you are in town, let me come to see you." But he insisted on coming to my office, and in a short while showed up. As I went around my desk to greet him, I saw a giant of a man who appeared to be twenty to twenty-five years my senior, possibly sixty-four years old, but a tremendous man, great height, broad shoulders, heavyset—obviously a man who indulged himself in the pleasures of life. He sat down, saying, "I congratulate you on your victory on Court House Square."

I thanked him, admitting that it had been quite a fight, when he asked if I had any idea who financed the different organizations that fought Webb & Knapp. I had to plead ignorance, at which he gave a half-smile, saying, "I come from the school of life that says when you lose to a man you don't fight him anymore, you join him. I'd like to know if you'd like to join me in continuing to develop Denver; I'll help you, and you help me." I said this would be a great thing, that I would be happy to do it, and we began to lay plans for working in tandem. We agreed that I would throw Court House Square into a combined operation with him, including some good property he held on Denver's Broadway and Seventeenth Avenue across the street from the famous Brown Palace Hotel, which he now owned. Eventually, at his urging, I agreed that we should develop the Broadway property first, though I could continue to line things up for a massive project on Court House Square.

We both recognized that there was a need for modern office space in Denver and agreed on the idea of the modern skyscraper. I had Pei draw up the plans, but the Korean War prevented us from immediately getting to work on construction. Boettcher and I kept in close touch on overall plans, however, and Arthur G. Rydstrom, one of his senior vice-presidents, and heir apparent, was also brought into our planning. It was not until 1953, however, that we were lined up and ready to go with a new office building. Then I received a startling jolt and setback. Pei and I had, from the beginning, designed our building for steel. It turned out that Boettcher, who was head of the local cement industry, wanted it in concrete, but by the time this came out it was too late to make a change. Boettcher said, "Much as I like you, and I am going to grant that you were not sufficiently aware—and maybe I was stupid, I didn't watch the plans—but as head of the cement industry, I can't be connected with a steel building. I can't go on with it. I'll buy you out, or you buy me out." This being the case, I named a price; he could buy or sell. He decided to sell, and I took over.

That is the official story. It is the explanation that Boettcher gave to me and which he later gave to the press. I was both fond and respectful of Boettcher, who stood head, shoulders, and barrel chest above the provincial crowd around him, but he was a strong Denver man with local ties and was exposed to local prejudices and pressures. Many years after this event, and after Boettcher's death, I heard that some people who were quite close to him were much against his involvement with me and with Webb & Knapp. But if this or other factors contributed to his decision to bow out of our partnership, I never knew of them. Though we had no further business connections, we remained friends, and when he died in 1957, I felt a loss. I also got a surprise, for the man I had assumed was a vigorous sixty-four when I met him in 1950 had been an even more vigorous seventy-five and had died at eighty-two.

It was in April, 1953, that Boettcher broke up our combine. Moving ahead on our own, we broke ground for the new building in May. To carry on the project, I turned to the George A. Fuller Construction Company of New York, who joined me as a partner. We finished that building ahead of schedule in July, 1955, and what we turned out was, and is, one of the finest architectural projects in the country, which, in part because of its special emphasis on site planning, won all manner of awards. The building was a lovely, clean-lined thing on stilts, which instead of the usual shops, stores, and entrance corridors on the ground floor, provided an open lobby which seemed part of the open courtyard on the north side of the main tower. Situated at the base of a moderate slope, this court was terraced. Fountains, a reflecting pool (in which we placed live trout), and walkways eased the way for both the eye and spirit of passersby. Alongside the main tower and at the level of the upper terrace we placed an open-structured office building under a wide, arched roof. We completely rebuilt a three-story building that fenced in the north side of the court so that it harmonized with the whole, and wound up with a pleasing combination of structures, public places, and walks. It was an office complex much ahead of its time that has withstood time's passing.

We paid a price for this pioneering. When it came time to finance the basic mortgage for Mile High Center, we were penalized for not having rental properties on the ground floor. The local realtors who were doing the appraising for the insurance companies we turned to for financing, just could not bring themselves to understand how a building that had terraces rather than stores on the ground floor could more than make up for this loss of rental space by charging higher rentals for the upper floors. They could not believe that there was prestige connected with having offices in a beautiful building. In Denver, as elsewhere, we eventually proved that beauty can be good economics. We got an unheard-of $5.85-per-square-foot rental for the two top floors, and even at this writing Mile High Center boasts one of the lowest vacancy ratios in town.

As Mile High Center neared completion, it became a favorite spot for Denverites to point out with pride to visitors. One block away and to the west, on Court Place, they could see and point out something that, in its way, was equally impressive. This was the five-story, sixty-five-foot-deep hole in the ground which we had dug out for Court House Square and which we were having trouble getting filled. But that is another story.

· 10 · Filling in Court House Square

It took Webb & Knapp four years to get control of Court House Square, and for almost five years after that, from 1950 through 1954, we ran it as a parking lot. This delay in construction was due to the Korean War and to our being drawn into the development of Mile High Center. Because of our partnership with the financially powerful Claude Boettcher, I expected to have little difficulty in eventually developing Court House Square, but one unexpected result of these delays was that Webb & Knapp became one of *The Denver Post's* favorite targets.

Every local newspaper cherishes at least one issue which is both safe and popular to attack. For the *Post's* sharpshooters on nearby California and Fifteenth streets, we provided an ideal target. Each year we did not build on Court House Square, we were obliged to pay a $25,000 surcharge to the City of Denver for not having started construction. The $90,000 in yearly revenues from parking more than covered this annual charge, so we paid the fine and played for time and took the editorial consequences. On long winter afternoons, when lacking other distractions, the editors of the *Post* could always create a little excitement by firing a broadside at the stationary target of Court House Square. "Let's Have the New Building," said one of the early and more moderate editorials of 1951, but this was merely a ranging shot. With practice the California Street snipers became more and more lively and imaginative in their efforts. After a series of demands that the mayor take action against our delays at the square, *Post* editorials with such titles as "A Good Square Deal," "Operation Peeled Potato," and "Dreams of Glory" kept fitfully agitating for a people's war against us. I especially remember one long and richly sarcastic editorial titled "Parking Lot Bill." This last editorial, which

by some coincidence appeared just a month before the formal announcement of our breakup with Boettcher, spoke of me as "Parking
Lot Bill," the air-castle builder. Commenting that I had turned down
a reported two million dollars for the property, which the *Post* felt
should never have been sold in the first place, they went on to say
I had picked it up for a mere $818,000 and furthermore had not ful-
filled my commitment to build. The editorial went on to note that
perhaps in two more years, when Mile High Center was finished,
"Parking Lot Bill" would get around to building Court House Square.
It would take another four years, they said, to have something visible
on the ground that had so trustingly been sold to me. "We can't wait,"
said the editorial in closing.

I had long since learned to put up with a certain amount of
scoffing, but as I am a man who likes to get things done, I was more
upset by the delays we were faced with at Court House Square than
by any of my critics. Meanwhile, I *was* in the midst of complicated
transactions in Denver, which were the result of the sudden breakup
of my association with Boettcher. Coming at the touchy time it did,
that last editorial hurt, but there was nothing very dramatic I could
say or do. We carried on with the construction of Mile High Center;
I announced that we would begin construction at the square by 1954,
and redoubled my now single-handed efforts at setting up a workable
situation for the square.

What we needed for that square was a large department store, a
magnet to pull shoppers out of their old shopping habits and walking
patterns downtown and put them into new ones around our property.
Part of our problem, however, was that there were three such people-
pullers already in existence in Denver. One was the Denver Dry
Goods Co., four blocks below Court House Square at Sixteenth and
California streets. Two blocks below that, at Sixteenth and Champa
streets, was a May Company store, and Daniels and Fisher lay yet
another two blocks downtown, at Sixteenth and Arapahoe streets.
Together these three establishments defined the east-west axis of
Denver's shopping district and threatened dangerous competition to
any newcomer moving into the far edge of things at Court House
Square. Although I had persuaded Macy's and, later, Gimbels to set
up branches at our new Roosevelt Field shopping center on Long

Island, neither they nor any other major chain was interested in opening a store in Denver. Neither were any of the local stores willing to
move to our site. I was blocked in all my moves. That is, I was
blocked until I broke from the established pattern of play by taking
a gamble that solved two problems and set Denver businessmen agog.

I bought the Daniels and Fisher store.

Daniels and Fisher, known throughout the region as Denver's
quality store, catered to those with taste and money. It was to Daniels
and Fisher, for instance, that well-to-do ranchers from as far away as
Wyoming, Montana, and Idaho might bring their families once or twice
a year to stock up on a thousand dollars' worth of goods. But Daniels
and Fisher, a Neiman-Marcus without oil in its backyard (or flair
in its front office), was beginning to falter, partly because of its poor
location. Though the store had helped pioneer the original south-
eastward growth of Denver by moving in 1875 to what was then the
edge of town, more than seventy-five years had now passed. Even in
slow-paced Denver there had been changes. Daniels and Fisher was
now the lonely western anchor of top-level real-estate locations and
was being hurt by the decaying properties around it. The store's un-
interested third-generation owners lacked the talent or drive to stay
in control and make changes. But by moving to Court House Square,
Daniels and Fisher would be able to leapfrog past its competition and
into a new place of prominence. A move by this store from one end
of Sixteenth Street to the other would shift the polarity of Denver
shopping patterns as surely and swiftly as a moving magnet under a
map of Denver would shift scattered iron filings through its paper
streets. It was for this reason that I bought the store.

Control of Daniels and Fisher cost roughly 1.6 million dollars in
cash, which I raised in New York. Then, in mid-1954, having negotiated a lease for Daniels and Fisher at Court House Square, I got my
cash out by selling to a combine of Midwestern purchasers: Jerome
Nye and Younker Bros., who operated stores throughout Texas and
the Midwest. The new owners had both the capital and the managerial
talent to run a competitive enterprise, and I, for the price of a little
effort and ingenuity, had solved two problems: I now had a tenant—
and a favorable pattern of pedestrian traffic for Court House Square.

I was very pleased with our prospects, because back in New York

I had already arranged with the Statler Hotel chain for their leasing and operating a seven-hundred-room hotel in Denver, the hotel and department store to be built back-to-back on Court House Square. Things were looking so good for the square that I planned to have the project finished by the end of 1956 or early in 1957. After that it would be good-bye to Denver and on to the dozen other projects which I had in mind or were already under way.

One of these "other projects" was acquisition and operation of the Statler Hotels, whose management I had negotiated so successfully with as regards Denver. The Statler chain, another closely held company with absentee ownership, had been quietly on the market for some time. Our takeover talks with management had gone so well that we had agreed on price—seventy-six million dollars, or fifty dollars per share—and I had lined up sources for the necessary funds. The deal, already known to the press, needed only a formal stockholders' approval, which was less than a week in the offing, when Conrad Hilton and a group of backers intruded. Moving swiftly and silently on my flank, they bought half the stock in the hotel chain, at the same fifty dollars per share, by dealing directly and secretly with a key number of owners, trustees, and heirs. Rather than get into a stock fight, I wired Hilton congratulations on his maneuver and urged that he keep the excellent management already running the hotels. Later I tried to purchase the Statler chain from Hilton for eighty-six million dollars, which would have given him an immediate ten-million-dollar profit, but he turned me down. I tried to get him to go ahead with the Statler plan for a Denver hotel, but here, too, I was rebuffed. The net result for Denver was a ceasefire on further developments till we could find a hotel, but true to my promise, we began to dig in Court House Square.

Toward the end of 1954 we put up a fence and began excavating the ground in part of Court House Square. The really serious digging got under way in 1956, at which point, with Mile High Center completed, the more than six acres of the square looked like a very promising bomb crater. We kept digging through 1956, during which time men working on three-shift basis had pulled out 421,000 tons of material, and in the course of all this digging we had a little fun.

At first the engineers had recommended that we drive sixty-foot piles into the ground for our building supports, because the square, situated over a prehistoric stream bed, was sixty feet or more above bedrock. They suggested piling because it would cost only one million dollars to drive piles, as against three million to excavate. But I had them test-core the fill for sand and gravel that we might use for our concrete and for the prefabricated mosaic surface of our buildings. It turned out that if we used our own material, we could save one million dollars in construction costs. This meant excavating would really cost only two million, while at the same time opening up an enormous space beneath the plaza for a profitable garage. Thus demonstrating the difference between an engineer and an entrepreneur, I told them to excavate, but since we were in Rocky Mountain gold country, over an old creek bed, I also had them test their core samples for gold. If they found gold, we could run it through a sluice while washing off the fill for its sand and gravel. They did find gold. We announced discovery of a small gold-bearing stratum of sand under the square, and this brought on a two- or three-day furor that must have had the old-time miners roaring in their graves. Denver's new mayor, Quigg Newton, immediately announced that any gold under the square should belong to the city. The next day the town district attorney jumped up to second this claim, and I, playing my part, publicly warned off any and all politicians and claim-jumpers. Then, of course, I cautioned local citizens not to start digging up their backyards unless they needed the hole, because we really weren't getting much gold from the site. Things quieted down. In all, we got fifty thousand dollars or so from our "mine," and I got one good nugget, which Marion had a duplicate cast from. I use these now as cufflinks and am no longer sure which is the original.

But as we poured the foundations for the square, which gradually rose toward ground level and above, the department-store deal I had so foresightedly arranged with Daniels and Fisher became unglued at the edges.

The post-Korean War recession had arrived, and the new owners at Daniels and Fisher were worried about expansion into a new store at Court House Square. I kept on building the store while looking about for some solution. I thought a merger between two Denver stores might be the answer, but the men who controlled the Denver Dry Goods Co. were reluctant to give up their good location. The May Company seemed even more set against a merger deal, but a refurbished and relocated Daniels and Fisher store under new management was a loaded gun pointed right at the heart of the May Company store, which would be left as anchor store in the "old" downtown. And, as I had made it my business to learn, the May Company had been busily branching out over the country and was now facing special difficulties. In the wake of recent expansions, the aggressive management at the May Company were discovering that bumping hard against entrenched, locally owned stores, in the farm belt, could be very painful. Younkers, meanwhile, bothered by the May Company incursions in Iowa, were nervous about future lumps they might take from their Daniels and Fisher incursions into Denver. It was an interesting case study of strategy, tactics, and painful stalemate in geographical warfare, which I eventually resolved for both parties. After a series of negotiations the May-Younkers confrontation was eased, when the May Company, raising the white flag in Iowa, gave up its store there to Younkers. Younkers, in turn, allowed the May Company to take over the Daniels and Fisher store in Denver. As part of the deal, the May Company, once it merged with Daniels and Fisher, would move into Court House Square. Webb & Knapp would take over both the old Daniels and Fisher and the vacated May Company properties in the same way auto dealers take in second-hand cars as trade-ins.

The May Company, recognizing that my own needs for a lessee were urgent, proved very tough bargainers. Though the shell of the new department store was now seventy-five-percent complete, they whittled down the terms of the lease, added to the costs of the building and by demanding more space than we had planned for the original Daniels and Fisher building, necessitated a basic change in plans for the square. Instead of having a hotel and department store back-to-back, we now had to plan for a five-story department store situated across the street from the hotel on Court Place and connected to the hotel both by an underground tunnel and by a covered overpass. Another proviso of the May Company deal was that we could not lease their old building to another department store.

On the other side of the coin, we now had a very powerful retail operation going for us on Court House Square and an arrangement whereby we would share in the profits from the new store. My only problem now was that of getting a hotel under way in the square, but when I say *only* problem I mean my only problem in Denver.

Elsewhere, I was involved in dozens of activities which I hoped would result in Webb & Knapp's becoming the greatest and most productive real-estate company in the world. These non-Denver activities were so extensive, numerous, and important that Denver can be properly viewed only in perspective with all of Webb & Knapp. Every single year, regardless of whether our operations in Denver moved ahead or were delayed, the firm of Webb & Knapp, as I shall show in the subsequent chapters, grew, changed, and was active, literally all over the map. Suffice for now to say that many of our deals were interrelated.

It was in 1955, for instance, that I met with a singularly impressive man, and later a most loyal friend, Robert R. Young, the fighting financier who headed the Alleghany Corporation. In 1956 Alleghany lent us twenty million dollars. It was this money that permitted us to go on with our Denver project, as well as others that might otherwise have been washed out. But when Young first met me, it was his railroad chief, Alfred Perlman, who was able to tell him something of who we were. This was because of what we had done and were doing in Perlman's home town, Denver.

At this time I was putting in forty thousand miles or more of traveling per year. Much of this was in our own plane, for by 1957 we owned and operated a DC-3 picked up from Robert Young. At first we took over the plane as a favor to Young; some of his dissident stockholders had attacked his having a company plane as an extravagance, although today, of course, it is considered a necessary convenience for a man in his position. We gave Mr. Young full access to the plane whenever he needed it, but in the course of trips up, down, and across the Atlantic seaboard as well as to the Midwest, that hard-worked plane became well-nigh indispensable to Webb & Knapp. Our pilot was Donald Gex, a competent and gracious gentleman who now flies for Peter Grace of W. R. Grace and Company. With its small galley, well-stocked bar, and comfortable office space, our DC-3 provided an excellent way of doing business while getting to where business was. On trips to Denver, which was far for a slow-moving DC-3, I traveled by faster, if less commodious, commercial airlines but even here there was a certain pattern to my trips. Normally I was accompanied by two, three, or more aides. We went first class. If, as often happened, there was an empty seat beside me, I would dump any papers I was carrying on this seat, making it a form of office desk, or I might call one or another associate over to sit beside me for a talk, the stewardesses, meanwhile, seeing to it that our high-ball glasses did not get too dry.

On arrival at Denver our party would be greeted at the gates by a group from our local office plus a number of reporters and photographers and maybe one or two business people with whom we were currently dealing. Striding along with this group in tow while playing a game of queries and quips with newsmen, we usually stopped for a while at the airline's hospitality room for a more formal press conference. Then, out in front of the terminal I would climb into the waiting limousine, chauffeured by the driver-superintendent who was always assigned to me, and we would wheel into town.

One particularly useful aspect of being in Denver is that I could rise at six or seven in the morning and, because of the difference between Mountain and Eastern time, call New York to catch people just as they came into their offices, but in Denver official business began with an eight-o'clock breakfast and command performance for our staff. Here, over a breakfast of melon or grapefruit, scrambled eggs and bacon, and English muffins, topped off with a spoonful of honey, we would go over details of local operations and get the word on any new development in town. As word of our business breakfasts got around, more and more Denver realtors and businessmen made it a habit to drop in on us. These extended sessions might wind up at 9:30 or later, after which I would get out to the building site or visit around town. Our local people were trained and primed so they were aware who owned what, who their bankers were, who was buying, who was selling, and what the status was of any major and many minor properties in town. A trip through town with them thus became an automatic real-estate reconnaissance trip. Not uncommonly I would be asked to make a speech to some local group; sometimes there was some small ceremony at one of our own properties. Webb & Knapp had so many projects going in so many other places that I seldom stayed in Denver more than one or two days at a stretch, and often, if running late, we (courtesy of the mayor's office) would leave town for the airport behind a pair of siren-equipped motorcycle troopers.

It was in the course of one such visit in 1956 that, while sitting in my hotel room getting a haircut, I bought half-ownership of the new local television station, KBTV, from its promoter-owner, John Mullins. Mullins is a shrewd, hard-line show-business type from the West Coast who was easy to get along with. Though the station seemed promising, he could raise no local money, which came as no surprise to me. He seemed to know his field and have plenty of imagination. So I joined him as a partner for $750,000 in what proved a very good investment. John drew me into a number of convivial escapades of one type or another.

One of my Denver forays ended up on the front page of *The Rocky Mountain News*, which, ironically, did not perturb me but did disturb and annoy Palmer Hoyt, publisher of *The Denver Post*. Since this incident has become part of the underground legend, I may as well tell it.

Newspapers and local publicity have always been important to Webb & Knapp operations, and though we had started out with opposition, dislike, and distrust on the part of *The Denver Post*, we always got generous support from even-tempered Jack Foster of *The Rocky Mountain News*, for whose backing I was grateful.

I also struck up a good friendship with the town's third force in publishing, Gene Cervi, founder and publisher of Cervi's *Rocky Mountain Journal*. Cervi is a delightful and spontaneous companion, and the very caricature of a crusading, liberal publisher. If hemlock were still in fashion, a certain percentage of Denver's would-be autocrats would be all for having Gene quaff a cup just for his health, but their votes would be negated by the others, who were too curious to see what he might say next. Almost by definition, this rebel with two hundred causes was on the outs with the town's inner circle. Seeing in me a challenger of local vested interests as well as of Denver's status quo, he gave us strong support. This backing did me no good among local establishment circles, where from time to time we endeavored to develop a little financial backing, but I was glad of it nonetheless, and Cervi's weekly paper did help counteract the bad image of us that the *Post* for so long projected to the general public.

The *Post*, in time, underwent a turnabout in its attitude toward Webb & Knapp. Palmer Hoyt, one of the finest newspapermen in the country, had been extremely skeptical of me, but we wound up great friends with a mutual feeling of respect, because Webb & Knapp did deliver to Denver the things he hoped we would, but didn't believe we could. At first, I am sure, he could not help but be influenced in his judgments by the people he associated with socially, but eventually he saw that they were the ones who should be criticized and that we were the ones who should be supported. He courageously reversed his stand. The change began when he realized that I would put up a hotel, though I inadvertently put this developing friendship to the test while playing hooky with my TV partner, John Mullins.

Once a year *The Denver Post* collects a chosen assortment of Western businessmen, politicians, and personalities, hires a train, and takes its guests up to Cheyenne, Wyoming, for a gala "Frontier Days" festival. Through a careful selection of guests, this junket has over the years become a prestigious affair and a great promotional device for *The Denver Post*. Palmer Hoyt graciously invited me to attend this gathering of regional influentials. I was then pouring millions of dollars into Denver developments to create a renaissance in that town, while developing dozens of other projects around the country. I'm not sure if I was there as a local businessman or outside luminary, but Palmer, now an ally, wanted to expose me to leading regional business people, and vice versa. Because I was grateful for his efforts and because I always enjoy that kind of gathering, I was delighted to accept. I showed up for the trip in Western costume complete with a red vest, my grandfather's Colt .45 pistols, and a Rocky Mountain miner's thirst.

We had a convivial trip up to Cheyenne, but pleading the fact I had to get back to New York for a conference at J. P. Morgan's, I did not stay for the whole of the program. Instead, I caught a flight back to Denver where I would take the plane to New York. Now, as it happened, a man who sat next to me on the plane to Denver was Grady Maples, a local radio announcer. We got to talking, and he mentioned that a nudist group were holding a wedding ceremony that day. He was to cover the event and asked if I wanted to stop by with him. Life is short, its possible experiences many, and since I had time between planes, I agreed on impulse. We arrived on the scene, I still in my cowboy dress, to find the wedding party present in the altogether. The local photographers spotted me, but I declined to have any pictures taken. I jocularly announced that I would not disrobe and was in fact there as a member of the working press—as consultant to Grady. It turned out, however, that the one ringer in this nudist group was a genuine pro, "$50,000 Treasure Chest, Rose Lee," a professional stripper so named because she had insured each of her beauties for fifty thousand dollars. Miss Lee was not averse to publicity: that's why she was there. While I was talking to someone, I heard my name called, turned around, and was confronted by a "$50,000 Treasure Chest" and a battery of cameras.

Those pictures got to New York as fast as I did, and the next day I had been preceded into Morgan's executive offices by an appropriately illustrated story in the newspapers. A part of me figured, "Here is where every bank note is called and I'm out of business." Every major officer of the bank, including old man Whitney, Henry Alexander, and Tommy Lamont, arrived, and I thought they all were there to get the money I owed them before I could get out of the room. As it turned out, they were only gathering around to chuckle over my personal description of the happening out West. I had no problem whatever in renewing the notes and in actually getting some more money.

In Denver, the *Post* carried a sober account of its Frontier Days get-together in Wyoming, of which I was an announced honored guest, while *The Rocky Mountain News* gleefully produced a picture of me à la cowboy and some of the wedding guests al fresco.

Palmer Hoyt was not amused. I must admit that I was more amused than upset by the juxtaposition of my presence at two such different forms of tribal rites in modern-day America; I knew that once the tut-tutting died down, nothing important would be changed in my life or in Denver's future, which was looking most rosy.

· 11 · From Court House Square to Zeckendorf Plaza and Back

BY THE mid-1950's a building boom, instigated by us, was under way in Denver. It began quite soon after our first "discovery" of the town in the late 1940's. The Texas Murchisons, in the form of John Murchison, followed us there. At one point he tried to buy Court House Square from me, but I was not selling, and what he did instead was buy up the choice site of the Denver Club at Seventeenth and Glenarm Place for an office building. The Denver Club, established in a fine old red-sandstone building with a pleasant lawn around it, was controlled by the old bulls who owned and ran the town. As a group they were much against change, and suspicious of outsiders, but Murchison's Texas money evidently dazzled them. For various considerations plus a ninety-nine-year lease on the top two floors of the proposed new Murchison building, the Denver Club gave up their distinctive quarters to the demolition crews.

Sad to say, the once exclusive and distinctive Denver Club has over the years been losing its position to other luncheon clubs in newer, better buildings, for, as I had predicted, new structures continued to rise in downtown Denver. After Mile High Center was finished, the newly merged Denver U.S. National Bank moved its headquarters to our new site and subsequently moved to the forefront of the local bank industry. Not to be outdone, the staid First National Bank moved into the office building that the Murchisons put up. In typical bankers' follow-the-leader style, the Colorado Federal Savings and Loan and the Western Federal Savings and Loan also moved into new buildings. More important, in some senses, some 153 oil companies eventually set up offices in Denver, attracting yet more services and industries to the town and bringing in independent money, new jobs, and new attitudes to once-closed-in Denver. It was not, however, till I finished the project at Court House Square—by putting up a modern convention hotel—that the town could be considered metropolitan. Getting that hotel started out as a problem, became a preoccupation, and finally turned into a near-obsession.

At first the immediate problems of the project were minor, and some were ludicrous. At one point, for instance, the Walter S. Cheesman Realty Company, owners of the Republic Building just across Sixteenth Street from the square, agitated to have us take out special insurance in case the great hole we had dug should swallow their building. Most of us were amused at this case of highly placed ignorance. At another point in the construction process we faced a strike, but strikes are not uncommon in construction projects. Potentially more serious was a local law prohibiting the sale of liquor within five hundred feet of a university. A hotel that can't sell liquor can't survive, and since Denver University held property just across the street from the proposed hotel, this could put us out of business. Fortunately, Colorado's governor, Edwin C. Johnson, although a dry, was too much of a realist and a politician not to see that there had to be a change in the law. With the help of the lieutenant governor we were able to get remedial legislation that permitted liquor at the hotel.

A quite expensive obstacle, in terms of cash outlay, followed the signing of the May Company–Daniels and Fisher deal when we turned Court House Square over to the department store. I then began planning for the hotel to rise alongside Court Place. When in my eagerness to get on with the project I let word of this slip out, the extra properties we needed, owned by Denver University, were under negotiation in the $250,000 range. Immediately, the school's administrators jacked their asking price to $600,000. It was only when I seriously threatened to walk out on the whole deal that they agreed on a final price of $500,000 for the properties. From a narrow, merchant's point of view, the university's opportunistic sharp trading was excusable and in some eyes laudable, but this local highwayman's toll was, in a sense, my own doing. In Denver, I should by now have known what to expect.

A far more irritating roadblock was thrown up in front of us by our friendly local banker, old John Evans of the First National Bank.

When we were first buying property on Court Place, we took over some mortgages held by the First National. The entrances and exits to the great two thousand-car garage we planned to construct under Court House Square were designed to pass below the street, under the hotel site alongside Court Place, and then up to the street level. As part of the strictly private financing of this great project, we had arranged a loan from the Chase Manhattan Bank for the garage. Part of the boilerplate, or small print, of the loan agreement asked for a right of easement from the basic mortgage holder of the property, the First National Bank of Denver. This meant that if anything went wrong with our developing the property and Chase had to take over, they would still have access to the entrances and exits to the underground garage. This is a fairly common, almost routine, courtesy that mortgage holders normally give without a second thought. Francis X. Wallace, our legal representative and office chief in Denver, called a senior bank officer of the First National about this matter and received an oral okay. But when Wallace got over to the bank with the necessary papers, the highly embarrassed executive recanted; John Evans of the First National would not grant his fellow bankers at the Chase rights of easement over that property.

When Wallace telephoned me with this present from Denver's leading businessman, I snapped, "Well, you tell that so-and-so that . . . ," but Wallace, who has a sense of humor, said, "Bill, I'm in Evans' office, you tell him," which, with a few modifications, I did. Of course, this blocking from a petty local banker could not stop us. Somewhere I dug up the cash to buy out these stick-in-the-craw mortgages, and we got on with the job of building Denver a hotel.

We needed an affiliation with a national hotel chain in order to get proper financing for finishing the project. Through 1957 we talked of setting up a Webb & Knapp hotel, but since the chain we were building up was largely a New York one, mortgagers were not willing to offer as much financing as we needed. The Equitable Insurance Company, for instance, at one point offered sixteen million dollars, but I knew we could do better, and kept trying.

Finally, in early 1958, with the hotel now rising four stories above ground and our out-of-pocket expenditures at the eleven-million-dollar level, I persuaded Conrad Hilton to take up the lease for the hotel by offering him a most attractive deal. After making a number of changes in I. M. Pei's plans in respect to size of rooms and layout of kitchens and public rooms, he signed. On the strength of this lease, the Prudential Life Insurance Company gave us twenty-two million dollars in financing. Now we could move with dispatch on the hotel. Move we did, and at last, after almost fifteen years, our Denver ventures were coming to a close.

While the hotel was under construction, we sold Mile High Center to its principal tenant, the Denver U.S. National Bank, for sixteen million dollars. Meanwhile, I had tried to get the May Company to ease the terms in our agreement, which stated that when we took over their building at Sixteenth and Champa streets for two million dollars, we could not lease to another department store. The May Company adamantly refused to change its contract and waited for their two-million-dollar cash payment to come due. We didn't have the money, nor had we a snowflake's chance of raising anything close to it. With Webb & Knapp strained tight for cash, the problem of where to scrape up two million more dollars hung over my desk during the day, followed me to bed at night, and greeted me when I woke up. But one morning at six o'clock my bedside phone rang. It was Wallace, our Denver lawyer, saying, "Bill, you don't have to take that building."

"How is that?" I wanted to know.

"There is a lousy two-foot overhang on the edge of the lot. It clouds the title, and that is just enough so we can refuse the building."

Ironically, this escape hatch had in effect been put there by the May Company. Under the standard "good-faith" contract which we normally used, the matter of an overhang in some section of the property would not have invalidated our agreement. But the May Company had been such tight, ungenerous bargainers, and their lawyers had written up such a hard-nosed, detail-crammed contract, that our people, in reply, had felt obliged to put in an equally detailed boilerplate specifying, among other things, that the title to the property must be unequivocably clear.

Soon after this, when no less than a four-man delegation of lawyers for the May Company stalked into our Denver office to enjoy the drama of presenting the deed for the Champa Street building, and to demand their two million dollars, we gave them a surprise ending. After the visitors had served their papers, Wallace called in his secretary and dictated his own papers rejecting the old May building and stating his grounds. When he was done, there was a long silence. Finally the chief of the visiting lawyers, gesturing at the deed lying on the desk, said plaintively, "But what am I going to do with this?"

Looking up from his chair, my man, keeping an utterly straight face, asked, "Do you really want me to tell you?"

That was in November, 1959. I'm told the other lawyer has not spoken to Wallace since.

In March, 1960 at the newly developed area around old Court House Square, we put up a plaque naming it Zeckendorf Plaza, and here, as previously in Mile High Center, Pei and his associates had proved themselves master architects. The relationship of buildings, forms, and spaces in that plaza, the play of height to mass and of textured stone to golden anodized aluminum in the interconnected hotel and department store, worked well. The generous setback of the skating rink combined visually with the hyperbolic paraboloid entrance to the department store and the hotel to give the city a focal point such as it never had before.

The hotel itself opened, with appropriate fanfare, in April, 1960. I was there, of course, but not in the happiest of moods. *The Denver Post*, I remember, was running a special supplement for the occasion and came to us seeking advertising. By this time we had poured some forty-three million dollars into Zeckendorf Plaza. Twenty million of this, in the form of equity financing, was our own hard cash. There was not a dollar of local money in the project; the rest of Denver, while now profiting from the overall effect of our development, had never seen fit to invest in its own possibilities, and in fact had not at first believed in them. I felt we had done just about enough for Denver for the time being, and was against taking out any ads at all. But then they showed me a picture taken from Fifteenth Street, looking northeast down Court Place. This photo showed the new May–Daniels and Fisher store on the left, with its overpass connection to the hotel at the right, while two blocks straight down, at the end of the street, was Mile High Center. The caption read: "They Said It Couldn't Be Done."

I bought that ad: it said it all.

In the afternoon Conrad Hilton and I raised the flag at the hotel's opening ceremonies, but my job was now done, and I did not stay for the later festivities. This would be Hilton's usual opening-night show, for which he had arrived primed with a planeload of dancing girls and captive celebrities. By the time it started, I was halfway to New York.

My next official visit to Denver would be in February, 1961, to address the Tenth Annual Building Industry Conference, but before touching on this visit, I should continue with a Denver windup.

In June, 1961, we turned over ownership of Zeckendorf Plaza to the Alleghany Corporation in settlement of a Webb & Knapp twenty-million-dollar debt to that organization. We took a lease on the property, paying a stiff one million dollars in rent. And there we took a loss, having to pay out more rent than the property could produce. This happened because the May Company did a disappointing business in their new store. No sooner had they closed their deal with us than, as if scorning profits from their new store, they embarked on a program to decentralize business in the downtown area, and ended by hurting all business in the Zeckendorf Plaza area, their own included. Hilton Hotels Corporation never made good at the hotel. The Brown Palace Hotel which had the goodwill of the public, added an annex. Because of the Brown's annex and the rise of various motor hotels, the Hilton remains Denver's much-needed and often-used convention hotel but it took many years before it made it on a bread-and-butter-transients basis. So, financially, our project, with its profit-sharing arrangement with tenants, did not succeed. It was an architectural triumph. It was a redevelopment triumph, and the community gained enormously by it; the project stabilized downtown and drew in new businesses and opportunities, but it did not succeed for the developer-promoters, ourselves.

In July, 1964, Webb & Knapp lost its lease at Zeckendorf Plaza in a default judgment for nonpayment of the Alleghany Corporation lease. In October of that year, the new owners at Alleghany changed the name from Zeckendorf Plaza to Court Place, and that, I assumed, was the end of the Denver story.

In February, 1966, however, after the collapse of Webb & Knapp, at a time when we were getting a new, comeback company, General

Property Corp., under way, I received a letter inviting me to Denver. The city planned to name a small park after me and to give me an award as the man who had done the most for Denver. It seems that following an article in *The Denver Post* about our comeback efforts, a number of private citizens and then the city council decided to make this gesture. They were much aware of the changes that had come to Denver in our wake, and perhaps a bit annoyed at the sudden erasure of the name Zeckendorf Plaza. The park is a modest triangle of ground at the intersection of Speer Boulevard and Seventh Avenue, but as a postscript of acknowledgment, not from the powers that be but from the citizenry of Denver, it is one of my most cherished accolades. Not to be outdone in graciousness of gesture, as president of the Marion and William Zeckendorf Foundation, I donated funds for a work of sculpture for the park, to be dedicated to the early pioneers of Colorado. The work, to be chosen by a competition of local artists, provided a five-thousand-dollar prize to the winner, Susan Pozzeba, a talented young sculptress. In a brief but moving ceremony in April, 1968, the semiabstract statuary was unveiled and arrangements made for an inscription to be added in memory of my dear Marion.

My final comment on Denver's ruling circle, however, was given back in 1961 at the Building Industry Conference. At that time, speaking of the city's plans for a redevelopment of parts of the oldest section of town, I said that the project would not work unless it were large enough to be self-sustaining, a minimum of seventy-five acres. I added that with the shortsighted second-rate leadership dominating the Denver business community, the project would probably come to little as far as aesthetics or economics were concerned. Developments and lack of developments to date in Denver tend to bear me out. And now, recalling that speech, the gist of which the *Post* agreed with in an editorial, I am reminded of other remarks and the subsequent furor back in the late 1940's. This was when B. B. Harding made his famous faux pas and unkind judgments of Denver's Chamber of Commerce and the city fathers. I must admit that what I was saying, though in less direct language, was pretty much what B. B. had been telling us all along.

I could speak with such feeling and authority of Denver and its leadership because of what, against odds, we had done in that town and because of what I had discovered could be done elsewhere. At that time, in Canada, joined with some truly powerful and dynamic men of vision, we were creating Place Ville-Marie, which would turn Montreal into the principal city of Canada. Meanwhile, we were also involved in multiple other deals about which I was beginning to discover some generalities.

· 12 · Warp, Woof, and Some Emerging Patterns

FROM THE VERY beginnings of my ascendancy at Webb & Knapp, I made a practice of keeping the momentum going by constantly developing new projects, some of which might bear fruit and some of which might not, and some of which might divide and interact upon other deals over the years.

Meanwhile, the fifteen years we spent in Denver are something of a yardstick against which we can measure various changes in the company as well as our varying types of projects. For example, between the time of our first involvement in Denver in 1945 and the start of Mile High Center in 1953, Webb & Knapp changed from a partnership, to sole ownership, to a publicly held company. We acquired capital and staff; great holdings, such as the Graybar and Chrysler buildings in New York; an extensive reputation; an enormous momentum in the marketplace. During this time we ventured into an even greater variety of deals. Many were prosaic, the acquisition or resale of another piece of land or a building, some were more exotic, and a few were whimsical.

During the late 1940's, for instance, suspecting that there would be a worldwide shortage of tanker bottoms, I had put Webb & Knapp into the shipping business. We acquired four T–4 tankers and a number of C–2 cargo ships which we chartered out. In the mid-1950's we sold off our ships at a gain, making me one of few men in the world ever to buy from and then sell back ships to Greeks at a profit.

Again, aware of the choking effect which the automobile was having upon our cities, Webb & Knapp spent over a quarter of a million dollars on research and development of an automated parking system I had conceived—but the thing proved too complex and costly to be usable. I had turned down an opportunity to back Rodgers and

Hammerstein's hit musical *Oklahoma!*, which was the only poor advice Marion ever gave me. Somewhere along the line, though, we acquired a profitable piece of the Broadway show *Gentlemen Prefer Blondes*. At one point in time it looked as if we would take over the Brooklyn Dodgers. John Galbreath, the real-estate builder and investor and an owner of the Pittsburgh Pirates, brought his friend Branch Rickey into my office with an offer to sell Rickey's twenty-five-percent share in the club. The instant that word of these negotiations got out, our switchboard was jammed with calls from friends angling for box seats, but I never had to test their love by a refusal. I bid one million dollars. Rickey's partners had the right to match my offer. They did so, and I lost my chance at a lifetime supply of player-autographed baseballs. Suspecting this might happen, however, I had made my offer conditional on a $50,000 agents' fee if my bid were matched by Rickey's partners. In effect, I got a five percent commission for getting Rickey a sale. This took place in 1950, when we still expected to be finished in Denver very shortly.

During 1953 we took on the construction of forty Safeway Stores across the country, and bought Charlie Chaplin's Hollywood studio. That was the year I also got talked into backing a movie, *The Joe Louis Story*, and in which we picked up the air rights over the Pennsylvania Railroad's tracks and its terminal in Manhattan.

The year 1954 was equally busy, and its curious high points were a series of meetings involving Laurance Rockefeller, General Electric Company, Lehman Brothers, and others in secret negotiations with the famous and eccentric Howard Hughes for the purpose of buying out his multimillion-dollar industrial holdings.

In 1955 there was the less frustrating and quite profitable partnership I organized of the Rockefeller Bros. Corp. and various Texas investors to buy and develop the 2,500-acre Waggoner Ranch between Dallas and Fort Worth as an industrial center. That same year, working now with David Rockefeller and the Chase Manhattan Bank, I began the Wall Street Maneuver, a five-year operation during which Webb & Knapp moved the headquarters of many of New York's greatest banks but kept these banks still within the Wall Street area. As a result of this game of musical banks, at which we profited to the tune of many millions, the Wall Street area, which was in grave danger of being abandoned for midtown New York, became stabilized.

In 1956, as our excavation in Denver reached its greatest depth, I became involved in a curious series of negotiations, which were never completed, involving great acreage in Cuba which Fulgencio Batista, the "president" and dictator of Cuba, cut himself in as a silent partner. By 1956 we were also seriously involved in an urban-development project in Montreal, which in time surpassed even our Denver developments, and in 1956 we opened Roosevelt Field, the country's largest (125 acre) suburban shopping center.

If in 1955 and 1956 we had pulled in our horns and nursed only a few key projects along, I could have settled back as a multimillionaire and staid property holder. But with all of America before us and with so many useful things waiting to be done, I no more knew how to settle down to mere money counting than a bee in clover knows how to doze in the sun. Instead, I shuttled my men, and traveled myself, back and forth across the nation looking for projects, people, money, and ideas to bring together. We had discovered that in many cases it takes only a relatively little bit of seed money, plus quantities of effort and imagination, to get a worthwhile project under way. I was expanding Webb & Knapp from the management, purchasing, and packaging of real estate, at which we were now past masters, into new fields, in which we were pioneers.

By the end of 1957, for example, we had sold off the Chrysler Building and our highly profitable Thirty-fourth Street building on the block between Macy's and Gimbels. We made these sales partly to meet debts and partly to generate cash for other, newer projects, many in the special field of government-sponsored urban redevelopment. Webb & Knapp had entered this field by initiating a multimillion-dollar, five-hundred-acre redevelopment project in Southwest Washington, D.C. We were now in many other cities as well. In New York City, Robert Moses had called on us to bid on several projects. We were working on Kips Bay, Park West Village, and Lincoln Center, of which more later. We were involved in a project in Chicago and were talking to key officials in St. Louis, Boston, Hartford, Providence, Cincinnati, Cleveland, and at least a half-dozen other cities.

By the close of 1957 we were also embarked on a hotel-acquisition program. Blocked in our 1954 attempt to get a hotel in Denver by the Statler chain, we were now creating a new Zeckendorf hotel chain. At one point, mostly through ownership of New York hotels, we would be one of the biggest (8,000 rooms) hotel groups in the nation.

Between 1949 and 1957 Webb & Knapp's staff multiplied sixfold, from 40 to 240. As the biggest, most aggressive real-estate firm in the country, we inadvertently became the prime research-and-management training school of the industry; dozens of our alumni now hold eminent positions in the industry all over the country and in Canada.

Our brilliant counsel, Maurice Iserman, and his key assistant, H. Jackson Sillcocks, had assembled a group of smart aggressive young lawyers who soon became the most expert and fastest-moving practitioners in business, and by now Webb & Knapp closings had become famous industry "happenings." The fifty-two million-dollar Chrysler-Graybar closing, for instance, took three days and the concerted efforts of ninety-seven participants. Between closing out old mortgages, setting out new ones, checking existing leases, fitting in new ones, arranging sales and leasebacks, plus exchanges of stock and the transfer of funds, the sequential strands of logic and procedure in a deal could become as intertwined as spaghetti on a plate.

Like directors at a rehearsal, Iserman and his team would often stage a dry run before a big closing. At the actual affair, participants would then move from one room to another signing and exchanging papers and checks in a real-life game of Monopoly. At one closing, as the work wore on in a limbo of its own, the Chase Bank suddenly found itself lending several times more than the legal limit permitted it in any one operation. Had the transactions broken down at that instant, it would have been quite embarrassing, but they did not. By day's end enough loans had been called and settled so that the Chase was once more safely within its limits.

By now my son was another key figure in the company. He had grown up with Webb & Knapp. He was the ten-year-old messenger who delivered the final papers to Mrs. Clews Spencer when we sold her property in 1940. Through high school and early college he worked with us during vacations, and after his military service in Korea he had joined us full time. He learned quickly and accepted responsibility. I gave him all the exposure I could; he was my companion and adviser on all new developments.

What I was consciously doing at Webb & Knapp was creating an integrated real-estate and development company with its own construction division, an excellent design staff, and experienced specialists not only in trading or packaging or managing of real estate but also in urban development and in the economics and design of shopping centers. No such thing had ever existed before, but then, neither had the kinds of projects we undertook.

Meanwhile, although individual projects intermittently took up important parts of my time, they were never more than one part of an interconnected latticework of money, men, and real estate. At the center of this formation, keeping it together and keeping it growing by constantly phoning or visiting prospects, channeling funds from spot to spot for maximum usage, or riding the lawyers to get the red tape out from underfoot, I lived and loved a hyperactive sixteen-hour day.

In the midst of all this action, though not always entirely at a conscious level, I had been developing some special techniques which set the pattern and provided much of the color in our operations. For instance, in more than two decades of tailoring projects to suit the special needs of specific investors, we created the groundwork for what would amount to a quantum jump in the financing of real estate. I invented the "Hawaiian Technique," so called because the idea came to me while I was casting for fish on a Hawaiian beach.

This was in 1953, and Webb & Knapp was in process of buying 1 Park Avenue, a twenty-five-story showroom and office building. The sales price to us was ten million dollars, or ten times the million-dollar yearly earnings of the property. With first and second mortgages we could raise as much as eight million toward the purchase price, but this still left two million of equity to go. Though we did not have the money, the papers were in process of being drawn up when Marion and I went on vacation to Hawaii.

Charley Boettcher, the son of Claude Boettcher, then my partner in Denver, a man of about my own age, had a beautiful Japanese-style house on the windward side of the island of Oahu, with an excellent wine cellar and a very pleasant Japanese couple in attendance. He invited us to make use of the place, and we did. The house had beach frontage, and I went surf fishing each morning before breakfast. While casting out into the rough surf, I continually found myself casting about in my own mind for some proper method of financing the purchase and arranging the sale of 1 Park Avenue. Generally in real estate there are two types of funding—mortgages and equity. We needed more of both, and there was no visible way to get either, but I was sure that if we could get commitments from investors to purchase the building from us once we had it, this could create the financing by which Webb & Knapp would be able to acquire the building in the first place.

Standing out in the sun, in my bare feet and shorts I thought enviously about how an investment banker acquiring a ten-million-dollar industrial corporation has a much easier time of it than a real-estate man buying a ten-million-dollar building. The investment banker can divide and sell the ownership and rights in a corporation in a great many ways, a piece at a time. For instance, he can sell first-mortgage bonds to an insurance company, at the prime rate of interest. He could also offer debentures, which, though they take a second position to the bonds, offer a higher rate of interest in compensation. For investors interested in a speculative fillip (in case the company does very well), there are convertible debentures that can be turned into common stock. He can issue preferred shares (convertible or straight), which tend to be especially attractive to corporate investors, because preferred dividends passing from one corporation to another are taxed only seven percent. Finally, there is the common stock, the basic equity of a corporation, but the availability of capital does not stop there; there are also bank loans, accounts receivable (which may be financed with a factor), warrants to buy stock, and various other ways to draw investment capital into a corporation. In fact, investment bankers have over the generations invented as many ways of catering to investors as there are investors with particular personal needs, whims, or tax requirements.

While hauling in an empty line from the Hawaiian seaside, it occurred to me that if an investment banker did not have all these ways to reach various kinds of investors, he would be in just as difficult a position as I was with 1 Park Avenue. If he had to sell a corporation in toto, to one buyer, an investment banker would not get nearly as much money as he did by dividing it up for special customers . . . the lucky devil.

This kind of thinking was not really getting me anywhere; I pulled back with my rod and cast way out into the water again. Then an idea came to me: "Why can't we break the property up, just the way an investment banker does?"

With a corporate financial structure as my model, I began mentally to divide up 1 Park Avenue to see how and at what price the building might appeal to various kinds of investors. As the pieces and the arithmetic began to dovetail, I forgot my fishing or even where I was until I suddenly realized I was standing on a Hawaiian beach, in water up to my ankles, with a useless rod and reel in my hands. I went into the house, and in the course of two hours on the telephone I began to make the first application of what was to become known in the trade as the Hawaiian Technique.

In practice, because it involves a long chain of interconnected events and multiple side branches, the Hawaiian Technique can become as complex as some of the long molecule chains chemists work with and link together to concoct new products. In essence, however, like most good ideas, it is simple. I determined how it could work, in the case of 1 Park Avenue, which earned one million dollars in rentals a year and had a ten-million-dollar price tag on it.

Though most homeowners don't think of it this way, a major urban property breaks naturally into two parts—the land, and a lease which gives you a right to the use of the land. A building usually comes with this lease, but as the basic leaseholder and building owner you can alter, tear down, or rebuild on your site in any way you want—as long as you pay your ground rent for the land.

Now, considering only the land, I determined that $250,000 of the total million-dollar income of the property should go to the ground rent. This ground rent, since it must be paid before any other expenses, is the safest of all possible incomes to the property. Capitalized at the rate of five percent, therefore, the ground should be worth five million dollars. I could try to find a buyer directly at this price, or I might do something else: since ground income is so sure, a mortgage on the ground (which would have first call on the already ultrasafe ground rent) would be even more secure. I should have little trouble finding an insurance company or pension fund willing to take a four-percent return for such a safe risk and could therefore sell them a mortgage on the ground for three million dollars which would eat up $120,000 of the land's total income. The remaining $130,000 of income capitalized at the rate of 6½ percent would be worth two million, and for this sum I would sell the land to an institutional or individual investor.

The land mortgagor and land owner would be our equivalent of a corporation's bond and debenture holders, and at this point, having first mortgaged and then sold off our land, we would have five million dollars, plus a building and, of course, a basic lease giving us undisturbed use of the property.

The earnings on this property, after payment of ground rent, would be one million dollars, minus $250,000, or $750,000. The job now was to properly fraction and sell this leasehold and its income so as to attract particular buyers. What I did, basically, was to create two leases, an inner (or sandwich) lease, and outer (or operating) lease. Whoever purchased the operating lease would, in effect, be the manager of the building. He would solicit tenants and collect rents. He would get one million dollars in income, pay $750,000 in rent, and keep $250,000 for himself. The holder of the inner lease would, in effect, be the owner of the building. He would get $750,000 in rent, pay $250,000 to the owner of the land, and keep $500,000 for himself.

Before selling the inner lease and its $500,000 income, however, I could readily mortgage it with a leasehold first mortgage of 6½ percent for four million dollars. The mortgage payments on this would come to $270,000 per year plus two percent or $80,000 per year for amortization. This would leave $500,000 minus $350,000, or $150,000, to the building owner. Capitalizing this $150,000 at an attractive six percent, I would readily find a buyer for 2.5 million dollars. Thus the inner lease would bring me four million dollars when mortgaged, plus 2.5 million when sold.

As for the operating lease, with its $250,000 income, we could, at a seven-percent return to investors, get a price of almost 3.6 million dollars. If we provided the financing, by taking back a mortgage, it might be even higher, but holding things as is (in this simplified case), it turns out we have arranged to: (1) sell and mortgage the land (for five million dollars), (2) sell and mortgage the inner lease (for 6.5 million dollars), and (3) sell an operating lease (for 3.6 million dollars). All for a grand total of 15.1 million dollars on a purchase price to us of ten million.

In this profitably fractioned property, the holder of the operating (or outer) lease, who acted as manager of the building, in that his costs were fixed (at $750,000), was in a position not unlike that of a common stockholder. He was relatively secure against inflation, and if he could increase sales or rentals, his income would rise phenomenally; a ten-percent rise in rentals, for instance, would give him a forty-percent rise in income.

The building owner, or innerlease holder, would be in a cash position much like that of a preferred stockholder, with fixed income but with tax advantages even better than those available to corporations that pay only seven percent of their preferred dividends. This, because the building owner can write off the annual depreciation of the building against his cash income from the structure. What with the accelerated depreciation, such investors would be able to pocket their $230,000 income with no tax—and to garner extra tax credits against other income—until such time, of course, as yearly depreciation on the building began to equal amortization payments. At this point the individual owner would likely want to sell his interest in the building (paying only twenty-five percent in capital gains if he sold at a profit), to wind up with an excellent net return.

These, as with a great many other tax possibilities that we realized for investors, were perfectly legal and well within the concepts and spirit of the law as it existed then. They also led to much new legislation, however, because the Internal Revenue Service, upset about the amount of money they were not getting, instituted new rulings to plug the new holes we had discovered.

The example of property-fractioning I have given above is a simplified one. In an actual case there might be quite a number of individual variations and many more investors. For instance, in an inner (or sandwich) lease, aside from the first mortgage we might create a two-million-dollar second mortgage, this second mortgage to pay interest but no amortization, till the first mortgage had been paid off. Or we might create a dormant mortgage which did not pay anything for twenty-five years. Only after the first mortgage was paid would this dormant mortgage take over, but then, as a first mortgage, it would acquire full value. One might be able to sell such a mortgage for, say, $750,000 to a man who wants to give it to his children twenty-five years hence.

Similarly, the operating (or outer) lease, instead of being sold outright, might be mortgaged, broken into subleases or subsubleases, hedged against various possibilities, and sold to as many as ten or twelve different investors.

The Hawaiian Technique was so flexible that it became a very powerful tool which often could make two plus two equal to four plus one plus two plus more. I was not the first one to package real-estate deals for particular customers or to use a sale-and-leaseback technique (I, for one, had been doing just such things since the 1930's), but this was the first time anyone consciously and deliberately fractioned a great property off beforehand in order to tap many markets at once. We used the technique with 1407 Broadway, with West Thirty-fourth Street, with the Graybar Building, and with just about every other one of our major properties. The Hawaiian Technique, because it permitted us to anticipate and make early use of the future earnings of our properties, became the principal tool of Webb & Knapp expansion. And, as the technique spread and was adapted by others, it brought a new liquidity and flexibility to real-estate financing in general.

An interesting little transaction which took place a little before the time of my Hawaiian interlude, but which is important because it had roots even further back, and flowerings far forward, was my purchase of McCreery's Department Store on Thirty-fourth Street. This deal came to us on a Friday afternoon in 1951, when I got a call from Robert McKim, chairman of the board of the Associated Dry Goods Company, the owners of McCreery's Department Store.

"I'd like to see you tomorrow, Bill," he said.

At that time we had not yet moved to Beekman Place, nor had we acquired our place in Greenwich. I said, "Sure, Bob, I'll be working tomorrow . . . but I'll be at my apartment at 30 East Seventy-second Street."

"I'll be there at ten-thirty."

McKim showed up as promised. It was a sunny day, I was out on the terrace picking up a little tan, and he joined me. I knew that McCreery's was not going well, but this was quickly verified when McKim explained his visit by asking me if I wanted to buy McCreery's.

"Sure."

"What will you pay for it?"

"I'll pay five and a quarter million dollars."

Looking a little flabbergasted, McKim said, "Do you know anything about it?"

"I've never been in the store."

"How did you come to that price?" he asked.

"Well, that's my business...."

I might have gone on to say I was offering five and a quarter million because that is what I thought the land was worth, but, shaking his head wonderingly, McKim said, "Bill, our book value is five million four hundred and fifty thousand dollars. If you pay that, you can own it."

"We'll buy it, if you will take a million dollars down and the balance in a year or two at two-percent interest, so we can turn around and lease the property to someone else."

"You've got a deal," said McKim.

Part of the deal was that he and his people had to get out of the store by title date. We did not want the heartache and problems of discharging hundreds of employees; that was his job. He agreed to make his severance arrangements, and tucked away at the corner of my mind I had a pretty good idea of who I would be able to get in as a new tenant for the place. The tenant I had in mind was Ohrbach's. I knew they were getting restless down on Fourteenth Street because of a deal that had come up eight or ten years previously when I was acting for the Astor estate. Astor owned the middle one of a three-building property occupied by Ohrbach's. In the process of generating cash for Astor so he could buy properties elsewhere, I had gone to Nathan Ohrbach with a very attractive proposition. Ohrbach's rent to Astor was seventy-two thousand dollars per year. I told Ohrbach that if he would give us a first mortgage of $900,000 and one dollar in cash we would give him the property. The mortgage would be at two-percent interest (in the early 1940's, interest was very low, but this was phenomenally so). I had so designed the package that this two-percent interest plus amortization of the mortgage would be covered by the rent Ohrbach was already paying. In other words, Ohrbach without having to go into his pocket for a single extra penny, would wind up owning his store. For our part, we would hock that mortgage, take the cash, and invest it in profitable out-of-town properties I had been scouting. It was an attractive deal all around, especially for Ohrbach, but he could not see it; he was afraid he was being cheated and so turned me down. I gave Ohrbach thirty days to think it over, but he again turned me down, and I put the parcel on the market. Quite soon a man named Weinstein from Brooklyn bought the property for $1,150,000 (the $72,000 rental represented a nice return on this investment). That might have been the last you would hear of the deal— except for one thing: Mr. Weinstein was the owner of Brooklyn's Mays Department Store, which is not to be confused with the national department store chain mentioned in my Denver chapter. What Weinstein wanted was a merger with Ohrbach. Over the years since that purchase, Ohrbach had held Weinstein off, but that lease was going to run out someday, and Ohrbach was understandably nervous about having a landlord who, if the occasion arose, could apply excruciating pressure. As a result, in 1951 I did not have too much trouble making a deal to move Ohrbach's to Thirty-fourth Street at a yearly rental of $435,000 against a percentage of sales and with a negative covenant against their establishing another store within a specific mileage of the Thirty-fourth Street site.

On the strength of this lease I was able to borrow enough money from the Central Savings Bank to pay McKim his 5.45 million dollars.

As my friend Jim Lee at the Central Bank put it, "I don't care what you paid for it, what matters is the value of the building now. If you created a new value by getting a good lease, we will lend on that value." He gave us the money at four-percent interest, and we were able to acquire a most profitable property with no actual equity investment of our own.

About a year later, however, a broker representing James Butler (a scion of the family that owned the Yonkers Race Track) came in looking for another kind of deal. Some years ago the Butlers had bought property on the edge of New York, in a place called Baychester for a new race track which they had never been able to build. They owned four hundred acres; the family wanted to swap that land for some income-producing property.

I said, "I have just the thing you want. . . . I'll give you Ohrbach's on Thirty-fourth Street. It'll give you $150,000 a year income after paying the charges on a 5.4-million-dollar mortgage."

The Butlers liked that, and we made a deal. They felt safe about their income, and I felt safe because it occurred to me that it is pretty hard to go wrong when you trade one acre in New York City (with a 5.4-million-dollar plaster on it) for four hundred acres in New York City free and clear. It was in Baychester that we later built the Freedomland Amusement Park, which is another, later, and different kind of story. It is in Baychester that the United Housing Foundation, a labor-financed group, is building Co-Op City. Co-Op City, the largest housing project in the world, will, at a cost of over 350 million dollars, house 16,500 families (75,000 people). It is the last great work of an amazing man, a Russian immigrant named Abraham Kazan, now eighty-one years old.

I have always been rather fond of Baychester; its acreage and potential for development pleased me. It was the similar lure of an enormous acreage near an urban area that attracted me to the Great Southwest project which was organized between Dallas and Fort Worth in Texas, but this later venture also illustrates another point.

Sometime early in 1955, Bob Anderson, formerly the Secretary of the Air Force and subsequently the Secretary of the Treasury, stopped by my office for lunch. Anderson, a Texan, was a trustee and executive officer of the Waggoner estate, which, with its million-acre ranch, is one of the greatest land holdings in the world. But Anderson wanted to talk about a much smaller Waggoner ranch, the family's 2,500-acre quarter-horse breeding-and-racing ranch along Route 80 between Dallas and Fort Worth.

Dallas and Fort Worth are rival and quite different cities. Dallas is a relatively sophisticated city of great wealth which thinks of itself as a Southern city. Fort Worth, on the other hand, is where the West begins. The competitive fires between these two cities were fanned by Amon Carter, publisher of Fort Worth's main newspaper, a banker, and wealthy civic booster who, if he went to Dallas, conspicuously brought his own lunch in a paper bag. I am told he was responsible for a sign in the Fort Worth airport men's room saying, "Please flush the toilet, Dallas needs the water." Carter affected Western attire, even in his evening clothes, and wore six-shooters on his side on visits to New York.

In spite of the carefully nurtured rivalry between the two cities, it was obvious that a megalopolis would grow up between them. There were excellent rail connections between the two cities. With Route 80 getting crowded, one knew a new turnpike would eventually be constructed. A new airport somewhere between the two cities was also in order, and at two thousand dollars an acre, or five million for the whole, the Waggoner ranch was a good buy. We would acquire it—plus more land—create an industrial and distribution center, and by planning and accelerating that which was inevitable, we would create new values and profits.

It is always wise when dealing away from home to have influential local partners. Through Anderson I had met Toddie Lee Wynne and his nephew Angus Wynne. The Wynnes, who were in oil and Dallas real estate, were eager to help develop the Waggoner land. They brought in a number of top Dallas and Fort Worth businessmen as fellow investors. For my part, I brought in Rockefeller Bros., their family investment company. In due course, the Great Southwest Corp. we organized developed the corridor between and helped join these two great cities. Land value, as we anticipated, boomed. Stock in the venture that once sold for one dollar later sold for ninety and promised to climb much higher, though Webb & Knapp, in order to generate cash for yet other developments, profitably sold out its share long before this climb.

Typically, as we had in the past, we sold out sooner than we might have liked to because of the lure and pull of other projects. Meanwhile, as regards the speed and ease of getting this project moving, the principal explanation lies in the fact we had the right number and right kinds of partners at our side.

"Mr. Real Estate" -- In <u>ZECKENDORF</u>, his autobiography, William Zeckendorf replays the real-life game of Monopoly that made him king of the largest real estate empire in history. The book is published by Holt, Rinehart and Winston, Inc.   HRW Photo.

Even before the Civil War, Zeckendorfs were coining money. The author's grandfather, William Zeckendorf, printed his own money for his flourishing mercantile business in the Arizona Territory. This enterprising pioneer became a member of both the Territorial and State legislatures and an aide-de camp to General Nelson Miles.

Arthur and Bertha (known as "Birdie") Zeckendorf, the author's parents.

A close and relaxed family, the author still remembers that his younger sister "won most of the battles" with him.

William Zeckendorf, Jr., and his sister Susan, the author's children. William, Jr., and Susan's husband, Ronald Nicholson, are now the author's partners in the General Property Corporation, a real estate firm which was formed after the collapse of Webb & Knapp.

Marion Zeckendorf, to whom this book is dedicated, at opening night at the Metropolitan Opera. She was to die tragically a few years later in an airplane crash.

William Zeckendorf in his unique igloo-shaped, teakwood office designed by I. M. Pei.

William Zeckendorf's penthouse offices at 383 Madison Avenue, New York. His private dining room is the circular struc_ ture atop the penthouse.

I. M. Pei, the talented and visionary architect who, along with the author, conceived and guided so many of the Webb & Knapp projects.

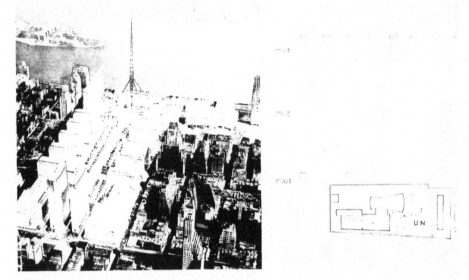

An architect's drawing of Zeckendorf's conception of an adequate approach to the United Nations buildings in New York. It involved the redesigning of two full city blocks east and west, and four full city blocks north and south. On the right is a diagram showing the plan adopted by New York City for an approach to the United Nations. It simply consisted of widening 47th Street. (See cross-hatching.)

30 Rockefeller Plaza
New York 20, N.Y.

December 17, 1946

Dear Mr. Zeckendorf:

I want to express to you and your associates my sincere appreciation for the important part you have played in making it possible for the United Nations to select New York City as its permanent home.

It was your vision and courage in assembling the East River property that made it possible for the site to be offered for what may become the capital of the world. Your original suggestion to Mayor O'Dwyer on Saturday, December seventh, to abandon the carefully conceived plans which you and your associates had prepared was an outstanding demonstration of public spirited citizenship. The farsighted and effective cooperation of the Mayor and Commissioner Moses made it possible to realize what I hope will be a factor in the future success of the world organization.

It has been a privilege for my family and me to work with you in this effort.

Sincerely,

Nelson A. Rockefeller

Mr. William Zeckendorf
Executive Vice President
Webb & Knapp
383 Madison Avenue
New York New York

A view of tenements which still front on the approach to the United Nations as a result of the plan finally adopted by the City of New York. It was the Rockefeller family and William Zeckendorf who finally brought the capital of the world to New York. Zeckendorf offered the East River acreage to the UN and the Rockefellers paid the minimal cost. The letter on the right reflects the high hopes and public spiritedness of the day.

Above, the *big hole* at Denver where the 23-story Mile High Center was to rise and generate a whole new era of city planning in that midwestern city. At the upper right of the photograph is the legendary Brown Palace Hotel, whose original owner was the husband of the "unsinkable Molly Brown." On the right a view of the finished Mile High Center, Denver. Below another view of the Mile High Center and Plaza in Denver.

At the centennial celebration marking the founding of the original Zeckendorf store in Tucson, the *Daily Citizen* spoofs the Zeckendorf proclivity for buying huge tracts of land at the drop of a homburg hat. It was the author's grandfather, also William Zeckendorf, who established the store which was the foundation of the family fortunes.

The tracks of the Canadian National Railroad as they cut through central Montreal. This is the area that Zeckendorf redeveloped as Place Ville-Marie.

The aerial view is of the finished Place Ville-Marie.

Above is a typical scene of the Southwest section of Washington, D.C., before Webb & Knapp redevelopment. 76% of the dwellings were substandard: 44% without baths, 27% with outside toilets, 70% with no central heating and 20% without electricity. These blocks, renamed L'Enfant Plaza by Zeckendorf, were part of the former slum area and have now become one of the most desirable real estate sections of the nation's capital.

The traditional kiss on the cheek for the author after he was made a Chevalier of the French Legion of Honor.

William Zeckendorf, his son and General Douglas MacArthur during the ceremony at which the General received an honorary degree from Long Island University. Zeckendorf was then the Chairman of the Board of Trustees of the University.

A pre-Revolutionary House in Philadelphia which was restored by Webb & Knapp during their Society Hill project.

The same house as it is today. The adjoining houses were also restored.

A part of Society Hill in Philadelphia as seen from the restored eighteenth-century Powill House.

The author and his son stand on the porch of a replica of the original Zeckendorf store which was built as part of the celebration of the opening of Century City in California.

Century City, complete unto itself, on the former 20th Century-Fox lot. The few remaining studios may be seen at lower right of picture.

At the top we see the financial district of New York City before Zeckendorf's famous Wall Street Maneuver. Below is the same view of Lower Manhattan, after the Wall Street Maneuver.

The author with Crown Princess Beatrix of the Netherlands who visited New York on the occasion of the celebration of the 350th anniversary of the discovery of the Hudson River.

Georgé Cserna

Kips Bay Plaza in New York City, then a revolutionary concept of apartment dwellings involving glass walls from floor to ceiling. The open, uncluttered plaza is a basic design employed by Webb & Knapp.

Using pads of lined sheets of paper, Zeckendorf makes a rough (and usually final) draft of any deal. These four pages illustrate the bewildering sale, resale and re-resale of the same piece of property, involving many millions of dollars.

The beginning of the end: a last minute attempt of the author's to stop the fall of Webb & Knapp by auctioning off various properties.

An architect's conception of the Zeckendorf plan for two miles of the Staten Island waterfront, which also involves a containership port.

A floating dock and a small jet and private airport for New York's Hudson River. Yet another Zeckendorf project of today.

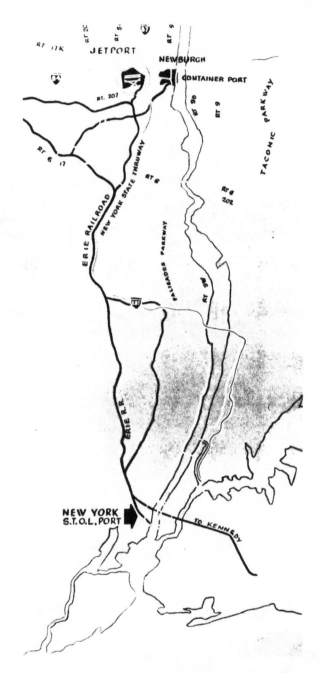

One of the author's latest projects is to convert Stewart Air Force Base into the fourth New York jetport. The Erie Railroad and the New York State Thruway both service the former base. The airfield and the equipment, of course, are already there.

• 13 • People and Places

A CITIZEN of a small town can, through circumstances or design, come to know almost everyone in the community. On the upper levels of our own business-oriented society it is the same. The threads of mutual acquaintanceship spread everywhere. In some cases they work and weave together as tightly as a piece of waterproof cloth. At other times they scatter out like the strings of an unfinished net, but each strand is somewhere connected to others.

What I did in the course of my work was continuously pick out and weave together a great variety of these strands. Whenever possible I made use of existing connections between people. At other times I created new ones. And deals that did not go through, every bit as much as deals accomplished, can usefully illustrate how, at the top, what one might call the "village system" of contacts operates.

For example, sometime after the American Broadcasting Company bought our West Side Riding Academy for its television studios at a handsome price, ABC's chairman, Ed Noble, called, inviting me to lunch at "21." There, after a pleasant meal and a bit of verbal sparring, he said, "Bill, I invited you to lunch because you are the first man to make any money on television—by selling us that studio. You must be doing something right, so I'd like you to join the board of directors and help us out." Noble also offered me some potentially lucrative options on ABC stock, but as it turned out, his invitation was less of an honor to me than an admission of desperation on the part of the company. I joined the board and for the next ninety days found myself working almost exclusively for ABC, which was in terrible shape. A multimillion-dollar bank loan was being called, with no cash in hand to pay it, and ABC's facilities situation around the country was chaotic. Through Charlie Stewart at Bankers Trust I was able to help ABC refloat its loan. Then, by arranging sales and leasebacks of ABC's California properties with my friends at Mutual Life, I solved the company's most pressing cash problems. Within six months, thanks in large part to these manuevers, ABC had a fairly presentable balance sheet, and I was Noble's favorite board member.

Not long after this, however, Noble called a special meeting to announce a proposed merger with Paramount Pictures Corp. This was the theater chain which was half of the old Paramount movie empire that had been broken up by an antitrust decree. The theater company was cash-rich. And, as Noble put it, "I'm like a fellow who owns a giant circus except all I've got is a great big tent and no players, no actors. . . ."

He thought Paramount would help him there, but I said, "These fellows are just a bunch of theater owners who are in trouble themselves—because of television. They're not producers. All you'll wind up with is an even bigger tent than before—and still no players." But Noble wanted to get his hands on Paramount's cash, and the discussion went back and forth.

Finally I said, "Well, if you must have a merger, right this minute I can think of a much better match. Merge with International Telephone & Telegraph Company. They have money, they could be to you what RCA is to NBC." Noble's curiosity was piqued, but he doubted that ITT would be interested. "Give me an hour," I said. He agreed.

During a Cuba vacation with Fred Ecker of Met Life, I had met Sothenes Behn, the international financier and chairman of ITT. Now I called Behn. At my request for an immediate meeting, the ITT chairman invited me to see him and General Harrison, the company president. I drove downtown, walked into the dark-paneled executive offices, and Behn said, "What is it, Bill?"

I replied, "Here's the deal . . . ," and outlined ABC's situation. ITT, with most of its holdings then spread overseas, was very much interested in balancing these properties with U.S. investments, and that very afternoon I arranged an offer of a share-for-share exchange of stock between the two companies.

Noble, however, only used the ITT offer to further his bargaining with Paramount and then closed that deal. When this occurred, I felt obliged to turn in my resignation as a director. The stock options once promised me, and which I had more than earned, were never again mentioned by Noble. I could, I suppose, have made things a bit embarrassing for him on this score, but I didn't. At that time I had enjoyed my maneuverings for ABC. I was sorry that what would have been the best long-term deal for ABC was spurned, but, where it counted, it was known how and by whom ABC's short-term fortunes had been brightened. My repute as honest broker and corporate negotiator continued to grow sufficiently, so that a few years later I found myself in another and quite different sort of nondeal involving Howard Hughes.

Howard Hughes, an industrial genius and paradoxical man, has been phenomenally successful. He has also produced some disastrously costly movies. He was known as a famous Hollywood Don Juan who collected and discarded beautiful women the way boys collect and discard model airplanes. For the past twenty years he has also managed to live as a traveling recluse, a sort of peripatetic Trappist. He deals with his various company managers only intermittently, sometimes through handwritten notes, at other times through obscure intermediaries, midnight phone calls, or summonses to secret, out-of-the-way meeting places.

The last time I saw Howard, he had already surrounded himself with the phalanx of competent, honest, and thoroughly humorless young Mormons who served as the gate-keepers, errand boys, and contact men. Through them he wards off and deals with much of the rest of the world.

The first time I met Hughes, in the early 1950's, was in Florida, where we had talked about his buying the 63,000-acre Indian Trail Ranch that Webb & Knapp controlled. At one point, I also offered to swap our 12,000-acre Mountain Park property in Los Angeles for his RKO Theatre stock. Nothing came of these brief encounters, all of which had taken place in motels, beachside shacks, and the like. These meetings, I presume, helped set things up for the following episode.

It started in October, 1954, with a telephone call from Spyros Skouras, suggesting we have lunch. I had met Spyros, a stocky, gravel-voiced Greek, when he was chief of Twentieth Century-Fox during my earlier California reconnaissances. Spyros, who had long been a friend and, as much as anyone could be, a confidant of Howard

Hughes, hoarsely announced at our lunch: "I've been talking with Howard Hughes, and he is ready to make a change. He wants to retire from business and devote his time and money to medical research. . . ." Spyros continued for a time building on this theme and the vast extent of Hughes' holdings. Finally he said, "You are a man who is always dealing with money people. Can you find a group big enough to handle this thing?"

I immediately replied, "It sounds like a Rockefeller proposition . . . they have the money. They would also be interested from the standpoint of their own foundation work, Laurance Rockefeller especially. They are backing lots of research in cancer. Do you want me to try it?"

He said yes, so I called Laurance Rockefeller for an appointment. We met, and I told him the story. He asked, "Do you think Hughes really means it?" I said I thought Hughes meant it because Spyros thought he meant it, and it was the kind of thing an eccentric like Hughes might do. The only way to know for sure, however, was to go to California and find out. Rockefeller agreed to come along, and through Spyros I arranged for a meeting, while quietly lining up some other backers who might have a special interest in some part of Hughes' holdings.

Rockefeller, my son, and I flew out to Los Angeles. There we met Spyros. The four of us lunched in the terrace dining room of the Beverly Hills Hotel, where, I suppose, we were all scrutinized by Hughes or his agents. In any event, we found ourselves programmed into a script that only the members of various undergrounds, portions of the CIA, the NKVD, and perhaps the Minutemen would normally take seriously. At precisely 1:30 Spyros was to get up and take a taxicab to a predetermined place, where he would be met and then taken to the rendezvous. At 1:50 Rockefeller and I were to go to a certain intersection, where a man wearing a red shirt with an open collar would contact us and drive us to the rendezvous. The meeting was to be attended by Spyros, Rockefeller, and me. There was no provision for my son's being there, but I thought I'd bring him along for the experience.

At 1:50 Rockefeller, my son, and I got up and walked over to the nearby corner. A man with a red shirt, open at the collar, came up, looked us over, and said, "Follow me." We did, for about a block, where he climbed into a 1932 Chevrolet jalopy, something the Okies might have used on the trek west twenty years ago. The car was dusty blue in color, some of the windows were cracked, the fenders looked as if they had been battered in and hammered out more than once, and the rugs in the back had been worn through. It was quite a sight to see the immaculate Rockefeller get into this wreck. It wasn't a very large car, and maybe my squeezing into place amused him as well. At any rate we got rolling, and after a time found ourselves in a seedy section of town. We stopped in front of a four-story building, a one-time private home that looked as if it had been converted into a flop-house, except that the building was now being patrolled. Four or five young, neatly dressed, rather good-looking men, all with crew-cuts, continually walked around the place. These were Hughes' Mormon entourage, and as we pulled up one of them came over and said, "Mr. Hughes has called the meeting off."

I said, "Why?"

"Sir, just you and Mr. Rockefeller were supposed to come to this meeting. You have a third party here, and Mr. Hughes feels that is a breach of the understanding."

"The third party is my son."

"It doesn't make any difference who he is."

I turned and said, "All right, Bill, you go back to the hotel, and we'll carry on."

The young guard said, "Wait a minute, I have to find out if Mr. Hughes will still go through with the meeting." We sat out in the hot sun till our native guide came back to say that Hughes would see us. We then climbed up to the top floor of the building and down to the end of a long hallway, where our escort rapped on the door with a distinct pattern of knocks. The door opened, and there stood Howard Hughes, looking exactly as he has often been shown in news-papers and magazines: six-foot-three, slender, youthful-looking, he had a three-day growth of beard, wore a V-neck shirt, soiled sport trousers, and dirty tennis shoes. The only thing neat about him was his hair, which was combed straight back, covering a balding head. He was around fifty-two years old at the time. As we stepped into this hideaway office, I introduced Rockefeller and joshed Howard a bit about his not buying the Webb & Knapp Mountain Park property, which was fast rising in value. We all seated ourselves. Hughes, who wore a hearing aid, pointed the speaker at whoever was talking. After a bit, and in the most casual way, he asked, "What do you fellows want?" Since it was Hughes who had approached us through Spyros, and since polite indirection had done nothing for me in previous meetings, I decided to be blunt, saying, "Howard, you know damn well what we want. We didn't come three thousand miles to admire your old trousers and sport shirt, or because we like this part of town; we came here to buy. I was told by Spyros that you were ready to sell."

"Oh," he said, "I told Spyros I'd *listen* to something."

I said, "If that is the way things are going to go, we've wasted our time. Either you are talking in good faith or not. Spyros says that you want to sell out and devote the rest of your life to science and the interests of humanity. Is that true? If it isn't, we may as well leave."

"I said something like that to Spyros."

I turned to Spyros and said, "Before we go any further, suppose you tell Howard what you told me."

Spyros, hoarse voice, Greek accent, and all, has tremendous charm and is very persuasive. He soon got the meeting on a much better footing, and it began to go along more easily. Rockefeller, who up to this time had said very little, now spoke up, saying that he had come there only because I asked him to. If a deal required capital financing, he would be interested in helping, but he did not come out there just to make money. He was interested in getting new money for cancer research. Hughes replied that he was interested in backing a great research foundation and that he had already established one foundation which was doing great things in medical research and would do more. Then, turning his hearing aid toward me, he said, "What do you have in mind for buying me out at . . . as long as you are here?"

I said, "Let's analyze what we are talking about, and I'll make you an offer. We are talking about Hughes Tool Company and Hughes Aircraft. We are talking about RKO, your real estate in Tucson, plus the brewery in Texas, and we are talking about TWA. That's your portfolio, isn't it?"

He said, "Generally speaking, that's it."

I said, "I'm recommending that we pay three hundred and fifty million dollars for all that."

"You don't know what you're talking about."

"Maybe . . . maybe I don't know anything about it. Let's assume I don't. But you do know all about it. Will you take three hundred and fifty million dollars? You can have a check for it."

"Where is the check?"

"Well, I have a letter and a check. I have a cashier's check for nineteen and a half million, plus a letter from Sloan Cole, who is chairman of the board of the Bankers Trust Company, stating that the check is for the purpose of making a down payment for the acquisition of your holdings. The amount is nineteen and a half million not because it bears any relationship to a price that might be negotiated, but because it is the maximum the bank can lend in one single transaction, being ten percent of their capital. Here it is," I said, and reached over to hand him the letter. He put up his hands, saying, "Don't give it to me, don't ask me to touch it."

"I didn't ask you to touch it, I want you to see it."

Hughes is the most suspicious man in the world. Maybe he was afraid that taking the letter might be tantamount to acceptance, or perhaps it was his morbid fear of bacteria that kept him from touching the letter. Up until this time he had been slouching on the edge of the couch, sometimes crossing his legs, occasionally leaning forward to shift his weight, but with never a change in facial expression. Now he leaned forward to read the letter I held out to him.

Finally he said, "I won't take it."

"Why not?"

"It's not enough."

"What is enough?"

"I won't tell you."

"*Do* you want to sell?"

"Under certain circumstances."

"What circumstances?"

"If the price is right."

"What price?"

"The price that you might offer me. If it is enough, I'll sell."

"Now you are getting me to bid blind. . . . I'm willing to match a bid of tabled stakes, but I don't like to shoot blanks. Are we fifty million dollars apart?"

Hughes said, "No."

"Do you mean it's less?"

He said, "No, I mean more."

For a man who supposedly wanted to get down to serious business, Hughes was acting like the original coy mistress, but I kept trying. I said, "Are we one hundred million dollars off?"

"Are you offering it?"

"No, I am asking."

He said, "I told you . . . I won't tell you."

"All right, I'll find out. I am offering you four hundred and fifty million; will you take it?"

"No. . . ."

"Howard, just exactly what do you want?"

"I won't tell you."

"Howard, take it or leave it, five hundred million."

He said, "I leave it."

"Howard," I replied, making no effort to hide my exasperation, "I think you invited us out here to give you a free *appraisal.* I don't think you were ever sincere."

He said, "Think what you like," then added, "I'll tell you what we'll do. I don't want to talk anymore today. We'll all go down to Las Vegas and talk down there."

Rockefeller said he couldn't go to Las Vegas, he had to get back to New York. Spyros said that he and I would go.

"Can I bring my son?" I asked.

Hughes agreed to this. And then, as if we were ten-year-old members of the latest Post Toasties secret membership club with "super" clues and passwords, four grown men who among them commanded or could influence a significant share of American wealth, sat there with never a smile, as Hughes programmed a properly secret rendezvous.

Spyros, my son, and I were to meet Hughes at midnight at a semiabandoned airport on the outskirts of Los Angeles. He would fly us to Las Vegas, but would arrange that we be driven to town in separate cars. Once in Las Vegas, we must go directly to our rooms. Under no circumstances were we to leave them during daylight, when we might be seen and start rumors.

At midnight we arrived at the deserted airport, which was entirely dark. A Constellation, a plane which Hughes had helped design, bulked in the gloom, and a guard with a flashlight told us to wait. We waited till Hughes, accompanied by another young guard, drove up in a little car. Guided by flashlights, we climbed into the darkened Constellation. Hughes checked her out, revved her up, and we took off. He did the flying. In Las Vegas we were met by several Hughes cars, driven by another group of Daddy Warbucks' monosyllabic young men, and taken to our hotel, where we had already been checked in. At this point, if Orphan Annie (accompanied by her dog, Sandy) had now shown up offering drinks, I would not even have blinked. Nothing of the sort happened, however, and we had to order our own drinks. It was late, and with Spyros' remonstrances to "humor" Howard still ringing in my ears, I went to bed.

The next day at about one o'clock Hughes called. We met in his suite, and he began our discussions by saying, "I am willing to review the situation further only if you offer more cash on the barrelhead."

"What kind of money?" I asked.

"Oh, perhaps one hundred million dollars more."

"Well, that casts quite a new light on this thing. We'll have to get backers into it. I'll have to return to New York and let you know."

Then he said, "Never mind, we'll just forget it. The deal is off."

I told him this was a very shabby way to treat people. We exchanged some more words, but the deal was kept alive by Spyros, and after I returned to New York a number of other negotiations went on. By the time it wound up, the list of supporting characters included the chairman of General Electric, the chief of Lockheed Aircraft, one of the heads of Blythe & Co., the head of Allen & Co., a senior partner of Lehman Bros., and a senior partner of Lazard Freres. Spyros, however, fell sick about this time and had to undergo an operation. That delayed things. Lehman and Meyer, of Lazard Freres, eventually did go out west on their own for a meeting with Hughes, but they were interested only in part of his kingdom. They offered, I think, to buy Hughes Tool. Eventually the whole deal died away. I was not surprised. After those first meetings with Hughes, I never thought he was serious. I think he was trying to find out what he was worth for tax purposes, perhaps in order to make gifts to a foundation. One of the best ways to determine the value of vast holdings is to have someone make you a bona-fide offer for them. However, Hughes' TWA situation was already getting a little sticky, Hughes Aircraft had been having management troubles, and his bankers at Irving Trust had found themselves way overboard on loans to TWA and were pressuring for changes. Hughes may have been checking out a financial countermaneuver. We'll probably never know exactly what he was up to.

At this writing Hughes is in the process of preparing the greatest supersonic jet port in the world in Las Vegas. I sincerely hope it comes off. Hughes is eccentric, but he has always been his own man, and he has great vision.

Some time after the Hughes episode, I was involved in another quite different kind of adventure. In 1948 I got a call from my old Depression-days friend and mentor Jim Lee at the Chase. He and Mrs. Lee were to attend the opening of *South Pacific* with us, but two of his granddaughters would be in town from school in Boston, could we get two extra tickets? Lee Shubert let me have two extra tickets. The young ladies, girls in their teens, joined us for dinner at Le Pavillon, and from there we went to see Mary Martin and Ezio Pinza's magical triumph. Jim Lee's granddaughters, two of the loveliest young women I have even seen, later acquired a certain fame. One of them, Lee, after a marriage to one of the Canfields of the publishing family, married a member of the deposed Polish nobility to acquire a coat of jet-set glamour as Princess Radziwill. The other, Jackie, became Jacqueline Kennedy.

I was not to see Jacqueline again for many years, until as Mrs. Kennedy, she interviewed Pei as a possible architect for the John F. Kennedy Memorial in Boston, but in 1956 I not quite inadvertently blocked a power play by one of her in-laws against another New England–New York family, the Reids, then owners of the New York *Herald Tribune*.

Early in the fall of 1956 I received a call from Mrs. Helen Reid, asking for an appointment. I offered to go visit her, but she insisted she would call on me, and came in soon after. Even before sitting down, she said, "Bill, I need your advice. Would you recommend that I sell my plant for 1.75 million dollars and then lease it back?"

Helping her to a chair, I said, "That depends on the terms of the lease and how badly you need the money."

"The interest would be eight percent."

Since at that time money was averaging between four and five percent, I told her it was a low price for her property and a very high rate of interest, then asked, "By the way, who are you selling to?"

"I don't know whom I am selling to."

"Who is the real-estate broker. Is there one?"

"Yes. John J. Reynolds."

"In that case, Helen, I am going to ask you a very simple question: Would you sell your newspaper to Joseph P. Kennedy for $1.75 million dollars?"

"What do you mean?" she said.

I said, "I mean he's your customer. He is giving you just a little less money than you need—to force you to go broke. He has set the interest rate just a little too high to make sure that you do. Not only will he have your plant, but he will also have your paper, all through a very low-cost real-estate purchase."

"Do you really think that?"

"I don't think it; I know it!"

"How do you know?"

"Because that's the way Kennedy does business."

She said, "What am I to do?"

"You must need the money very badly, Helen."

"I do, very badly."

"Is this life or death?"

She nodded. "Just about."

Sometime during the 1930's the *Herald Tribune* had begun to fall seriously behind *The New York Times* in general performance, but its owners and managers could not or would not see that any change was needed. Then, in the mid-1950's, the widowed Mrs. Reid and her two sons found themselves in control of a paper that was losing readership and money. They were trying to turn the property around, with Helen Reid and her eldest son acting as editors-in-chief. Looking at the paper, one could tell they were not doing very well. It was a privately owned company, however, and until now I had not realized she was up against the wall.

"Well," I said, "life or death is another story, but before you give up the ghost, why don't we . . . Have you tried to sell the paper?"

"Yes, but I can't find a decent buyer or a decent bid."

"Then I am going to make a suggestion. The first thing we ought to do is explore the possibility of legitimate finance. I'll make some appointments up in the Connecticut valley, up around Hartford, where you've some of the last remaining old-style Republicans. I am sure they all read the *Herald Tribune* and would not want to see it go out of business. I'll call my friends at Connecticut General . . . and two other institutions."

Over the phone I made appointments for the two of us and arranged to pick her up in my car at six o'clock on a September morning for the drive to Hartford. The appointed morning was also the morning Hurricane Betsy, one of the two worst hurricanes we ever had, came to New York. When I got up and looked out, the plants on our terrace were lying flat from the force of the wind, but I called for Mrs. Reid anyway. Like two characters in a melodrama, we drove through the heart of the storm in order to keep our appointment with fate. Through the slanting rain we could see trees breaking apart in the wind. Our driver had trouble keeping even my heavy limousine in lane, but we did get to Hartford, and we did get a loan offer of two million dollars at five-percent interest. I told Mrs. Reid not to accept it right away. We went back to New York, and I arranged yet another appointment with the Massachusetts Mutual, who were in Springfield. The president of the company, Peter Comack, said he would be glad to meet with us, but on the day appointed for our visit, a second storm, Hurricane Carla, made her appearance. Again we drove north through ominous weather, but again we were rewarded; the Massachusetts Mutual were very sympathetic. They offered Mrs. Reid 2.25 million dollars at 4½-percent interest, which for a specialty property such as a newspaper building is very handsome, and which, compared to Kennedy's offer of 1.75 million dollars at eight percent, was magnificent.

Under Mrs. Reid's son's leadership, the paper for a time made a comeback, until, while still convalescent, it was shot out of the sky by its own striking employees.

Ironically, if I had not helped Mrs. Reid, the *Herald Tribune* might still be around today. I am sure that Joe Kennedy planned to take over the paper and use it as a vehicle for pushing the political careers of his sons. The Kennedys undoubtedly would have pumped in vital injections of talent, which, along with money, would have saved the paper, but I could not let anyone who had turned to me for assistance be taken by a maneuver such as Joe Kennedy had in mind for the Reids.

A continuing series of minor forays and adventures can keep life interesting and sometimes exciting. I certainly got more pleasure from helping Helen Reid out of a tight corner than I would from buying and selling a particular piece of land, but I never let myself forget that these interesting side ventures came about because of our efforts and successes in various major projects. Such a project, and in some respects our greatest adventure of all, was located in Montreal and began in 1955.

· 14 · Change Comes to Canada

THROUGH THE mid- and late 1950's Montreal, although nominally the
financial and commercial capital of modern Canada, had little wealth,
dynamism, or modernity to show to the casual visitor. The sure indicator of a town's fortunes, its business district, was especially dowdy.
True, the St. James Street area, Montreal's equivalent of London's
financial center, the City, was packed to capacity and overflowing, but
new office space was being constructed at the rate of only 300,000
square feet per year. No major building had been built for over fifty
years, and most large companies had their offices scattered throughout
various buildings. Many of these great corporations were quietly in
the process of moving their headquarters to booming Toronto. The
whole of Montreal real estate was under a pall. It did not help any that
Montreal had for generations been burdened by city administrations
second to none, not even to Boston's, for venality and ineptness. The
town seemed to be at the start of a long, downhill slide.

When we announced plans to build a 3.5-million-square-foot
office complex, centered about an open plaza with a forty-two story,
cruciform tower, in mid-Montreal, few people believed us, and of
those who did, the majority were horrified. Conventional thinking
held that such a project would not only fail but would depress the
local real-estate market for another generation. Naturally, we went
ahead with the project.

We were able to go ahead because I met and worked in Montreal
with four men, three particularly strong ones, and one particularly
wise one. The first key man was Donald Gordon, president of the
Canadian National Railways, on whose land we worked. Gordon is a
Scot, a tall man, perhaps six-foot-four, and one of the few men I know
who could outdrink me; when he was one-third through, I would
have had it. Second was James Muir, president of the Royal Bank of
Canada. Another Scotsman, Muir was a fierce and egotistical man who

in another age would have been chieftain of a fighting clan. In our time he had to settle for control of Canada's largest, most aggressive bank. Third, a cool-headed and formidable leader of another sort, was Montreal's new mayor, Jean Drapeau. His Worship is a French Canadian, and a political Hercules. He assigned himself the task of first cleaning up, then revitalizing Montreal, and has just about succeeded. The fourth man was Lazarus Phillips, a counselor and the highly respected confidant of many. Phillips was the official leader of the long-established, somewhat introverted Jewish community in Montreal.

The stars must have been right when we met, for each of these men had individual visions about Montreal which matched mine, so we could work together. Each of these leaders laid something, sometimes something as subtle and precious as his reputation, on the line to make our project go. But I was the entrepreneur–risk-taker. I took the multimillion-dollar gamble, which nobody else in that country was willing to take, on Canada and on Montreal's vitality. I was the one who determined that the only way to make the gamble pay was by concentrating it in one massive, imaginative building, and because of what we did, Montreal and Canada will never be quite the same again.

For all its eventual great success and for all the enduring friendships that grew out of our Canadian adventures, it was no honeyed love feast which we seated ourselves at in Montreal. This, possibly the greatest of our ventures, had more than its share of tension and drama, though it began quietly enough around the table at my New York office. Here two visitors were Senator Thomas Viene and Rudolph Lemire, both Canadians and residents of Montreal. The senator was a most distinguished man, a bon vivant of considerable charm and sophistication, as well as an astute practitioner in the field of French-Canadian politics. Lemire, his associate, was a competent and articulate real-estate man. My guests had with them a map showing the holdings of the Canadian National Railways (CNR) in Montreal. They suggested that we acquire the lease and build up these twenty-two acres of downtown land. On this centrally located property, just north of the main station, was the "hole," a great, soot-stained, angry-looking, open cut where railroad tracks ran out of a three-mile tunnel under Mount Royal. Since the 1920's the CNR had devised a number of grandiose plans to cover the scars and develop the air rights around this equivalent of New York's Grand Central Station, but nothing came of them. During the depression, the CNR deepened parts of the "hole," and during World War II it had built a new station, but this is as far as it got.

The CNR is the survivor of a number of bankrupt railroads whose stock was taken over by the government after the end of World War I. A "Crown Property," it is operated like a private company, but its directors are appointed by the government. In 1950, when Donald, a banker, took over as president, the CNR tried once again to get a large-scale project under way on its land. Finding no interested developers among well-to-do, ultraconservative English Canadians, Gordon turned to Lazarus Phillips to see if someone in the Jewish community might be interested in a major project on the property. Here, too, he drew a blank. No one in Canada would tackle the job. But, my visitors suggested, maybe Webb & Knapp would be interested.

Any real-estate man is interested in twenty-two acres of singly owned midtown city property. What was frightening most people off was its size, plus the owner's insistence on an overall rather than a piecemeal development. But it was this very aspect of the situation that intrigued me. I decided I had better take a firsthand look at the area and meet this fellow Gordon. I called up, and then flew up with my son. Gordon walked us around for a look at the site and a view of the city. What I saw persuaded me. As Gordon now says, "I thought I was going to have to sell Zeckendorf, but after a walk around the place he was selling me."

A few weeks later Gordon came down to New York. He wanted to see what sort of outfit we had and whether we were big enough to take on the job he had in mind. Webb & Knapp in 1955 was already deep in the enormous southwest Washington urban-redevelopment project, and looking into projects in other cities. We were about to commence the Wall Street Maneuver, which would keep Chase and most other major banks still headquartered in the Wall Street area. Seeing our 240-man staff at work and the plans and models of projects already under way gave him plenty to think about. So, I suppose, did the constant flow of business calls coming to me over the phone. Naturally, he had made inquiries among the banking and insurance people about our past and present projects. The critical factor, however, was his reaction to me and my reaction to him. Here we hit a happy note. It was hard not to like and respect a man as forceful as Gordon. During the day, over drinks at lunch, and later in the evening, I recognized that here was a strong man with whom one could deal confidently. The clincher for an eventual agreement came when I suggested that Webb & Knapp, at our own expense, design a plan for the entire Canadian National Railways holdings in Montreal.

Gordon raised his brows a bit and asked, "Without obligation?" I answered, "That's right."

He replied, "Based on that, of course I will."

We promised an integrated development plan for his whole property. The CNR was then building a great new convention hotel on part of the site. We came to some early conclusions about the hotel vis-à-vis our location. "Project Canada" was now under way. And now that we were to become Canadian investors, I began to learn my first lessons about things Canadian and about the facts of life in part-English, part-French, bilingual Montreal.

Like a great many of my fellow citizens, I had long thought of Canada, when I thought of it at all, as an extension of the United States. I very soon discovered that Canadians rightly resent this inaccurate generalization and that they have a unique culture; in fact, they have two, which often clash. It is useful at times to think of Canada as two countries enfolded in one nation. I consciously say "enfolded" rather than "mixed" or "blended." Although French settlers founded Canada, English settlers then took over and developed it. Today, Canadians of French descent account for three-quarters of the population of the province of Quebec, but Quebec is only one of ten provinces and two territories. French Canadians represent only one-third of Canada's population of twenty million. For a mixed bag of historical, political, and cultural reasons, control of commerce and industry in Canada today lies almost entirely in the hands of the English, meaning Canadians of English, Scottish, or Irish descent. These key leaders, who went to school together or have known each other socially for many years, tend to form a close-knit group which is conservative in both thought and deed. However, it must be remembered that U.S. firms control over fifty percent of the country's manufacturing and resource-development assets.

Montreal is an island tucked far inland at the meeting of the Ottawa and St. Lawrence rivers six hundred navigable miles from the sea. The first European settlement in the area was named Ville Marie by its founding group of missionary priests and nuns. It was taken over by soldiers, fur trappers, and merchants, rebuilt, renamed Montreal, and, thanks to the St. Lawrence, which gave access to the Great Lakes and the center of the continent, became the greatest port in North America. For two hundred years Montreal completely overshadowed New York as a port and metropolis. It was not till after the opening of the Erie Canal and the subsequent development of U.S. railroads that a great flow of Western goods and produce down the Hudson Valley allowed New York to pass its northern rival, and permitted John Jacob Astor, whose descendants I dealt with, to multiply his fortune via New York real estate.

Pei's partner and one-time student, Henry Cobb, was to be the architect in charge of our Canadian venture. I suspected that a New England Yankee might get along well in old Montreal, and twenty-eight-year-old Henry, a bright, very talented, and most circumspect young man, was the scion of an old Boston family.

Soon after our first New York meeting with Gordon, Cobb and I flew up to confer at the site. The "hole" Gordon wanted to fill was just north of the railroad station, the principal department stores, and the St. James Street financial area. A great, new building complex, a sort of Rockefeller Center-cum-Grand Central Station, could create a new center of gravity and focal point for the city. This location would provide the "centricity" which Montreal needed, and which we needed, to make the project click. I was enthusiastic, made no bones about letting the CNR know how we felt, and gladly committed Webb & Knapp to the $250,000 it would take to draw comprehensive plans.

By late winter and early spring of 1956, Cobb was ready with preliminary plans for Montreal. He and Vincent Ponte, our city planner, as well as some *Look*-magazine people who were doing a story on Webb & Knapp, flew up to Montreal with me in our DC-3. Circling the city at a few thousand feet, I looked over the site while studying Cobb's designs. Because we were concerned about the conservative atmosphere that pervaded Montreal, Cobb had prepared a step-by-step design. On an elevated platform plaza over the "hole," he set two rectangular towers plus a number of lower, subsidiary buildings. In this way, only after the first tower was successful would we need to put money down for the second structure. It was a competent and a pleasant design, but as I stood up in the steeply banked airplane, and looked out of the windows to the winter-gripped city below, I was dissatisfied. Something was missing. Here lay this unexploited but potentially fabulous site which only we could develop, but what we proposed to develop lacked power. As I began to sense what was missing, I said, "Henry, I want to tell you something . . . you don't make 'melly' out of a blue white diamond." The minute I explained that "melly" are merely the bits and chips left over when a great diamond has been cut, he saw what I meant. He, too, recognized that we needed something with enough critical mass to force changes on Montreal. By critical mass I mean not only the physical but also the emotional and the aesthetic impact of a truly successful building complex. We then and there set out the final specifications, within which Cobb was free to design as his genius dictated. I told him we wanted a major building of at least 1.5 million square feet total area, with at least 35,000 square feet per floor. It must be designed to provide corporate identity for more than one major tenant. Given these directions, Cobb went off to produce the plans of the great cruciform building that now so powerfully dominates downtown Montreal. This was the design that I took to Gordon. What we determined on that airplane was the most crucial decision of the whole Montreal project.

Through early 1956 Gordon and I held a series of meetings to hammer out just how we would work with one another on the project. Gordon is a man blessed not only with self-confidence but also with humor, which made these planning and bargaining sessions highly enjoyable for us all. Cobb sat in on all of these conferences so as to be aware both of the economics and of the nuance of attitude on which any agreement was reached. Normally such agreements are long and involved treatises which lawyers concoct with legal language which consumes page after page, but by now Gordon and I knew and trusted each other so fully that what we produced was a concise two-page affair in simple English. A key part of this final agreement was the master site plan, which we were to produce in six months.

That master site plan proved to be the conceptual basis not only of our venture but also of all following ventures in mid-Montreal. Rather than conceive of our giant building complex as an isolated venture, I had Cobb and Ponte plan it in context with the whole of the CNR's twenty-two acres, and, most important, with the surrounding area which we would affect. The plan, which was devised in close collaboration with Montreal's City Planning Commission, included marketing studies, traffic studies and details of proposed street widenings, underground parking, and pedestrian and vehicular crossovers. It involved studies and projections of peak-hour and off-hour pedestrian flow through various routes, the interactions between various routes, and detailed cost estimates of the various elements of the plan. That plan is what sold Gordon. As he says, with a faint Scottish burr, "When I saw the model, well . . . it was very handsome, but it was not necessarily real. Then I went over the plan, and that convinced me."

Gordon was impressed, but he was still Gordon. He had his engineers go over the details of that plan for six months. He formally accepted it in September, 1957. The Canadian government, which owns the CNR, approved the plan in December, 1957, and that month we signed a lease for our project, which I estimated would cost one hundred million dollars in total.

During this time I was moving on the financial and corporate front. In November, 1955, we had formed a new company, Webb & Knapp (Canada) Limited. One of the first things we did after that was establish relations with a Canadian bank, and I use the singular advisedly. This is because in Canada, unlike the United States, banking is a membership business. Once you are affiliated with one particular bank, that bank expects you to be loyal to it and to bank exclusively with it, or almost so. In exchange it gives its loyalty to you and will support you in your efforts. The bank we joined was the Royal Bank of Canada, which, more accurately, meant James Muir. When John

McCloy, chairman of the Chase, heard that we were starting up a Canadian company, he had introduced us to Muir, the most powerful and controversial figure in Canadian banking. A dominant and domineering man who kept his aides in a constant state of terror, Muir was a tough competitor who had driven his bank from the second rank to the head of the industry. The Bank of Montreal, which for the previous hundred years had been the biggest in Canada, was now number two, and Muir did all he could to slow or crowd his prime competitors. Muir, a great sports fan, and a stout drinker (when he drank), laced his everyday speech with profanity worthy of a sergeant major. Highly dogmatic, he kept things simple: if you were his friend, you could do no wrong; if you were his enemy, you could do no right. If you were worth considering at all, you were in one category or the other. We became good friends because, although I could yell back at him when it suited, I was genuinely fond of this outspoken ruffian, and he liked and approved of what we were trying to do in Canada. He was of tremendous financial and psychological help from the beginning. So, too, was one of his directors, scholarly, quiet-spoken Lazarus Phillips, who gained and kept Muir's confidence through his own integrity and keen intellect. When we bought the solidly built Dominion Square Building for our Canadian company, the purchase was financed by the Royal Bank. Muir and Phillips gave good backing and advice in this and all our other Canadian projects.

In the meantime, armed with our basic agreement with Gordon, we set out to lay a monetary base for our new Canadian company. Graham Mattison, a lawyer and driving force in the New York investment firm of Dominick & Dominick, handled this job. His company, which had a strong branch office in Montreal, created a consortium of Canadian merchant banks to underwrite a package of bonds, convertible debentures, and common stocks, most of which Mattison was able to place through banking connections in Switzerland. This issue brought in some twenty-five million dollars which almost immediately began bearing interest at 5½ percent. Since we had no income to speak of in Canada, we went out looking for short-term investments where we could put the money to work and draw it out later for the project. For instance, we used some ten million dollars of this new money to buy a group of some 277 gas stations owned by a new oil company in Canada, Petrofina. We leased these stations back to Petrofina for ten percent, which, right away, gave us one million dollars a year against our interest payments, and we later quite profitably sold off the stations as we needed money for construction in Montreal.

At the start of the winter of 1957–1958 we had a lease and we had a wonderful plan, we had a great hole in the ground ready for filling, we even had a name for the project: Place Ville-Marie. But when we went looking for tenants, every major company in Canada turned us down.

We were in trouble from the beginning, because we were strangers and foreigners. And later the Montreal establishment would be spiritually in arms against us, because, to round out the property around the "hole," we had, in "collaboration" with Mayor Drapeau and the City of Montreal, arranged to expropriate and demolish the venerable St. James Club. This stately watering spot was established in 1863 in a fine building on the corner of Dorchester and University streets. There, for ninety-four years, some of Montreal's most solidly established English Canadians and their fathers and grandfathers before them had been quietly spending the afternoons and escaping their womenfolk in the evenings. Quite apart from this desecration and razing of a local temple and wildlife refuge, our project was originally resented because it threatened the stuffily stable state of affairs down at St. James Street, where every major bank and company was located. Not only did these gentlemen not like to see their ancient, dark-paneled offices made obsolete, but the very idea of a shift to center-town offices struck many as dangerously radical. The banks that competed fiercely with Muir's Royal Bank were most reluctant to advise their clientele to aid any allies of his. But essentially our trouble was that nobody, not even Muir's friends, actually believed we would ever put up a project as big as we said we would. No matter where we went, we were turned down. Du Pont of Canada gave us a particularly haughty rejection, and Canadian Industries Limited, though we offered them five million dollars for their old building as an incentive to move to our new tower, also showed us the door.

If we couldn't get a major tenant, we couldn't get mortgage

financing from an insurance company. This meant we couldn't get any interim bank loans to finance construction—and this meant that we and Place Ville-Marie were dead. All that winter of 1957–1958 I kept trying, but the ironclad faith of the local business community that we could not get going kept anyone from committing themselves as tenants. Meanwhile, the "hole" kept getting bigger. We kept digging, putting up scaffolding, and working the architects, if for no other reason than the psychological impact on the community; but the local business community were not impressed. By late winter we were four million dollars out of pocket, with nothing to show but the air in the hole we had broadened. The cold Canadian front we were encountering had reached deep into my bones and into my pockets. Numbed by months of this exposure, I did not know where to turn next, until one gray day, walking by the black-and-white, soil-and-snow landscape of the site with my son, I had a thought.

I said to him, "You know why we are not getting anywhere with this damn thing? Because we are tied in with a powerhouse like Jim Muir. His enemies are not going to take a lease in there. And we haven't gotten anywhere with his friends because they don't believe we are going to build. There is a lot of prejudice and antipathy in Canada, particularly in Montreal. They don't want Americans, and especially an American Jew [myself] with a Chinese [Pei] for his top architect. These guys are provincial as hell . . . and they don't like it; we are interfering with their nice infield way of life. . . . I'm going to call Muir."

That weekend, calling from my home in Greenwich, I got Muir on the phone and said, "Jim, you know we are not getting anywhere with this damn renting."

He roared back, "Why the hell should you get anywhere? That goddamn Chinaman is stopping you."

"No, you're stopping us."

"I'm stopping you?"

"Jim, your enemies, the ones who hate you, won't take space here. The ones who love you don't believe in us. There is a gang-up on the part of the other banks, the Bank of Montreal, the Imperial Bank, the Canadian Bank of Commerce, the Bank of Nova Scotia, Toronto Dominion . . ."

He said, "You're crazy."

"I'm not crazy."

Then he said, "Well, what do you want me to do about it?"

"Move."

"I should move? Move? You're mad."

"Move, Jim. We'll call the new tower the Royal Bank of Canada Building in Place Ville-Marie. You will be king of the hill, towering over the whole of Montreal. The business will come to you."

"You're out of your mind. We have the biggest bank in Canada in the biggest bank building in Canada."

I said, "I'll buy it from you."

"You've got no money to buy it, you _____ Jew."

"Now, look here Jim, think this over. I'm coming up tomorrow morning to a directors' meeting."

"Och," he interrupted, "I'm going to England. I don't get back for two weeks. Forget about it."

"No, you think it over, Jim. Call me tomorrow and tell me how you feel about it."

I arrived at our Canadian office at 9:30 next morning, and there were three calls from Muir. When I called him back I said, "Why don't you go to England, and appoint three members of your staff to study this thing while you're gone? We'll have three members of our staff work with them, and when you get back, you'll have a report on it. If it's no good, you don't have to do it. If it's good, you'll do it."

"Well," he said, "all right, I'll do it, I'll appoint three people, but you are crazy anyway." And he hung up.

We put the team together, and when Muir got back in two weeks, they made a report. It was affirmative, and three weeks after that we started drawing up the leases, which involved our buying their building and their moving into the tower. That started the Royal Bank of Canada Building going.

I have often noticed, but never been so rash as to delve into it too deeply, the traditional similarity of bank, temple, and cathedral interiors. This deistic design style has begun to fade in the United States, but in Canada no self-respecting bank would ever move into a building that did not boast a great cathedral of a banking hall. Fitting a properly gigantic Canadian banking hall into Cobb's stark new building was a desperate problem until he conceived of the four great, blocky quadrants now at the base of the structure. These quadrants, which, happily, visually stabilized and accentuated the structure of the building, were conceived of and readied for presentation to Muir in six hectic weeks. As Muir walked into the conference room to look over the plans, the finishing touches were just going onto the last drawing. Muir liked that. He also liked the plans and, typical of the man, rather than consult with his directors about a move, he called them together, announced his plans, and then led them out to look at a model of the bank's future home. This was in May, 1958.

With this coup dangling from my belt, I went down to see my friend Fred Ecker of Metropolitan Life, to borrow seventy-five million dollars. The complex would cost one hundred million, of which we had twenty-five million. When I came in the door, Ecker grinned and said, "Bill, what in hell are you ever coming to see me for?"

"Because you said if I got a top tenant you would be interested in financing us in Canada. Now I have the Royal Bank for seven floors, and I want seventy-five million dollars."

"Seventy-five million! That's more money than there is in Canada."

Ecker lent me fifty million—with strings. He wouldn't lend the money on just the Royal Bank lease, I had to get another one. So I went to see Nat Davis, who is chairman of the board and president of Aluminium Limited and a nephew of Arthur Vining Davis of Alcoa.

Davis, a handsome, slender, youthful-looking man who stems from a top Pittsburgh family, is smart and tough. As regards Canada, Davis was nominally a member of the opposite camp, a director of the Bank of Montreal, but as an American he didn't think as clannishly or at least not as much so as many of the people around him. He was interested in doing the best thing he could for his company, and this is what I was counting on. I told him that we wanted to rent him major space in our building. He countered by saying that they were thinking of putting up their own building. The fact that they were even thinking of putting up new offices gave me hope, and I argued my case with renewed enthusiasm. We made layouts showing what their new quarters would be like. We made great concessions and expensive additions on interior design; I just had to get Davis in as tenant to crack that fifty-million-dollar nut Fred Ecker was holding out for us. For three months I romanced Aluminium, calling on Davis again and again, and he was very tough, but finally I said, "This building is going to be such a great . . . so fantastic a structure that you just can't afford not to be in it."

He said, "What do you mean?"

I told him that we were going to put up the greatest showcase for aluminum in all the history of Canada, if not the whole world.

"How will you do that?" he asked.

And I answered, "We are going to have to sheath this thing with some kind of metal. If you are in this building, it will be aluminum. If you are not, it might be something else. Let's assume it is something else—wouldn't that be an opportunity for your competition? Like, for example, copper, or bronze, or steel? Or, let's assume it is aluminum and you don't move into it. This would be a terrible negation of your own product." Of all the arguments I could bring to bear, that one, I think, is what made it. At last, in September, 1958, he agreed to move.

These two key leases were good-sized deals in themselves. The Royal Bank's lease provided 2.6 million dollars a year in rent for fifty years. Aluminium Limited's was two million dollars a year for twenty years. Next we got in the Montreal Trust Company at $750,000 per year. This came to fruition after Don Kerlin at the Trust had turned us down, but I got him on the phone, saying, "Don, I know you have said no, and I know that you mean no . . . but let's talk for a minute. . . ," and the logic of what was now taking place in Montreal was so persuasive that Kerlin took that lease and was glad of it ever after. Later we made a fine deal for another $750,000 with Trans Canada Airlines, now Air Canada, and with names such as these lined up, all Montreal now realized that our project was no dream but a great reality. The great freeze-out of 1957–1958 had cracked and thawed, and the city would never be the same.

Since we had only twenty-five million dollars of our own money and fifty million promised from Metropolitan Life, we were twenty-five million short of our project cost estimates, but I gave the go-ahead signal. My observation has always been that after a certain key point you must move ahead as if a project were assured—in order to assure it—because if you wait around for all the pieces of the puzzle to fit before closing a deal, you can wait forever. Counting on our own abilities and the evident worth of the project to bring in the additional capital we needed, we let the first construction contracts.

Within two years we did get new capital, and I must give credit to my son for finding it and bringing it in. With Muir and other key tenants signed up, the project began to look a little more interesting to investors. I had been trying, with little success, to find secondary financing for the property. Then my son set up a twenty-five-million-dollar deal with Jock Cotton, the British financier who later backed the Pan Am Building in New York. Bill had visited Cotton in London to discuss the project with him. Cotton seemed interested, and Bill traveled on to Nassau, where he and Cotton drew up a memo of understanding contingent upon the Bank of England's approving this outflow of cash from Britain. On a hunch that something might just possibly go wrong, Bill also called on Kenneth Keith of the London merchant bank of Phillip, Hill, Higginson and Erlanger (now Hill Samuel) to tell him of the impending deal. When, as it developed, the Bank of England did turn down Cotton's application to export capital to Canada, Bill visited Henry Moore, chairman of Phillip, Hill, Higginson and Erlanger. Over lunch at the Savoy, Moore said he felt he could get a clearance for the export of money to Canada and was interested in joining with us on the project. Negotiations went on for many months. Jim Muir and Lazarus Phillips joined these talks, and the net result was that in 1960 a new company, Trizec Corp., jointly owned by Webb & Knapp (Canada) and a British investment group, took over the Montreal property, providing the new company with twenty-two million dollars in construction capital.

While the British negotiations were under way, I arranged a second mortgage at a walloping interest rate, because it would be far less costly to keep the project going, even at high interest rates, than to temporarily close it down. As soon as the new financing came in, we cleaned up this short-term loan, and I could devote myself to other opportunities and crises in other locales.

Montreal, like Denver before it, was never more than one bright aspect of a constantly shifting kaleidoscope. We had started investing throughout Canada in order to keep our twenty-five million dollars in new capital busy. By the end of 1959 we had the first of a series of regional shopping centers under construction in downtown London, Ontario. A second such shopping center, Brentwood, was under way in Vancouver, as was a four-hundred-acre industrial park. We had acquired control of a hyperactive company, Toronto Industrial Lease-holds, which had contracts for over a million square feet of industrial construction throughout Canada, and we were developing a combina-tion industrial and housing development called Flemington Park in North York, Ontario. In all, we had made outlays of 11.5 million dollars on our various projects and expected to spend twenty-five million more the next year.

In the United States our urban-redevelopment projects in New York, Washington, Chicago, Pittsburgh, and Philadelphia were now in various stages of development. We were both buying and selling—and then leasing back—hotels around New York. We had acquired, very profitably, the great land holdings of the Godchaux Sugar Co. of Louisiana. In partnership with the Aluminum Company of America we had acquired 260 acres of land in Los Angeles from Spyros Skouras at Twentieth Century-Fox and were building Century City. Our Wall Street Manuever, before phasing out, would bring the U.S. Steel Corp. into New York real estate by their purchase of a great block of land downtown. It would also lead to our pioneering in the upper Sixth Avenue area, locating a hotel and office buildings there, rivaling our previous work on Park Avenue.

With all these activities in hand, I got to Montreal no oftener than to our great project in Denver. Montreal, however, was at all times the greater and more intricate, and therefore more interesting, enterprise.

Much of the intricacy and interest of Montreal flowed from the curious, unwritten rules of coexistence between the French and English of Canada, and we soon learned how important these rules were.

• 15 • Maneuvers and Battles for Place Ville-Marie

WEBB & KNAPP brought a very youthful team to Canada. Cobb, as I mentioned, was only twenty-eight years old. Our town planner, Vincent Ponte, also a former student of Pei's, was little over thirty when I first met him in 1955. Arnold Gorman, resident architect on the project, and also from Pei's office, was in the same age bracket. Our Canadian architects, the now deservedly well-known firm of Affleck, Desbarats, Dimkaopoulos, Lebensold & Sise, consisted of five young men a few years out of school. At the time we came to Montreal this group shared offices over a pizza parlor near McGill University but were not organized as a company. Quinton Carlson, our construction supervisor, was a thirty-year-old engineer. Our Canadian contractor had placed another young engineer, Tom Phelan, in charge of their part of the operation. At Jim Muir's suggestion, we had taken on Leslie W. Haslett as executive vice-president in charge of our Montreal office. A very pleasant older man, Haslett was once a renowned cricket player for England and a member of the old-boy network. But the ramrod of the operation, and later also a vice-president, was David Owen, a young Canadian just out of law school. Working with him would be Fred Fleming to handle rentals, and serving as secretary, Jim Soden, a smart young lawyer from Lazarus Phillips' office.

I gave these young men all the work and responsibility they could handle, and more. All of them, drawing on their training at Webb & Knapp, later reached positions of national prominence in their industry. Such Webb & Knapp talent-seeding was not confined to Montreal. In every city where the company established a major presence, some of our alumni stayed to man posts at the top of their professions. However, the youthquake we instituted in stodgy old Montreal was an exceptional one.

Through the summer of 1955, although our talks with Gordon

were still in the early stages, I was on the alert for possible partners who might joint with us in Montreal or in other ventures. We had been approached by management of the Società Immobiliare, the construction and investment company which has headquarters in Rome and is partly owned by the Vatican. They wanted to talk about mutual projects, including one in Rome. Pei, my son, and I flew over there, and Pei spent a month working on some preliminary sketches for parts of EUR, a great housing and commercial project on the outskirts of Rome.

At the time I was led to believe that we would be able to do great things in partnership with Immobiliare, and our understanding was that when they came to North America it would be in partnership with us. In effect, it turned out that they were playing a Machiavellian game and had been picking our brains before moving in as our direct competitors both in Washington and in Montreal. Immobiliare also lured away one of my key vice-presidents, Nicolas Salgo, a young Hungarian who could play their kind of game at least as well as they and who has since made a fortune in the field of assembling corporate conglomerates.

In view of the ownership and connections of Immobiliare, I was naïvely unprepared for this about-face. Later, however, we did get a certain grim satisfaction from the fact that, though they picked our brains, the charming gentlemen from Immobiliare did not make very good use of their own. They came to Montreal with backing from a Belgian bank and with the architect Pier Luigi Nervi, but their project, Place Victoria, was ill-conceived and quite costly. It did not effectively tie itself into the existing communications system of which our project was the hub. Instead of going up at one master stroke, Place Victoria was built slowly and piecemeal. At this writing only one of three originally proposed towers has been completed; and this one tower is not filled, despite discounted rents.

One good thing that came from our Italian visit, however, was that Vince Ponte, then in Europe on a Fulbright scholarship, happened to be seated at a café on the popular Via Veneto one afternoon admiring some of the beautiful passing scenery. When he spotted Pei also walking by, Ponte ran out to say hello, and wound up going to work for us in Montreal. A talented planner with a sure command of French,

Ponte was soon well liked by officialdom in Montreal. He stayed there after our project was completed as site planner for a number of other projects. As co-developer, with Cobb, of our original master plan for Montreal, he possessed a depth of background and continuity from which the whole area profited.

However, the first employee of Webb & Knapp (Canada) was twenty-four-year-old David Owen, whom I met over the back fence of our estate in Greenwich, Connecticut. Sometime before we moved to Greenwich, Hans Tobeason had bought the Fruehauf estate, which adjoined ours. Toby and I became friends. David Owen, Toby's Canadian son-in-law, was a member of a well-established West Coast family. At the time our Canadian venture began, David had just graduated from Columbia Law School. We needed young Canadians of the right background, and I offered David a job. He took it, accepted responsibility fearlessly, and handled a variety of assignments with dispatch, sometimes too much dispatch. By 1958, when it came time to demolish some of the properties surrounding the "hole," we got a number of angry telephone calls; it turned out that our eager-beaver crews were illegally knocking down buildings we didn't even own yet, but this kind of schedule-pushing I can stand; it is the many delays that can sometimes plague a project which are painful.

For all my technically trained and talented young helpers, I was principal troubleshooter for Webb & Knapp and would not have it any other way. Financing and building a great project is a bit like building a road through mountain country; around every bend there is a surprise, and a great part of the excitement and interest in a development, aside from its conception, lies in the challenge of finding new ways around the many difficulties that crop up. In Montreal we had a fair sampling of every minor and major form of difficulty that a great project can encounter, some of which I shall now detail.

In the first category of predictable, avoidable trouble, I destroyed one thousand copies of the first brochure my aides put out on our Montreal project. The reason: in Canada just experiencing the first strong spasms of economic anti-Americanism, our brochure would have read like a version of "The Stars and Stripes Forever." Quite unconsciously, by what it did not say, this brochure dismissed Canada as a mere state, another Illinois or Colorado where Webb & Knapp of

New York operated. Such a pamphlet would have been a psychological and political disaster. I stopped its distribution and had a new broadsheet prepared. Turning the spotlight away from Webb & Knapp, New York, to Webb & Knapp (Canada), I laid special emphasis on our illustrious board of Canadian directors, our relationship with Gordon and with the CNR, and our plans for Canada. Brochure number two went forth to the press, the public, and investment world and was received quietly. It created no favorable breezes in the form of new investors, but since brochure number one would have whistled up a raging nationalist squall, I was content.

The niceties of nationalism, moreover, did not stop at things American vis-à-vis things Canadian. There is the complex and ever-present business of things French versus things English waiting to trap the unwary from the south. In Webb & Knapp's case, we were fortunate; the Montreal scene boasted of a number of chilling examples of knowledgeable men who, moving briskly through the maze of English-French relations, ran into sudden and painful obstructions. In fact, one of these examples was provided by the CNR and my estimable friend Donald Gordon when they were naming their new hotel.

The hotel was being built next to the proposed Place Ville-Marie. It was going to be the pride and flagship of the CNR's hotels. It also would have been the toast of Quebec province had not the CNR been hoist on an imperial petard. For weeks, as construction went on, the CNR directors thrashed about trying to ready a decision about the name of the new hotel. On their own, I am sure they would come up with a suitably French name, but in the meantime a great many volunteers joined this pleasurable pastime. One of the volunteers was Sir Vincent Massey, the governor general and Queen Elizabeth's official representative to Canada. On a visit to Britain, the governor general, in a fairly offhand way, wondered out loud if the Queen might wish to have the hotel named after her. In diplomacy, as in business, indirection can become a way of life, because certain kinds of official entanglements can thus be avoided, but there is also a constant danger of over-interpretation of signals. This now happened. No one in England, I am told, was that anxious to see a hotel named after the Queen, but they assumed the Canadians, as loyal ex-colonials, wished nothing more and had, with proper British understatement, just signaled as much. After due consideration, word was sent out that, yes, her Majesty would be pleased to grace a hotel with her name. And the CNR's decision was, in effect, made. For now, not to name the hotel after her would be an insult to the Queen, and to the Crown, which is *not* done. Thus painted into a corner, the CNR board stiffened their collective upper lip and announced the name of the new hotel—the Queen Elizabeth.

This incident is fairly typical of English-French relations, in that all the parties involved felt innocent, righteous, and put upon. When the hotel's name was announced, the hoots and howls of rage and frustration from French politicians and editors lasted for months. To the French this was just one more bitterly resented, politically exploitable instance of arrogance on the part of the English. To many of the English, who, if the Queen's acceptance had been rejected would have been ten times more upset than the French, this was just one more instance of the overexcitable French seeking out and finding trouble where none existed.

As for the Americans, one crass executive of the Hilton chain tried to have the hotel named the Elizabeth Hilton.

To us, this was a lesson and a warning that whatever name we chose for our project, it had better be French—or there would be no project. I toyed with the name Place Renaissance, because we were dealing in a rebirth of Montreal, but finally chose Place Ville-Marie, evoking the beginnings of the city. Mayor Drapeau, delighted with the name, immediately checked with his Eminence, Montreal's cardinal, Paul-Emile Léger, who was equally enthusiastic. Boosted by this from both the church and the laity, we were just barely able to hurdle the next totally unexpected obstacle—the election of a new coalition federal government in Ottawa when the Liberal Party, after years in office was voted out. Flushed with victory and stuffed with their own economic-nationalist oratory, the new parliament looked on our "foreign" project through jaundiced eyes. A throw of the election dice had done us in, and the CNR was quietly advised to desist in its dalliance with the devilish foreigners from the south. And yet, we were a special case (no one else in the world was willing to tackle this project for the CNR), and we were in French Canada, another special case, where some of the French leadership had smiled upon our cause. Lazarus Phillips, that invaluable mediator, arranged for me to go to

Ottawa to visit with the politically powerful Louis St. Laurent of Quebec province. Maybe, with St. Laurent's help, something could yet be salvaged.

St. Laurent was most polite, but definitely cool. At the very start of our conversation he noted that the American economic presence was becoming increasingly unwelcome in Canada and that turning over twenty-two acres of CNR properties, Crown properties, to Americans, even if it were in Canada's long-term best interests, would be extremely difficult to support politically. Then he asked three questions:

First: what we were going to name the new development? Well, since I was dealing with a Frenchman, I immediately told him it would be called Place Ville-Marie, which the cardinal and all French Montreal were pleased with. At this he gave a very French arching of the eyebrows and sigh of relief, which said all by itself several separate paragraphs about the Queen Elizabeth Hotel, Montreal, Quebec, and English-French politics in Canada. Next, after a series of indirect questions, he asked two quite pointed ones: Would we be putting up a lot of small buildings to compete directly with going businesses in Montreal? The answer was no, we were going to put up one great structure that would be to Montreal what the Eiffel Tower was to Paris. Finally he wanted to know if we were going to insist on taking over the whole of the CNR's twenty-two acres for development. And here, sensing what was wanted, I again said no, our interest was in the tower project, a mere seven acres; all we asked for was the right to bid on any second-stage project. Meanwhile, we would contribute to the overall project by donating our master plan for the whole of the area to the CNR.

On hearing this last, St. Laurent said, "Mr. Zeckendorf, based on what you have told me, I now see things in a quite different light. I shall try to help you." The vote was close, but the government did give its approval, and we did get our lease.

In matters great as in matters small, around the world as in Montreal, I find it is not logic but emotions, sometimes carefully rationalized to resemble logic, that more often than not decide most issues.

We saw ample evidence of this in Canada in politics, in business, and in politics-verging-on-business, where I found a strangely strict, quid-pro-quo, favor-for-a-favor, an-eye-for-an-eye framework of English-French coexistence. Thus, before any street widening or property expropriations could be undertaken for Place Ville-Marie (which was considered to be in the English part of town), something had to be done in the French part of town. Therefore, the multimillion-dollar Berri Street tunnel and underpass had to be authorized by the City Council in order to clear the way for legislation aiding Place Ville-Marie.

Even the St. James Club episode, where Webb & Knapp publicly played the villain's role, fit into place as part of the meticulously scored Montreal game of tit-for-tat. In our early plans for Place Ville-Marie we very carefully skirted the sacrosanct site of the St. James Club, with the intention of building around it. After all, what newcomer seeking friends and favor would willfully disturb the office-hour rookery of some of the richest and most important old birds and most likely customers in town?

It just so happened, however, that the top French club had been razed in a previous street widening. Montreal's French administrators, after pointing out the evident flaws in our compromise site plans, flatly announced that if anything at all was to be razed for Place Ville-Marie, the St. James Club would have to be, too.

I dislike having to demolish such fine old buildings as the St. James Club, but, as I previously mentioned, since its razing did make good architectural sense and because I could find no workable alternative, we went ahead with the operation.

The club members naturally fought this move, but, local politics considered, it was no contest. A Montreal cartoonist, French of course, depicted a last battle with assorted club members umbrellas drawn, standing off the workmen and fending off the bulldozers with blasts from seltzer bottles. This pretty much told the story. I suspect poor Donald Gordon, a St. James member, may have suffered some cool moments during the last days of the club on its old site. I tried my best, and went to considerable expense, to turn a bad situation into a good one. The top floor of the great tower in Place Ville-Marie is two feet higher than the other floors. We designed this floor, along with its private elevator, as new quarters for the St. James Club. The club membership, however, could not bring themselves to join with Place

Ville-Marie. Instead they took quarters in a small, most unprepossessing and expensive new building diagonally across the street from their old quarters. The last I heard the St. James Club's operating costs had risen to the point that it was spending more than its annual income from dues.

Another, and quite different, instance of in-city infighting involved Jim Muir. The longer the Royal Bank could keep any competitors from making a similar move away from St. James Street and onto the high ground in midcity, the longer it would be able to reap the advantages of being the sole bank in a modern office and new location. Therefore, Muir never publicly announced that the Royal Bank would be moving its headquarters to Place Ville-Marie, announcing only that he would take space in the new building. Muir was particularly interested in foxing another Scottish money man, McKinnon of the Canadian Imperial Bank of Commerce. But McKinnon was not fooled for long, and working with local developers, the Imperial Bank pulled a sly maneuver of its own. It acquired from the Royal Bank the lease to a key property at Dorchester and Peel streets. They began erecting the high-rise Canadian Imperial Bank of Commerce Building, designed to compete with the Royal Bank in Place Ville-Marie.

When he learned of these plans, Muir called in the bank officer who, all unknowing, had turned over the lease to McKinnon, thus giving aid and succor to the enemy. He gave this executive such a fierce tongue-lashing that that night the shaken man toyed with thoughts of suicide. Fortunately, he went back to work instead, to find Muir still bubbling furiously in the morning but no longer emitting lava. Like it or not, we and the Royal Bank were face to face with some competition. Muir was especially delighted to learn that, by city regulations, his competitors had to provide suitably spacious parking facilities within five hundred feet of their building. If they could not, they would be required to dig down through solid rock for the four or more extra floors to supply the necessary parking area for their building. The only available parking site was the Tilden Garage, and Muir immediately had us buy it with his money. Eventually, I believe the Imperial Bank of Commerce, which was not without friends and influence in Montreal, was able to have the pertinent regulations "properly" interpreted so it did not have to dig quite so deeply and expensively as might have been the case. The quite handsome Imperial Bank of Commerce Building was completed almost at the same time as Place Ville-Marie and is now doing well. The Royal Bank building, as we first planned it, was to be the tallest such structure in the British Commonwealth. McKinnon pointedly designed his building to be a few feet taller than ours. We made no visible response, but I had Cobb design the top of the building so that, if we wished, we could add a few floors. Then, when the Bank of Commerce plans were finally frozen for construction, I added three extra floors, to once more make ours the tallest building in the Commonwealth.

The Bank of Commerce, however, was not our only competition. Back in 1955, during one of our first visits to Montreal, I had hosted a luncheon for a dozen of Montreal's top real-estate men. At some point between dessert and coffee I asked each of these gentlemen to give his estimate of the maximum amount of office space Montreal could assimilate in the next five years. They wrote their predictions on slips of paper, which I collected. Most estimates ranged from 300,000 to 750,000 square feet. I read these answers out. Then I cheerfully announced that we would soon be starting on a four-million-square-foot complex, which would be larger than the original Rockefeller Center. The faces at the table turned green with horror.

One of my guests that day was a local developer named Ionel Rudberg. Galvanized by our entry into his town, he did a wonderful thing: he set out to build a thirty-four story, 600,000-square-foot office tower at the corner of Dorchester and University streets and catercorner from our own complex. Rudberg's smaller structure was completed before our own. To what degree home-town boy Rudberg drew on Montreal's underlying xenophobia, I do not know but he soon found backing. Canadian Industries, Ltd., which had turned us down, signed a lease as principal tenants and the building was named after them. Between the Canadian Industries, Ltd., the Bank of Commerce, and our own Royal Bank buildings, we eventually had three million square feet of new office space simultaneously on the Montreal market. Because of this competition, Webb & Knapp had to offer more attractive and lower terms than might otherwise have been the case in order to fill Place Ville-Marie. As a partial palliative, the rise of two new buildings on our flanks definitely assured the shift of the business and financial community to midtown. All this was very good for Montreal, which did indeed begin to undergo a renaissance, but what followed next, an amputation of a minor Place Ville-Marie extension, was not good for anybody.

Rudberg, in order to get Canadian Industries, Ltd., as tenant for his new building, was forced to meet the exceedingly handsome trade-in offer of five million dollars which we, in trying to draw Canadian Industries to Place Ville-Marie, had made for their building. This building, at McGill College Avenue between Cathcart and St. Catherine streets, lay right beside our plaza and complex. Place Ville-Marie, like my concept of "X City," is set on a great, three-block-long, one-block wide platform. The buildings rise through this plaza. The plaza's long southern boundary, at busy Dorchester Street, flanks the Queen Elizabeth Hotel, while on the north, the platform stands fifteen feet above the elevation of quiet Cathcart Street. The center of the open portion of the plaza intersects the heartline of the city, McGill College Avenue. A man standing at the foot of Place Ville-Marie's cruciform tower can look north, along McGill College Avenue, across crowded St. Catherine Street, and directly onward to the bluff of Mount Royal—a perspective that provides a pleasant play for the senses. We decided to accentuate this pleasing geometry by widening McGill Avenue from Cathcart to St. Catherine streets, some 60 to 115 feet. Then, from the level of our plaza we would build a gradually sloping mall to the intersection of McGill and St. Catherine, the town's main shopping street. We visualized this combination causeway-promenade as the final link connecting Place Ville-Marie to the great department stores uptown and the commuter railroad and offices downtown. Though on a smaller scale, the mall was, in a way, reminiscent of the great approachway I had once tried to create for United Nations Plaza in New York.

This time, however, it was not a prideful Robert Moses but a worried Ionel Rudberg who blocked our way. He was worried about a possible five-million-dollar turkey, the Canadian Industries building, which he would soon have on his hands. He fought the proposed street widening and mall in City Council, and what transpired was a lively example of the effects of in-city politics and pressure on planning.

On the local political scene Mayor Drapeau had lost the 1957 election, to be replaced for one term by Sarto Fournior. Our relations with city hall were still excellent, and we had every hope of getting our project through. That is, we had such hopes until Rudberg pulled out his aces in the form of a multibarreled corporate cannon. He persuaded his friends at Canadian Industries, then still owning and occupying their old building, to write a letter protesting our causeway, stating that the rise of a ramp alongside them would adversely affect their building. That letter cowed our allies on the Montreal Council like General Wolfe's guns on the Plain of Abraham once quelled the French in Quebec. Under Mayor Drapeau and his associate Lucien Saulnier (who could look beyond an immediate skirmish to long-term goals and effects) we might have been able to hold our ground, but no ordinary mayor could whip his councilmen into line against one of the city's major employers and one of the nation's larger and more wealthy corporations.

The upshot of all this was that our opponents and enemies enjoyed a minor triumph and we were temporarily dismayed. But the real loser was the City of Montreal; it lost not only a delightful architectural flower but also the vital momentum for badly needed improvements and further widening along McGill Avenue. In spite of later great efforts by others, including my friends at Eaton's, the department-store chain, this momentum never built up, nor is it likely to do so for quite some time. (We dealt with Eaton's all over Canada, and I will later have more to say about this peculiar institution.)

In retrospect we now know that Rudberg's building would not have been hurt, but much helped, by the increased flow of traffic through and around our proposed mall at St. Catherine Street, but this, too, is now just so much blood under the bridge. The lesson is that in a city, a relatively minor investment in open space can pay off handsomely in better rents for whole blocks in the area—if the city and property owners can raise their eyes above and beyond the limits of their own sidewalks.

At the time of the incident, however, I expended little thought and even less emotion on mourning any loss to Montreal from our defeat in the City Council. I was too engrossed by another kind of discovery: our little setback with the city fathers was putting the whole of Place Ville-Marie in jeopardy.

It may at first seem unlikely that this relatively minor upset of our site plans could have seriously threatened the whole project, but such was the case. It came about because insurance companies, in the early negotiating stages, can be quite flexible about the details of a project, but become more and more rigid as an agreement reaches the signing stage. By the time an arrangement has been reached and written up into preliminary contract form insurance companies have developed a ritual inflexibility that only the priesthood of ancient Egypt may have been able to equal. Every income augury and cost incantation must be precisely spelled out, every minor detail of planning and construction must be exactly as prescribed by codicil, or the whole magical process of mortgages, loans, and grants will be contaminated by uncertainty, and the entire delicate process must be started up again from the beginning.

Our mall was to become a magnet for people (like the one I had created between Macy's and Gimbels on Thirty-fourth Street in New York). And our mall had just been blown out of existence. With an important subelement, one we had been touting as a profitable link to retailing, removed from our plan, I was in great fear of Metropolitan Life deciding to reconsider the whole matter of backing Place Ville-Marie. To forestall this, it was necessary that we persuade first ourselves—and then Metropolitan Life—that the mall was a piece of frosting. We had to convince ourselves that visitors drawn to Place Ville-Marie from St. Catherine Street by the mall would still go there by the lower-level route under the plaza, and that escalators could then take them up to the next level. We had to convince ourselves that there were advantages to the change (there were) and that the new lower-level, or promenade, route on which pedestrians would now tend to move would be a great windfall for the many shops on this level (which it was). Having convinced ourselves, we now had to convince our friends. Our associate architects, angry at the Council's blow against good design and a better city, were ready to march on City Hall in protest against the stupidity of the decision against us. But if we were to throw any more forces into the battle, the resulting publicity would only convince Metropolitan Life that the mall was indeed vital to the project. Then, if we lost, and the odds against us were great, we might lose not only the promenade but also the whole project. It took soft-spoken Henry Cobb five hours to do so, but he finally talked our allies out of staging a grand battle for a principle, in order to save a cause.

After a week with one foot in limbo we also convinced Metropolitan Life that the mall, though useful, was not vital, and Place Ville-Marie, sans sloping causeway, was once more on its way. Then the great steel crisis of 1959–1960 hit us like a torpedo in the bow. It put a five-million-dollar gap in our finances, and it is a profound tribute to the concept and basic design of Place Ville-Marie that we could keep going and eventually reach safe haven after such a blow.

Place Ville-Marie's cruciform tower contains forty-nine thousand tons of steel. A significant percentage of that steel was not necessary, but the putting in of that extra steel cost us five million dollars. The nominal cause of this staggering cost hike was a Quebec law aimed at questionable practices and ethics. This law puts responsibility for design of steel structures not only on the engineers and builder but also on the steel company that supplies the materials. Such a law can be useful in discouraging suppliers from providing inferior-quality products. However, this law, in effect, also puts the steel company in the designer's seat, with some built-in conflicts, for the objectives of the builder and those of his suppliers are necessarily opposite. In the case of Place Ville-Marie, for instance, this law and a number of other factors began to play one upon the other, to create our crisis. One prime factor was that our forty-five-story cruciform building was something new in the world, and calculations as to how winds would effect such a structure were quite abstruse. Another was that Canadian steel engineers, especially at that time, had had very little experience in high-rise technology. Like engineers the world over, they did not like to think they were behind anybody in anything, and made up for any insecurity by being hyperconservative as regards stress and safety margins. A third factor was that steel companies like to sell steel. They sell it by the ton and take pleasure in selling as many tons at a time as possible. So the situation all but reduced itself to the fact that ultraconservative engineers, whose chief interest was the sale of steel, had veto power on our designs.

When we originally contracted for our steel there was a recession under way and excess steel on hand, so we got the very favorable price of 280 dollars per ton. But now the recession was over, and the equivalent steel was getting 300 dollars or more per ton on the market.

Finally, there was a clause in our contract having to do with the complexity of the steel delivered to us. This clause opened up the possibility of renegotiations if this complexity were to increase beyond a given amount.

Our principal design consultants were a reputable New York firm who boasted a wealth of background in steel design. Their signature on a design would normally be quite enough to guarantee its acceptance in New York. In Canada, however, over the course of some six months of discussion, our consultant was not able to convince local designers that his stress formulas and designs should be accepted in Canada. Gradually, parts of the design began to change, more steel was added, more fabrication was called for.

Over a period of time, our local suppliers, because of their special legal position, were forcing a drastic redesign of the steelwork on the building. Finally, claiming that the forced design changes now made this an entirely new job, they upped the price, not of the extra steel, but of all the steel on the job, from the original 280 dollars to 320 dollars per ton.

When I finally realized that we were in the gentle hands of our suppliers, I tried everything I could think of to better the situation. But canceling the contract and turning to other sources would still mean steel at the market price. It would also be difficult and time-consuming and could subject us to legal harassment and delays. Further extensive delays would end up costing us more than would bowing to the new prices our suppliers insisted on using. In effect, we were trapped deep in a steel-lined box. All we could do about this was tap on the sides, note the watertight construction, and pour in enough more money to eventually float to the top. What with redesign, new construction to new specifications, and new prices, our Canadian steel crisis totaled up as a five-million-dollar misunderstanding.

At this point our British fellow investors of the Eagle Star and Covent Garden companies were in the process of joining with Webb & Knapp to form Trizec (Tri + Z for Zeckendorf + E for Eagle Star + C for Covent Garden) Corp. Trizec began as a fifty-fifty agreement between Webb & Knapp (Canada) and the British investors. Our partners, however, arranged to supply more capital, and credit for capital loans, in exchange for a proportionally greater interest in Trizec, with

Webb & Knapp holding the option of reacquiring its percentage of the ownership in the project upon repayment of its share of the loans and interest. So the project went on.

In the summer of 1961 the last piece of steelwork on the building was topped out. We had a ceremony with the mayor, Cardinal Léger, and a great many other guests and notables present, with one sad exception. This exception was my volcanic friend Jim Muir. Jim had died. The white-hot fires that had kept him fuming and roaring so impressively down on St. James Street went out before he could test his vocal effects at the new locale at Place Ville-Marie, but we thought and spoke of him. Then, in September, 1962, with Montreal's transformation and renaissance underway and with our great, masculine building standing up against the Montreal skyline like a man surrounded by boys, we held an official opening. Here I toasted Muir once more. He was not unlike the giant building which he, Gordon, Phillips, and I, with invaluable help from others, had gambled, cajoled, and fought to bring into reality.

At the time of the opening, only fifteen stores in the lower-level promenade under the plaza had been rented, and these (I must admit) largely to second-string retailers. At the opening, however, the town's top merchants came to look, and realized just what a magnet for people the promenade was going to be, and they began lining up for available space. Stores in the promenade that once went for six dollars per square foot now rent for fifteen dollars per square foot and find no dearth of tenants. As to the plaza, some had argued that in a city of long winters and strong winds its open space is wasted, but every city desperately needs well-planned open spaces. Besides, a basic element of the CNR's agreement with the city was the promise of a public space and plaza on the site—and the plaza does see use. After the building was completed, a fervent group of young French nationalists, in public protest against what they held to be the CNR's discrimination in the employment and advancement of French Canadians, held a noisy rally on the plaza. The climax of the meeting was the burning of an effigy of Donald Gordon. About Gordon's reactions to this display I have not inquired, but I do know that Henry Cobb, the architect, was delighted: the town plaza was serving its function.

Because of what we did at Place Ville-Marie, Montreal's financial center moved uptown. Shopping and commuting patterns in the city were drastically changed and improved, and helped make Montreal's fabulous Expo '67 possible. Because of the building and commercial expansion which we precipitated, the city received an unexpected windfall in tax revenues. With the help of these new tax moneys, Montreal was able to raise capital in New York for a subway system, the Metro. With a subway under construction, our practical but also visionary ally, Mayor Drapeau, (now back in office), was able to bid and win approval for a World's Fair which millions of people will remember as Montreal's architecturally delightful and intellectually disciplined gift to Canada and the world.

The new Montreal has something to offer to all metropolitan centers. Montreal has a city core so planned that the flow of pedestrian, auto, and other forms of traffic actually complement each other, to help make the center more usable and attractive. This "model" system grew out of and around our project, with its various and separate levels for train, truck, auto, and pedestrian traffic. In Montreal, which has seven months of winter weather, our wide, well-lighted pedestrian passageways offered a handy all-weather pathway so popular that some shops in the promenade found themselves doing business at the rate of four hundred dollars per square foot of space, compared to one hundred dollars in most successful shopping centers. The Metro was tied into this all-weather network. Other builders joined the system. As a result of both city and private planners tying into an existing "good thing," Montreal has become a place to which city administrators and planners come in search of lessons they can apply at home.

Finally, as regards Toronto, Montreal has once more moved several strides to the fore as Canada's true queen city.

I received verification of this during a visit to Toronto. I had been to Toronto a number of times trying to get a major project off the ground there. On this particular visit my son and I were invited to call on Fred Gardner, who was to greater Toronto what Bob Moses in his heyday had been to New York. He was a tremendously successful and productive public servant who knew how to overawe politicians and get things done. He redeveloped the water front and built multiple roads, parks, subways, and throughways, to bring some cohesion to

Toronto's urban sprawl. During our visit with him Gardner said, "I wanted to meet you to tell you something. . . . I am retiring. . . . I've been planning to do so for five years or more, but now I am doing so with a great deal of grief and worry. I was convinced once that Toronto had decisively passed Montreal to become the leading city in Canada. In fact, I was sure we could keep this position forever, because Montreal was asleep while we were growing. . . . You pulled Montreal ahead and now the momentum and initiative lie with them. You made one city of Canada pass the other and changed Canadian history."

I was touched, because this was a great as well as generous gentleman speaking to us. We had a great plan for Toronto which could do much for that city as we had done for Montreal, and I said, "Actually, Toronto's ripe for masterful development, but you need three or four big funerals here among your vested interests, because they are not about to make any imaginative moves."

"Name them," he said.

"I can't, because I'd be touching on areas that might hurt me," I replied, "but I'll tell you one thing; Eaton's is the biggest single stumbling block to progress in this city."

Eaton's is Canada's greatest store chain. Its sales of over one billion dollars per years would be the equivalent of ten billion dollars in the U.S. market. Eaton's is the Canadian Sears Roebuck plus the next six or seven largest U.S. store chains combined. This great enterprise, controlled by a single family, is headed by John David Eaton. Mr. Eaton is a merchant prince, but in pride of city or sense of service, no Medici. Almost by happenstance, Eaton's had a geographic stranglehold on the natural growth of Toronto, by virtue of the land space they owned in and around their store, which lies just to the north of the heart of town and in the line of natural growth from Lake Ontario. A greater part of this land lies idle, either as parking lots or as dusty, truck-chocked warehousing. Sprawled out like a great patch of crabgrass on a lawn, the Eaton holdings effectively choke any new growth trying to get under way alongside.

We had worked with Eaton's in establishing various shopping centers throughout Canada. In consultation with Eaton's and at considerable expense to Webb & Knapp, we also devised a plan for their Toronto holdings. Our development, centered about a beautiful open plaza to replace their present nest of buildings, included high-rise office buildings and a great new Eaton store. Aside from developing much new traffic for the store, our project promised impressive returns as a real-estate development. The management of the company, however, turned us down. John David Eaton would not even attend our presentation of the project, and the plan was aborted. As a result, Montreal has maintained its developmental lead, and Toronto lost out.

After we had left the Canadian scene, Eaton's, in part emboldened and in part stung by our example and commentary, did make a stab at rehabilitation of their properties along the lines recommended by us. Through lack of imagination and of boldness in execution the project died stillborn.

Three

▪ Prologue

By the late 1940's and early 1950's it was obvious that the central core of every one of our major cities was falling in on itself. During the 1930's there had been almost no new building and a cut in the maintenance of most older ones. Meanwhile, population continued to grow. With World War II, the country underwent some further population shifts to certain cities (i.e., near training camps or industrial centers), but shortages and controls curtailed construction of new buildings as well as the maintenance of old ones. In other words, the key cities grew more crowded and continued to deteriorate.

After the end of World War II one might have expected to see a wholesale revival in the cities, but a great percentage of those who could afford to moved to the suburbs, deserting the cities. Urban America became suburban America, and the new megalopolis flourished—in part at the expense of the cities. For instance, corporations that had originally established themselves in great cities to be near a supply of labor, sources of materials, customers, and a railhead, began building their new plants near the new homes outside of town.

The result of this outflow of people and absence of new industries was a loss of tax revenues and the creation of a vacuum, especially in the older residential and manufacturing sections of the cities. As a consequence, urban blight began to spread out of the ancient slums and into once pleasant residential neighborhoods.

Then, compounding their problems, the cities found themselves invaded by a postwar influx of rural Americans. These newcomers, the bulk of them unskilled laborers, had for several decades been leaving the farm country for work in the cities. The trend gained impetus during World War II, but after the war it became even more pronounced. Spilling out from the traditional ghettos where they first moved in with friends and relatives, the newcomers flowed into the partially evacuated nearby neighborhoods. This in turn accelerated the flight of the remaining old residents to the suburbs or other parts of town.

The newcomers, the majority of them uneducated and unskilled, had difficulty in finding good jobs and steady work. Because they were poor, they crowded together, which of itself tends to create a degree of urban blight. Besides this, the immigrants, many because they were ignorant and unaccustomed to the mores and disciplines of city living, others because they were exploited and resentful, and some because they were renters rather than owners, proved indifferent if not destructive caretakers of property.

Today some explosive events and television have made most of us dramatically aware of the situation which I have laid out in barest detail. The interrelated problems of jobs, housing, and education in the great cities we now recognize as the great challenge of our ultraurban society. In 1952 this was not the case. The outflow to the suburbs was too evident to be denied, but what this exodus meant and what the speed and size of the migrations to the cities foretold was something many tried to ignore or deny.

There was some awareness, though, and in 1949 a proposal, first broached in 1937 for the elimination of slum areas, was enacted by Congress. This act, a variant of the land subsidies through which our early railroads were built, was known as the Title I Urban Redevelopment Act. The basic idea of urban redevelopment was that a city, using its right of eminent domain, would acquire slum or blighted land at fair market prices to the owners. It would clear this land, then offer it to private developers at less than the cost to the city. On this low-cost land the developers could then erect low- and medium-income housing. One-third of the cost of the newly cleared land was to be borne by the city, and two-thirds by the federal government.

Title I was a good idea, but it did not work. The trouble was that the law concentrated only on housing. It takes much more than the razing of slums and putting up of clean new apartments to revitalize a great area stricken with a combination of social and economic ills: revitalizing parts of a city's core calls for a change in its human chemistry. The best way to achieve this is through new or better land use (as happened in Montreal). Housing can, and in most instances should be, a key part of this change, but you also have to create supporting commercial and aesthetic elements in the area or have them already available nearby, otherwise your housing will eventually succumb to the decay around it. The 1949 law took none of this into account.

Many cities, while much interested in Title I, were unwilling to commit their limited resources to take advantage of the new law, because major builders and institutional investors were leery of becoming involved in obviously complex and politically prickly projects in cities. These investors had become accustomed to getting Federal Housing Authority (FHA) mortgage insurance on all their projects. And the FHA, while freely funneling funds to the suburbs, treated proposals to build in slum areas with about as much enthusiasm as your maiden aunt getting an invitation to a strip tease show.

In response to the poor showing of Title I and the suggestions of a special commission appointed by President Eisenhower, Congress in 1954 passed further legislation enabling the FHA to insure urban developments by using formulas based on the value of property once a project was successfully completed. In other words, the FHA insurers were called upon to begin thinking and acting as propagators of seed money and not as money guardians. Also, under this new legislation, mixed commercial and residential developments were encouraged. Eventually things were so set up that sponsors need put up only three to five percent of the total cost of a development in cash. Thus, even though total profit on such developments might be held to a modest six percent, the relatively low amount of cash involved promised the sponsors great leverage on their investment.

With passage of the new law, numbers of major builders and investors developed an interest in urban redevelopment. A slow-moving but impressive procession of urban-redevelopment projects began to get under way across the nation, with Webb & Knapp sometimes twirling the baton, at other times beating the drums, and always leading the parade.

Billions of dollars were invested under the above-mentioned legislation. It is obvious that the urban-redevelopment programs of the 1950's were merely the forerunners of something much greater that is yet to come—the United States seriously directing itself to the task of rehabilitating and humanizing its cities. Meanwhile, there may at this time be some virtue in adding to the record something of what we did in urban redevelopment.

▪ 16 ▪ Washington, D.C.

LATE IN THE FALL of 1952, John Price Bell, my public-relations vice-president, flicking through a back issue of *The Architectural Forum* magazine, came across an illustrated article on Southwest Washington, D.C. The story dealt with the ancient slum by the Potomac that, spreading out of its old confines like a cancer, had begun to nibble at the very edges of Capitol Hill. Thus far, said the article, there had been much debate but no action to rehabilitate this enormous and growing area.

Bell knew I was interested in the great cities. On his own he flew to Washington. Taking a cab to the Southwest, he toured the site, returned to New York, and began promoting the project. I turned him down. Phil Graham, the publisher of *The Washington Post*, and that city's renaissance man-about-town-and-politics, had already tried to get me interested in the area. I had said no: I was not interested in becoming entangled in a government-involved project.

Nonetheless, Phil Graham kept in touch. He had read a speech I gave at the Harvard School of Design, which was reprinted in *The Atlantic Monthly*. The burden of my message was that city cores could and should be saved. I found myself being invited as a speaker to one or two Washington conferences and, once there, kept hearing more about their local project. With Bell still touting Southwest Washington and with Graham giving me arguments from my own speech, I began to undergo a change of heart. Besides, Eisenhower was now our President-elect. He, too, was reported to be very much in favor of redevelopment of the Southwest. With the backing of people such as Eisenhower and Graham, maybe something actually could be done in Washington. The least we could do, I decided, was take a look at the area.

Early that winter, Pei, Tex McCrary, our public-relations consultant, Bell, my son, and I flew down to Washington from New York.

We met with local officials. Then, by car and on foot, we toured the proposed redevelopment site. The end result of our walk in a slum was that it is now one of the most valuable pieces of Washington real estate. Parts of it are second only to Georgetown in residential snob appeal. The L'Enfant Plaza office center and its approach mall (which we conceived that day) are important tourist attractions and, in all, over half a billion in development funds were eventually attracted to the area. And yet, Southwest Washington was the most long, drawn-out, and frustrating of all our projects. Had we had a true idea of what it is really like to get a great, innovating project under way in Washington, we would never have tackled the job. Fortunately, we had only an inkling of what we were in for, and that was quite bad enough.

Just as I had previously found Denver to be a caricature of American cities, so too, at the other extreme, was Washington. Denver's problem was that it had no home-grown group capable of keeping a self-satisfied, second-rate establishment on the qui vive. Washington's trouble was that too many forces kept tugging it in separate directions —and, as regards civic government, it was a headless monster. With no mayor, no strong city officials, and a U.S. Congress intent on keeping things that way, the city could not move in any one direction for more than one month at a time. Technically Washington was run by three commissioners appointed by Congress. It was Congress that legislated for the district; the citizens did not vote. Actually, various administrative officers and members of boards and of the courts were appointed respectively by Congress, the President of the United States, and the U.S. Supreme Court. The U.S. Army Corps of Engineers, the U.S. Park Service, the Fine Arts Commission, the Planning Commission, and a dozen other agencies officially and unofficially also shared in the operation and control of various parts of the capital. Though they may have lacked broad executive power throughout the city, the members of these various groups had veto power over great parts of each other's operations. Builders couldn't build what the Planning Commission opposed. The Fine Arts Commission had to approve what the Planning Commission proposed—and so on. Given the above, it was axiomatic that back scratching was the order of the day in Washington. The time-honored way to kill many proposals was to send them to a committee for a time till they died or were emasculated beyond recognition. With changes in the national administration and in Congress, prospects of a given project changed drastically from year to year. One result of all this was that only innocuous projects tended to get through this forest of committees easily. The small amount of effective planning and governing done in Washington, D.C., was accomplished by a self-anointed coterie of well-to-do long-term residents and members of Congress who were, as long as they got nobody excited, permitted by the others to make this their hobby. Solid, stolid local stalwarts such as Ulysses S. Grant III sat on one commission after the other without ever upsetting anybody with new ideas.

Since Washington had always been a small noncity, a government employees' bedroom and retirement area, none of this mattered very much. The capital remained, at core, a small, semirural, semi-Southern city. Then, in quick succession, the New Deal, World War II, and the postwar mushroom growth of big government changed all this. New people, new or greatly expanded government agencies, and new problems began to crowd into town. Washington and its environs became a boom area. In real estate, the greatest growth took place in the towns and new suburbs that had begun to ring Washington the way weeds ring and eventually choke a shallow pond. There was migration of whites from parts of the city into the suburbs. There was also a migration of blacks from the rural South into the District. The city was changing, but in 1952 the town fathers still held the levers of power in Washington, feeling it was their duty to steadfastly ignore any change going on around them—and it was an impasse created by this resistance to change that brought Webb & Knapp to Washington.

The Redevelopment Land Agency, a new agency whose job it was to redevelop Washington's slums, had locked antlers with the National Capital Planning Commission over how this redevelopment job was to be done. At the time my associates and I were cruising through the proposed Southwest development site in 1952, the impasse was entering its second year.

On the map, the proposed site formed a giant five-hundred-acre triangle. The triangle's northern side ran parallel to Independence

Avenue and the great Washington Mall that lies between the Lincoln Memorial and Capitol Hill. On the westernmost side of the area lay the Potomac, whose potentially beautiful and valuable riverside land was cluttered by old warehouses, a produce and fish market, decayed wharves, and a few seafood restaurants. On the east the project was flanked by shabby homes slated for demolition and replacement by public housing. Independence Avenue was the project's northern boundary, but, in effect, it was the elevated tracks of the Pennsylvania Railroad, which rose just below the avenue and cross the river to Virginia, that form the visual and psychological boundaries of the area. The Chinese Wall effect of these tracks had, since the 1860's, separated and segregated Southwest Washington from the rest of the city. Once fashionable, the site had long ago become a workingman's and eventually a black man's ghetto. On our tour we found numbers of pleasant, tree-lined streets, but the houses were falling apart; porches sagged, windows were cracked, rain gutters hung awry, and the paint looked like something left over from the Civil War. Many homes had no running water and outdoor privies—all this within sight of the Capitol dome.

The Redevelopment Land Agency was headed by a volunteer chairman, John Remon, a wise and public-spirited executive of the phone company. What Remon and his executive assistant, John Searles, wanted to do was clear the site of old buildings. They planned to change the area's chemistry altogether by putting up high-rise residential buildings, upgrading the commercial areas, and developing the waterfront. In this way the Redevelopment Land Agency hoped to once more tie the Southwest into the city proper. The National Capital Planning Commission, however, felt that the Southwest, "traditionally a low-income area" (for "low-income" read "black") should remain so. Buildings and streets should be rehabilitated, but their general appearance not changed. In other words, the Southwest should be made into a poor, black Georgetown. What the commission was actually promoting was a policy of containment. Since the ghetto had long since broken out of its confines and was now flanking Capitol Hill and spreading out through the rest of town, this containment policy was obviously defunct. Besides, it takes enormous sums for house-to-house rehabilitation. The money that was available would rehabilitate only a small pocket of homes, which would, as has happened in other cities, soon be swept under by the tide of decay around them.

Nonetheless, without the blessings of the Planning Commission, the Redevelopment Land Agency could do nothing. With local pressure groups pushing to "get something done," seventy-five acres of land were being converted to government low-cost-housing projects. Such "relief housing" was the ultimate fate predicted by many Washingtonians for the entire project, because there was not a major builder in America who would touch a Title I project. It was at this point, however, that we entered the scene. The beleaguered Remon and his allies quickly flashed us eager messages of welcome.

Webb & Knapp announced its interest in taking on the entire Southwest redevelopment in March, 1953. We were too late to take over the seventy-five-acre Area B low-cost-housing development, but Pei went to work studying the remainder of the project site. In November, Redevelopment Land Agency chairman John Remon came to New York to see if we were really interested in the whole project. We gave him a couple of dry martinis and a good lunch in the tower dining room over my office. Then, as proof of our interest, we unveiled a master plan for the entire area.

The key to our plan was a three-hundred-foot-wide mall stretching south at right angles to Independence Avenue. The mall commenced across from the Smithsonian Institution at Tenth Street. This was the one spot where the railroad tracks dipped below the relatively high ground near Tenth Street. By constructing an esplanade, a form of land bridge, over the tracks, over the site of a proposed eight-lane expressway, and into the heart of the Southwest, we could literally reconnect this area to Washington proper. Think of the railroad tracks as a giant wall and the expressway as a river of cars. Our mall bridged both these obstacles. Alongside this mall, in the crescent-shaped island of land between the tracks and expressway, we proposed a special office, cultural, and entertainment center to be named L'Enfant Plaza, in honor of the original planner of Washington. To the west and north of L'Enfant Plaza we proposed a series of government office buildings. Below this business and cultural escarpment, and along the river, we planned a magnificent marina and recreation area. Finally, east of this waterfront we placed a combination of high-rise elevator buildings and, something new in urban redevelopment, a series of common-cornice-line townhouses. All but two major streets would be closed to through traffic. The existing rights of way, and the fine trees already on them, were to become local-access streets, pedestrian ways, and open courts.

Our plan, which went beyond anything that had yet been pro-posed, made an obvious unity of the Southwest and the rest of the city beyond. A jubilant Remon promised all the assistance and support he could muster. We consulted further on plans and strategy and prepared to move in 1954.

There was a four-part sequence and logic to our plan. A prime concern was to get a number of new government office buildings put up in the northern tier of the project along Independence Avenue and/or parts of our Tenth Street mall. These buildings would blend in with existing structures nearby. More important, the quick rise of various new offices in the Southwest would help the rental of new apartments in Area B, which was upgraded into middle-income hous-ing, and in the Town Center apartment complex Webb & Knapp would build. The rise of our new apartments would in turn give a boost to the buildings and activities planned for L'Enfant Plaza. A successful plaza would, in its turn, create a market for even more homes and apartments throughout the Southwest. This phased de-velopment of mutually supporting elements is part of what good planning is all about. But it was just as important to present our plans properly.

I had learned in Denver, and from our UN-approachway experi-ence, that the finest and most beneficial of plans can be quietly starved or publicly drawn and quartered unless powerful friends and the general public have rallied to its support. In the case of Washing-ton we had backing from key elements in the capital, but I wanted to be sure of enough public support to overawe the opposition. In January, 1954, we therefore launched a promotional and sales cam-paign. First we informally presented our plan to select members of the Washington Board of Trade. The next day we made a formal presentation of the project to the city commissioners, city officials, and the chiefs of a string of interested agencies—the Federal Housing Administration, the Housing and Home Finance Administration, and others. On February 15 we made another series of presentations and held a banquet at the Hotel Statler for members of Congress, their wives, and various civic leaders. Enthusiastic stories about our plan and our efforts blanketed local television, radio, and the newspapers. Up till that time the Southwest's redevelopment prospects were about as cheery as those of a terminal-ward TB patient's, but these presentations were like shots of a broad-spectrum antibiotic.

Webb & Knapp and the Redevelopment Land Agency next prepared a joint Memorandum of Understanding. By this agreement Webb & Knapp, entirely at its own expense, undertook to prepare a detailed master plan for the whole of the Southwest site. The Redevelopment Land Agency would not negotiate with other developers while our plan was in preparation. Upon acceptance of the plan by the City of Washington, Webb & Knapp would have the right to negotiate for fifty percent of the land involved. Those other developers who later joined the project would conform to the master plan. Meanwhile, the Redevelopment Land Agency would do all it could to assure acceptance of our all important Tenth Street mall. The memo specified that our entering the development depended upon acceptance of the mall.

In July we made a private presentation of the plan to President Eisenhower in the White House. He gave us his official blessings. Everywhere we had met kind words and promises of private and public support. True, some members of the Planning Commission had their noses out of joint, but they kept their own counsel. Through the rest of 1954 and part of 1955 our men worked with the Redevelopment Land Agency, the Planning Commission, and a dozen other departments and agencies through a coordinating committee, to forge the actual details of the plan. I had been hopeful we could break ground for the project by 1956. Then the silent opposition surfaced under the banner of the influential and prestigious Smithsonian Institution.

The Smithsonian, situated on the north side of Independence Avenue, considered the land south of the avenue as its domain. This was where we planned to put our mall, but now the Smithsonian moved to assert its territorial imperative and cranked out preliminary plans for a massive, vaguely airplane-shaped building which would be a new air museum. By right of institutional preeminence, they planned to place this new building athwart where our mall would touch Independence Avenue. We outlanders could adapt our mall accordingly or move it elsewhere. They did not care which.

I countered that it was our fondest hope that the Smithsonian build on either side of the mall but that they should not block it. The Planning Commission, however, immediately announced that in view of this conflict the entire matter of the mall would have to be reconsidered. A Planning Commission subcommittee headed by Conrad Wirth, director of the National Park Service, was appointed to look into the matter. The subcommittee met and suggested that we drastically shorten our mall, to branch its northern end out in a giant U, to sweep around both sides of the proposed air museum at Tenth and Independence. We once more explained how important it was to have a monumental connection from the Southwest to Washington proper. The subcommittee listened politely and in February, 1955, came out with another compromise solution. We should move our mall east to Ninth Street. True, this would put the mall below the grade of the railroad tracks, but this, they said, could be solved by moving and sinking the tracks. This new proposal would create enormous new costs, for which no funds were available. It would involve new planning, which would take at least two more years. The Southwest redevelopment might be delayed or crippled, but the Smithsonian must be left undisturbed. The Planning Commission, which had been putting off approval of our plan for a full year, gave an immediate "tentative approval" to the Wirth plan. To Washington insiders it was clear we had been mousetrapped.

Our agreement with the Redevelopment Land Agency, however, was perfectly clear: no mall, no Webb & Knapp. Webb & Knapp could live without the Southwest, but without us the now popular and much-needed development could not exist. We were anxious to cooperate with the city, but could also walk away from the situation with honor. There things stood, at another Washington impasse, and it took President Eisenhower to break the deadlock.

The President's chief interest, actually, was not primarily in the

redevelopment of the Southwest. What he wanted was a good relocation point for the tempos, the temporary office buildings put up on
the greensward of the great Washington Mall during World War I,
when Ike was a shavetail. These eyesores had survived World War I,
World War II, and the Korean conflict. With the everpresent office
shortage, they threatened to continue in perpetuity, and this irritated
Eisenhower. Our plan for the Southwest provided for office space
to which the tempos' occupants could move. But, before anything
could be done about the tempos, something would have to be done
about our plan. The President appointed George A. Garrett, a prominent Washington businessman, a former ambassador to Ireland, and
the president of the Federal City Council, as his special representative,
"to get the project moving again."

Henceforth Garrett sat in on all meetings of the Redevelopment
Land Agency, of the Planning Commission, and of the Wirth subcommittee on urban renewal. Garrett had no power or authority as
such; he was an observer. But if he lacked direct power, he had something else. Only in the harems of the ancient Turkish court, I am told,
were the nuances of place, position, and current favor more carefully
gauged than in modern Washington. Garrett, through a combination
of personality, social position, and recent Presidential anointment,
possessed all the above. His personal standing was such that he could
offset the influence of Chief Justice Earl Warren, who was chancellor
of the Smithsonian. Garrett's job was to prod and cajole enough
members of the Planning Commission, and their friends and adherents
around town, into a change in stance. Like some genial papal nuncio
dealing with quarrels among local bishops, Garrett first persuaded
people not to take an inflexible public position. Then he would
gradually bring them to a change in stance. This gentle process of
turning in place while maintaining "face" took time. Not till the end
of 1955, after a last-ditch effort by the Wirth committee to relocate
our mall all the way over to Eighth Street, did the Planning Commission give way. They then advised the Smithsonian to look elsewhere for an air-museum site. In April, 1956, our general plan, with
the mall narrowed to 250 feet, was formally approved. We were
now ready to go to work.

As per our agreement with the Redevelopment Land Agency, we

were granted negotiating rights to the Town Center shopping and apartment complex for the Southwest, the L'Enfant Plaza site, and the waterfront, these to be developed in that order of priority. These three areas represented fifty percent of the Southwest.

Meanwhile on the political front, with particular assistance from Representative James C. Auchincloss of New Jersey and senators Stuart Symington and Barry Goldwater, we had piloted a special government office lease-purchase bill through Congress. Given such a bill, the budget-conscious government, with a minimum outlay of cash, or delay in time, could move into and own much-needed office space in the Southwest triangle. This lease-purchase bill, Public Law 150, specified that four federal office buildings be lease-purchased by the General Services Administration in the Southwest.

All was going well with these plans until the next election shifted the balance of power in Congress from Republican to Democratic. Public Law 150 was on the books, and the General Services Administration could make use of it, but no such thing was about to happen now. The great Washington agencies are like placid herds that spend their time quietly grazing on and in turn fertilizing particular parts of the national economy. They count on their size and the milk they give to shield them from attack. They are fearful of very few creatures—except the Big Bear of Congress.

Though it never was mentioned in the debates, I suspected a lease-purchase arrangement, in that it would permit agencies to slip ever so slightly away from congressional control, would be looked upon askance by some politicians.

In the case of the Southwest, at the sound of the first angry snorts from the now powerful opposition congressmen, the General Services Administration took one frightened breath and froze. The Redevelopment Land Agency might appropriate all the land it wished, but the General Services Administration was not about to take possession or build on it until each building had been duly scrutinized, certified, and directly funded by Congress. As a result the high-priority government land acquired by the Redevelopment Land Agency for offices stayed bare for years, and when the Area B and our Town Center apartments were first erected, they rose up from the cleared landscape like lonely mesas on the Arizona desert.

In order to get some government offices to go into the Southwest, we needed congressional assistance. To help us find it, Garrett and his assistant, Yates Cooke, along with John Searles of the Redevelopment Land Agency, called on Congressman Albert Thomas of eastern Texas, who headed the House Appropriations subcommittee dealing with independent government offices. They had an introduction to Thomas from a friend of Eisenhower's, but for all their fine Washington and home-town references, my friends got a frosty reception. Thomas told his visitors that he resented Washington Chamber of Commerce types pressuring him. A desultory conversation nonetheless got under way. Somehow it came out that Thomas had an interest in the grain-futures market. Garrett allowed as to how he was a partner in the firm of Merrill Lynch, Pierce, Fenner & Beane. Thomas began to ask technical questions which my friend Garrett fielded with all the aplomb and jargon of an insider's insider. Nothing more was said about the Southwest. It was clear, however, that Thomas had begun to look upon Garrett as a friend to be cultivated. The visitors finally got up and said their good-byes. As they were leaving, Thomas called out, "I think maybe I can do something for you." He did. In due time the Space Agency building was authorized for the Southwest, and after that, others followed.

At this time I was flying into Washington four or five times a month in order to testify, plead, or prod for our cause. This was a complex, pioneering project. At one time Webb & Knapp was dealing with no fewer than twenty-seven separate Washington agencies, departments, or subdepartments. Most federal bureaucrats tend to deal with time as sedately as Chinese mandarins, and there were all manner of important distractions before them. For instance:

Should the Redevelopment Land Agency (which owned properties) or the Federal Housing Authority (which insured properties) determine the value of the land? This was a question of policy about which bureaucratic power revolved, and only after a tussle was it settled in favor of the Redevelopment Land Agency (though the Federal Housing Authority kept the option of second-guessing and in effect vetoing such Redevelopment Land Agency decisions).

There were legal points to be settled. Could the Redevelopment Land Agency expropriate land? Yes, said the Supreme Court.

Should the Redevelopment Land Agency have to pay full taxes to the District on properties it acquired? (It did.)

There were questions of philosophy: should the Redevelopment Land Agency be authorized to hire an architect to design the Tenth Street mall? The Federal Housing Authority did not think so and held up such authorization for five years before coming around to a more enlightened view.

It was agreed that the Redevelopment Land Agency would build the actual mall, but should the Redevelopment Land Agency or the Parks Service maintain pools, fountains, and shrubbery that the architects called for? This one was settled, after a period of time, in favor of the Redevelopment Land Agency.

A proposal that parking garages be built under the mall, operated by the City Parking Authority, was, after lobbying by city garage operators, stricken from the plan by special action in Congress. Instead, private parking facilities were organized under L'Enfant Plaza.

Each of these and dozens of other interagency questions had to be resolved and re-resolved. There were moments during these Washington years when I felt we were part of some mad surrealist's real-life Monopoly set: every time we were about to acquire a key property or pass "Go," the "Chance" card turned up reading "Go back three paces."

Our general plan had been approved in April, 1956. Five months later, in September, we presented the formal proposal for our first project, the Town Center shopping and apartment complex. Only nine months after this did the Redevelopment Land Agency approve our plan. For nine more months we bargained over land prices. Their appraisers reduced the per-square-foot figure from four dollars to two-fifty. It then took twelve months for the Housing and Home Finance Agency to approve this lease. Two more months passed before we had public hearings on the matter. There, difficulties raised by a local builder led to three more months' delay and an increase in price to three dollars per foot. It took seven more months before we started on construction. A hectic twelve months later, the first units in the Town Center were completed. By then, almost six years had somehow vanished down the drain, and we were still prisoners in the wonderful Washington time machine.

By 1960, though we had invested over half a million dollars in the Southwest, there was absolutely nothing on the ground to show for this investment. As previously, with Denver's Court House Square, we were beginning to get some crossfire from special critics, but the Southwest was too great a moral and emotional commitment for me to consider, even for a moment, pulling out. Besides, I knew we were making great progress. I could tell by the opposition we were meeting.

Curiously, the more progress we made, the more Webb & Knapp's position in the Southwest became subject to erosion. By this negative but sensitive barometer, things had begun to get stormy in 1958. This is when we discovered a number of special forays being launched against our position on the waterfront. Partly because of some of the difficulties we foresaw for this section, I had given it a low priority in the chain of development. Nevertheless, the owners of Hogate's, a riverside seafood restaurant that would be demolished and therefore have first rights for leasing space in the refurbished area, generously proposed to build a million-dollar planetarium near the overlook of the Tenth Street mall. All they asked, in return, was that this planetarium lie near the great, new Hogate's. This new restaurant (like the Arc de Triomphe on the Champs-Elysées) would be located at the end of the overlook itself. Roy Chalk, head of the D.C. Transit Company, similarly volunteered to build a grandiose colonial village, plus a boatel, convention hall, and other "attractions" for the waterfront. Along with a later, modified version of these plans, Chalk also requested permission to submit plans for developing L'Enfant Plaza. He could draw up such plans, he said, in ninety days.

In due time the Planning Commission, which does have its uses, formally rejected the Hogate proposal as "not fitting." Chalk's colonial-village and boatel schemes were similarly allowed to founder on their own weight. Chalk eventually did get a development site in the "open" area to the south of our own projects. Since his bus company had some car barns down there, this did give them a certain claim to preference in choice of developers in that area. The first we knew of his interest in the Southwest, however, was when we approached the bus company to arrange for service in the Southwest. We were given to understand that not much in the way of service would be forthcoming unless Mr. Chalk was allowed in for part of the action in our developments. When we countered that the D.C. Transit Company was a public utility and we could sue for service, we were invited to go ahead and do so; the case would take years —and in the meantime, just wait and see what kind of service we would get.

This, of course, was merely a kind of bargaining that some kinds of people feel it necessary to use. Webb & Knapp had been in successful deals with far stranger co-venturers than Mr. Chalk. We were always ready to welcome outside capital (under the proper circumstances). We did seriously discuss Chalk's joining with us in some portions of L'Enfant Plaza. In one instance his buses might have used part of the space under the plaza, but nothing came of these explorations.

But late in 1958 the Redevelopment Land Agency, suddenly a little frightened, and anxious now to get something moving in the area, turned over development rights in this section to a nonprofit corporation backed by the Federal City Council and headed by an ever so slightly embarrassed old ally of mine, George Garrett.

The rationale was that this "prestige" group would well defend and quickly develop the waterfront. As things turned out, neither this "new" effort nor others that followed could get off the ground. At this writing the waterfront has yet to be developed.

As partial compensation for losing the waterfront rights, we were granted two and one-half acres alongside the Tenth Street mall and opposite L'Enfant Plaza, but the important thing was that a precedent for altering our Memorandum of Understanding had now been set.

Not long after this, at the March, 1959, public hearing to consider our Town Center bid, another Washington stalwart strode out from behind the scenes to strike a blow for home-town interests. In a headline making pronunciamento, Morris Cafritz, a prominent Washington builder, denounced our $2.50-per-square-foot bid as a giveaway. From the floor he made a counter offer of three dollars per square foot. Since Cafritz had previously spurned several efforts by the Redevelopment Land Agency to interest him in the Southwest, had refused a partnership with us in the very Town Center project which he was now attacking, and had no plans in hand for his own Town Center, his offer was rejected.

Cafritz' proposal was never a serious one, but his spoiling maneuver did have one typical Washington effect. The Redevelopment Land Agency, made nervous by the publicity given the Cafritz offer, asked us to go along with a new, conditional arrangement. This was that if later the Federal Housing Authority, for its mortgage insurance purposes, were to place a three-dollar-per-square-foot value on the land, we would agree to pay this higher price and thus save the Redevelopment Land Agency the embarrassment of a discrepancy between the land value assigned by the Federal Housing Authority and that received by the Redevelopment Land Agency.

We reluctantly agreed to this. But then the Housing and Home Finance Agency, which supplies the Redevelopment Land Agency with its money, stepped in. Such a contingent agreement, they said, would be a *de facto* permitting of the Federal Housing Authority to set the Redevelopment Land Agency's land valuations. This should never be allowed. The contract, therefore, should be for two-fifty per foot as first agreed upon or for three dollars per foot but it should not be contingent upon decisions of some other agency. Predictably, price for the supermarket sections of the land was finally compromised at three dollars per square foot.

Joining what was beginning to look like a general assault, the General Accounting Office of the General Services Administration in June, 1957, issued a statement attacking the negotiation aspects of our Memorandum of Understanding with the Redevelopment Land Agency and suggesting that only competitive bidding should be allowed for redevelopment projects.

These general activities signaled a most important change. In 1954-1955, when the idea of a Southwest project seemed dangerously visionary, our Memorandum of Understanding with the Redevelopment Land Agency was seen as an instrument of advantage to Washington and as almost quixotic investment on the part of Webb & Knapp. Now, after years of pioneering effort, we had yet to make any money, but our special position and Memorandum of Understanding were subject to widespread attack.

What was happening was almost obvious. There might not be much showing on the Southwest grounds in the way of buildings, and this was leading to public criticism, but those who were sophisticated in these matters recognized that great values could now be created in the area. Local builders and financiers in Washington who had spurned the Southwest as too big or too speculative were eager now (and ready to knock off the originators, if necessary) to clamber aboard the Good Ship Lollipop.

While fending off the various assaults launched on our flanks and around the waterfront, we continued working hard on the central problem of making the whole of the Southwest viable. We encouraged local baseball promoters in their attempts to get a new stadium in the Southwest. When it seemed the CIA might build a headquarters in Washington, we did our best to get this cloak-and-dagger—and white-collar—employer into the Southwest, but we worked longest and hardest of all to attract the Washington Cultural Center. In combination with our proposed hotel and other public places, the Cultural Center would make the L'Enfant Plaza a sparkling, day-and-night people-magnet. Our keenest supporter and ally in these efforts was Phil Graham. In fact, it was he, working behind the scenes, who got his mother-in-law, Mrs. Agnes E. Meyer, owner of *The Washington Post*, appointed chairwoman of the commission to find a site for the Cultural Center. This idea was tactically brilliant but strategically disastrous. Mrs. Meyer was a splendidly self-assured American mother, with an all too conventional attitude toward the opinions of a mere son-in-law. Instead, she and her friends favored a proposed site in Foggy Bottom, alongside the Potomac and conveniently near, though not too near, fashionable Georgetown. In June, 1959, when we unveiled our formal proposal for L'Enfant Plaza, it was without the Cultural Center.

L'Enfant Plaza, as originally planned, would contain four office buildings, a one-thousand-room hotel, a theater, restaurants, stores, and four levels of parking beneath the plaza. One of the office buildings, the World Communications Center, would be graced by the Women's Press Club. Another, the Air Sciences building, was designed to fill the growing need of the aero and astronautical industries for Washington offices. Jim Dixon, husband of Jeane Dixon, the well-known soothsayer, was involved in lining up clients for this building, but psychic phenomena this close to home must not work. To the best of my knowledge, we had no clairvoyant help or warnings on the project.

The hotel, which was designed to overpass Ninth Street in the same way the UN building in New York overpasses the East River Drive, needed clearance from the Planning Commission and a special O.K. from Congress. A now familiar routine got under way again. Getting our proposed changes agreed to took one and a half years. Then came negotiations on land price. This took until April, 1961, when we agreed on a seven-million-dollar total, roughly twenty dollars per square foot. We went ahead with working plans for the area, finally focusing on a sixty-million-dollar, three-office-building project, plus hotel. However, a continuous series of discussions and changes on the details of the mall, and the plaza proper, both of which would be owned by the Redevelopment Land Agency, kept L'Enfant Plaza in a planner's limbo. This treadmill of haggling, hangfire, and uncertainty created a closed circle of inaction: The vagueness about plan details kept would-be lessees from committing themselves to plaza offices. This in turn kept mortgagors from committing themselves to finance the site—which kept Webb & Knapp from moving forward on the construction. This was a typical problem we had beaten many times before in many places, but from 1960 on, Webb & Knapp was so pressed for funds that I could not find the long-term cash to enable us to force the situation at L'Enfant Plaza. Besides, by this time, even I was leery of making heavy cash commitments that would be frozen during interminable months of bureaucratic and political deliberation. We had been discovering that in Washington even the most solid-seeming agreements cannot be counted upon until after they have been signed, and sometimes not then.

By the time our L'Enfant Plaza discussions were well under way, the Southwest had obviously turned that invisible corner which separates the world of possible developments from actual ones. Through 1960–1961 John Searles, concentrating now on the non-Webb & Knapp section of the Southwest, had established eight development sites south of M Street. Searles had come to a realization that to be successful the Southwest would have to be fashionable, which also means expensive. Therefore, after a politic arranging for one relatively low-cost co-operative to be built by Reynolds Aluminum Co., he deliberately sought out wealthy backers interested in luxury developments, people who would move into and induce others to follow them to the Southwest. This strategy worked. For instance, Sam Kaufmann, publisher of *The Washington Star*, became a leading booster, investor, and resident in the Southwest. The area in a few years became the most active construction site in the nation and eventually a prestige Washington address.

All this was as we had originally planned and predicted. Something which we did not plan and which we had long fought against and thought we had defeated became the victor. Up till 1962 the master plan for the Southwest called for the Navy Department, whose personnel occupied many of the tempos on the Great Mall, to occupy Federal Office Building No. 5. This important building was to consist of two structures, joined underground, that would *flank* the entrance to the Tenth Street Mall. But now the General Service Administration's architects, ignoring the master plan, designed a building that would straddle the mall, leaving a tunnel under the building as entranceway to the area. Ever so quietly, the General Service Administration, in executive (i.e., secret) sessions, gained quick approval for this change from both the Planning and the Fine Arts commissions, then in March of that year presented us with this *fait accompli*.

As a *Washington Post* editorial noted:

Tunnel to the Southwest

With an air of innocence, our public planners and redevelopers have agreed to undercut and diminish the splendid design for the future 10th Street mall. It was to have run grandly south from Constitution Avenue, flanked by big new buildings, to a dramatic plaza overlooking the Potomac. It was conceived as the commercial center of Southwest Washington, where hundreds of millions of dollars, some of it public money but most of it private, are being spent to replace slums. The 10th Street mall was to have been the gateway to the new Southwest.

Instead, under the current plan, it will be the tunnel to the new Southwest. The Government is now being encouraged to build its Federal Office Building Number Five in one vast continuous rectangle along Constitution Avenue, leaving a large hole in its middle for the 10th Street traffic to creep through. The Fine Arts Commission speaks of the "dramatic effect of passing through the arch and suddenly seeing a new vista open out." The Fine Arts Commission might more profitably contemplate the formidable barrier that this monolithic building would place, in every aesthetic sense, between Southwest and the rest of the city. If it is to work economically, Southwest must be an integral part of downtown Washington. Huge Federal office buildings can seal it off just as destructively as the railroad and the slums once did.

Why cannot the Government avail itself of an architect as gifted as I. M. Pei, who has been working for the private developers, to draw appropriate plans for the new Federal office building? The site is not so crowded that the Government is forced to use the air space over 10th Street. The city cannot expect private investors to put huge sums into redevelopment if the basic lines of the project are subject to change without notice.

And this change is particularly objectionable because it was hustled through the various public agencies surreptitiously. It was approved in each case behind closed doors as though the planners had guessed, correctly, that the alteration would not stand up to public inspection. At a meeting today the private developers are to discuss the mall with the public agencies. The proper solution is to return forthwith to the original designs. [*March 20, 1962.*]

We fought the new plan, but, caught unawares, found ourselves fighting in a Washington where the faith keepers of yesterday were no more. Of the original stalwarts who had believed in and helped us fight for an open mall, the majority were gone. John Remon and Phil Graham had died, one from advanced age and the other from suicide. Eisenhower had left, and Sam Spencer, the capable head of the District commissioners, had long since left that post. Even the Redevelopment Land Agency, now chaired by a most competent gentleman, Neville Miller, a one-time mayor of Louisville, Kentucky, had changed. John Searles, with whom we had had our differences, but who was an ally, had left in 1961. The Fine Arts and the Planning commissions were headed by new sets of political appointees. To these newcomers, anxious to wield their authority, the arguments and agreements of yesteryear were just so many myths and pieces of paper.

The Redevelopment Land Agency decided to assume a neutral stand on the mall issue. This was tantamount to bowing to the opposition. Webb & Knapp, its energies diverted by crises in a dozen

different areas, was in poor shape to move against a politically entrenched opposition. Even the fact that we had just signed for the
sixty-million-dollar L'Enfant Plaza development gave us no leverage:
it simply meant that any more delays than those we anticipated would
mean more expenses and trouble. It was ironic. In 1954–1955 Webb
& Knapp had been the linchpin that held everything together; without us there could be no Southwest project. In 1962 Webb & Knapp
was just one more contractor-developer under pressure from the
landowner and unable to prevent an architectural blunder.

In late 1963 and early 1964 Webb & Knapp negotiated the sale
of its Town Center development, plus a series of nearby townhouses
and walk-up apartments, to a group headed by Charles S. Bressler,
a local builder. By the end of 1964, we had almost arranged the sale
of our rights to and the detailed plans for L'Enfant Plaza to a suc-
cessor organization. This was L'Enfant Plaza Corp., of which George
Garrett, David Rockefeller, Lazard Freres, and others were principals,
and General Peter Quesada, one-time chief of the Tactical Air Command and member of the Civil Aeronautics Board, was chief administrator.

The Washington Star carried the following editorial:

Zeckendorf's Legacy

*When William Zeckendorf referred the other day to his
development rights in Southwest Washington, the last of which now
are being sold off, as "a legacy," there was no reason to doubt his
sincerity.*

*For the new Southwest is largely his conception. Its reconstruc-
tion, by a variety of other people, follows to a remarkable degree
the fine, imaginative plan he offered the city more than 10 years ago,
long before most of the slums in the disgraceful Southwest were
razed.*

*Mr. Zeckendorf's primary reason for entering the renewal pic-
ture was, of course, to make money. He believed that massive investment in urban renewal in Washington and other cities would, over
a period of time, pay off handsomely. In his case he guessed wrong
—partly because his whole financial empire is tottering; partly, no
doubt, because his chunk of the Southwest project was too large to*

bear the strain of the long wait for a fiscal return. And now that he is all washed up in the Southwest, or nearly so, one can look for very little good to be said about his role.

Well, just to set the record straight, there was a great deal of good. Redevelopment in Washington in the middle 50s was heading nowhere, and the Zeckendorf plan gave it a focus. Long before he had the opportunity to build anything, he had to fight for the plan's acceptance—for a longer time and at greater expense, perhaps, than any other developer could or would have done. He brought a superior brand of architectural and planning expertise to the city. And during these early years of controversy, everyone learned valuable lessons about the whole renewal process.

The flamboyant New Yorker, who was then at the crest of his wave, argued the possibilities for good in urban renewal at a time when the more popular position was to despair of cities as decent places to live. He gave Washingtonians more than a plan. He gave them, through the force of his personal enthusiasm, a greater faith in the future of their own city. [November 8, 1964.]

In 1966, almost a year after the fall of Webb & Knapp, and at a time when the Southwest's housing area was largely built or in active construction, ground was finally broken for the L'Enfant Plaza I had conceived twelve years previously in 1954. I was invited down to take part in the ceremonies. After a bit of ritual speech-making, the bulldozers started up, and symbolic digging commenced. It was a fine show, luncheon and drinks being served in a great tent, and at some point in the proceedings George Beveridge, a reporter from *The Washington Star*, asked, "Bill, how do you feel about all this; you conceiving the whole thing, bringing it along almost up to this very point, then having to watch other people take over your job and take the profit?"

"Can I talk off the record?"

"Of course."

"Well, what I say, and I don't think you will want to repeat, is: 'I'm the guy that got the girl pregnant. Those fellows you see around here are merely the obstetricians.'"

Beveridge kept his word. He did not quote me. His copy that afternoon read, ". . . Mr. Zeckendorf was beaming like a well-satisfied father watching the midwives at work. . . ."

In point of time and space, the Southwest was grandaddy to most other redevelopment projects in the United States. It was on the basis of and in spite of its Washington experience that Webb & Knapp determined to take on redevelopment work anywhere and everywhere in North America.

• 17 • Webb & Knapp's Peripatetic School of Urban Design

TROOPS OF PENGUINS, if they have been out of the water for a time, are very wary about diving into the sea; after all, there are often unfriendly creatures down there. Instead, these gregarious birds solemnly cluster around the edge of the ice, studying the water, leaning over the edge, backing away, bowing, and politely making room for anyone else who might want to step to the brink and maybe even test the water. Soon, building up excitement, the whole troop begins milling and shifting at the water's edge. As happens in crowds, even the politest of crowds, near a brink, someone sooner or later is jostled over the side. Once this happens, the whole troop stands still and watches. If their "volunteer" is attacked or gobbled up, his friends and relatives find some way to entertain themselves on shore for a while longer. If, on the other hand, the penguin goes through a series of aquabatics with no ill result, the whole gang of his fellows stage a swim-in.

Webb & Knapp was the great Emperor Penguin of urban redevelopment. We willingly and knowingly jumped into the water again and again in place after place to catch some wonderful fish and chase as many more.

In 1956 Webb & Knapp launched a nationwide urban-redevelopment campaign. Within four years we had bid on millions of dollars' worth of redevelopment work. We eventually went into actual construction in seven cities, to become the number-one Title I redeveloper in the country. In order to win contracts in seven cities, we had to submit proposals to at least fifteen cities. Before choosing fifteen cities in which we would offer to build, we had to study the possibilities in at least thirty cities, and we did the greater part of this investigatory and preparatory work in one great surge between 1956 and 1958. During this period a number of people in the industry took to calling Title I "The Zeckendorf Redevelopment Bill." They were only half-joking, and only half-wrong.

Since 1949 we had all known that sooner or later America would have to dive into the business of building in the cities with Title I, but no one seemed to know quite how to get started. You have to remember that through 1956 urban redevelopment was still something new and strange.

Robert Moses was possibly the only man in America who, when Title I came, was ready. As New York's coordinator of construction, director of parks, chief of the Triborough, and unofficial granter of patronage to local politicians, he had, beforehand, lined up support to pass the local and state legislation needed to implement Title I. As soon as the new law was passed, he and I put it to work rehabilitating one of the worst parts of Brooklyn. I was chairman of the board of trustees of Long Island University, then a diminutive and unaccredited school temporarily settled in a loft building in Brooklyn. Our university, then catering largely to ex-GIs, desperately needed an in-town campus plus more buildings. I donated the necessary extra funds to sponsor a Title I redevelopment project in the vicinity of the Brooklyn Navy Yard. With Moses' help and guidance, we cleaned out acres of asphalt jungle to put up various types of high-rise housing, a modest commercial development, and the beginnings of a Brooklyn campus for the university. This well-executed little exercise, however, was merely a warm-up for our later operations. My "donation" to LIU was a further means of inducing recently retired Admiral Connally to take over the school and begin the task of making it into a great university.

During this same period Webb & Knapp had learned how to create projects that mesh with the surrounding city. In our UN deal, at 1407 Broadway, at 112 West Thirty-fourth Street, in Denver, and in Montreal we had foreseen what would happen when, upon completion of our projects, key parts of a city would act upon each other in new ways. Naturally, we were interested in Title I projects; they offered a chance for more of the same, plus great investment leverage.

It turned out that most of the cities were as eager as we. In the case of Cincinnati, the town's mayor, Charles Taft, came down to Washington, met with our people there, and invited us to review possibilities in his city. On paper, Cincinnati had a relatively well-organized plan of development. We decided to try to do something in that town. In San Francisco it was my old friend and fellow investor Benjamin Swig, with whom we had acquired the Hotel St. Francis and the Fairmont in earlier days, who first drew us into that city. Swig, who was working on a modest six-block redevelopment plan of his own, was running into difficulties and invited us in to help out. By coincidence, it was in San Francisco, at a 1956 Municipal Association convention, where I was a speaker, that I met Mayor Anthony Celebrezze, of Cleveland. During dinner he told me of his hopes for a massive redevelopment in downtown Cleveland. After dinner we went up to his room to see plans and sketches he had with him, and this led to a 1957 Webb & Knapp foray into Cleveland.

When the City of Hartford invited us to take a look at their situation, we flew up there from New York in the early morning, and a quick tour decided me that we could try to do something in that town. Our Boston endeavors came about because of a speech I gave at MIT: I said Boston was a wonderful town, but due to its grim fiscal situation and outlook, its high tax rate and the indifferent attitude of too many key citizens, I would hate to own property there. The local newspapers naturally featured this portion of my talk. The town mayor, John Hynes, predictably took exception. He announced that vital changes were under way in Boston, and he only wished he could have the opportunity of explaining them to me. I took Hynes at his word. I sent him a short letter saying that given some promise of relief from the confiscatory tax rate in Boston, we could do something to rehabilitate the city's core and improve its finances. Hynes sent back a lengthy letter explaining how the city hoped to progress, and invited us to bid on a development project. I visited Boston. Hynes and I had a friendly meeting, and so began our adventures among the political Robin Hoods of Boston Common.

Our involvement in Pittsburgh followed a personal letter, in April, 1957, from B. A. Tompkins, one of my special vice-presidents, to General Richard Mellon of the Mellon Bank in Pittsburgh. On June 6, 1957, Mellon stopped in at our New York office to discuss development possibilities in Pittsburgh, with special emphasis on the ninety-five-acre Lower Hill Development to be built around a new civic auditorium. On June 12 Mayor David Lawrence of Pittsburgh also stopped by for an exploratory talk. By June 19, Tompkins, my son, and I were lunching with Mellon at his Pittsburgh headquarters. Eventually, via design competition against three other developers, Webb & Knapp was on its way to the three-building, twenty-million-dollar apartment project we started there.

Webb & Knapp's actual negotiations with any one city varied greatly, but there was a general pattern to the process. First came a rough screening of possible cities. From my own knowledge of a town, from our staff's informal visits with city officials, through map studies, and through a few telephone calls to local figures, we could decide what potential a city had and how ripe it was for development.

If after preliminary talks and studies things looked promising, we might arrange for a formal visit of inspection. These formal visitations were normally five- or six-man affairs. I would usually bring Pei, my son, Slayton, Tompkins, and two or more other planners and aides with me. We would arrive in our own plane, where we could get some work done during the journey; with a photographic map of a city in hand, we'd circle over the town, as we had done in Montreal. Once on the ground, we might be met by the mayor or members of his office, plus the local press. Climbing into waiting limousines, we would take a motorcycle-led trip to City Hall and then to the development area. On our first visit to Cincinnati, Mayor Taft also took me on a forty-minute helicopter tour of the town. In Cleveland, Mayor Celebrezze took all of us on a boat tour of his lakefront and river city, but an auto and foot tour was the principal part of this see-the-city ritual. These were working trips. I would ask questions: "Who owns that property?" "What volume do your department stores do here?" "What are your bankers doing to help?" "Who can you count on for backing?"

I would also make comments to the city officials: "You'll need a bigger area than this." "That factory there could move and do better on the edge of town." "I can envision a great mall and shopping center tying in to the center here."

And to Pei: "That street will have to be blocked." "Keep everything at an elevation, and the hotel and office tower can use the plaza."

These on-site tours were followed by a luncheon or dinner conference with local political and business figures. We would give an analysis of what the city could and should be doing in redevelopment. The city newspapers gave a great play to the whole performance. This general publicity was part of what the visits were all about. Then, the stage being set for phase two of the operation, we would leave.

During phase two we would seek to develop a Memorandum of Understanding (à la Washington), giving us certain rights and privileges in part of the development. In return, at no cost to the city, we would prepare a detailed master plan for the total area. This master plan was the key to the whole process. To create a plan we would (as in Montreal and Washington) send in teams of planners, engineers, and architects. They would analyze the total city. Next would come site planning and preliminary building designs, and finally we would build a three-dimensional model. All this work, plus the ultimate gilding of the lily with the model, might take six months to a year; it might cost $60,000 or $250,000 or more, but it was utterly necessary. And the model, in phase three of the process, became our most potent selling tool.

An amazing number of people have tremendous difficulty in reading a map or in visualizing structures—even from etchings. With our models, we could bring planners, businessmen, and laymen into a room and give them a three-dimensional sense of an actual development-to-be. We had our own model-building company, which worked for us full time, and these "toys" helped us win quite a few design contests. For instance, our Pittsburgh venture, the combination of high-rise apartment buildings and townhouses that we built in Chicago's Hyde Park, and the Society Hill development (three high-rise towers plus townhouses) that we put up in Philadelphia were all won in design competitions.

Webb & Knapp had by now evolved a pragmatic and consistent redevelopment philosophy, which our designs usually illustrated. For example, we had early determined that any urban renewal program must meet a number of criteria. One is that a project must reach a certain critical mass in order to generate a self-sustaining reaction. Second, the components of this mass must be properly balanced. For instance, it is usually a mistake to build only housing or only commercial projects in a given area. In any event, and this is the third and closely related element, the development must be properly connected to the city of which it is a part. City planners often concentrate projects in the very worst part of a city core but do not touch adjacent areas that are still more or less viable. In other words, they conceive of their projects as planners' ghettos or oases, with no real connection to the economic forces in a city. This is a grievous and substantial error. If it is to serve, a development must add to the existing or potential flow of business and people through an area. If this means expropriating and acquiring some nondeteriorated properties as a form of bridge between areas, so much the better for the best long-term results.

As it turned out, one of our functions in city after city was that of pointing out such planning gaps. Take the St. Louis Mill Creek project, an enormous rectangle of land to the west of the city's center and the river. The planning of this development was almost completely topsy-turvy. Commercial and residential areas were being so placed that they would almost automatically block, rather than augment, the actual and potential flow of people and commerce in that city. Usually we pointed out such planning flaws through countersuggestions or by stipulating certain minimum conditions under which we would tackle a project. In Hartford and in Cincinnati, as previously in Washington, D.C., we prodded local authorities into expanding projects in order to take full advantage of their potential. Often it was the planning rationale we provided, plus the publicity focused on it, that stimulated the public backing needed to carry forward these plans. Thus, in the course of our free-hand planning seminars and flying trips around the country, we became the construction-minded American mayor's friend, exemplar, and favorite lure. This last was because, whether or not we finally won the prize, we generated many kinds of activity. Word of our interest in a city project in time brought all manner of local as well as outside interests around to bid with or against us on a development. Like a gentleman caller with six younger brothers, we were sought after, not only for ourselves, but for those who tagged along behind us.

I am as fascinated by cities, how they grow and where they go, as by the men who make them go. It is the men, of course, who count for most; what they are, their city is. As a result, there were some cities where, for quite different reasons, we could never seriously consider working. In Dallas and Houston, for instance, local business groups were so confident in the future of their communities, so well heeled, and so eager to invest locally, that they felt they did not need and certainly did not want any outside help. The City of New Orleans similarly frowned on our approach, but since this was a town that desperately needed redevelopment, what we had here was a horse of another color.

New Orleans has by the grace of God inherited more natural advantages than any other city on the continent. It lies at the base of a great waterway that runs like a spine through the nation. It has water, inexhaustible quantities of water, for all possible uses. It has a great harbor; natural resources in the form of gas, oil, and sulfur; amazingly fertile soil; and plentiful labor. And yet, in the 1950's it was obviously one of these sad cities where an informal alliance between a moneyed clique and a venal political machine had kept the town in a comfortable-for-its-rulers state. The economic and behind-the-scenes control of New Orleans was for the most part in the hands of old-time, pre-Civil War landowners and families of entrenched capital, a great many living away from New Orleans as semiexpatriates. The major preoccupation of those establishment members in town seemed to be that of living from year to year for the next Mardi Gras. What success and prosperity came to New Orleans came not from the efforts of its elite but from the bountiful accident of geography and strategic location. The closely held power of the establishment has loosened of late. New leaders have come forth to challenge the once unassailable powerhouse headed by the Whitney Bank. For instance, Louis Russo, a Cajun who fought his way up from poverty to prominence in banking and in oil, is now a leader in that town. He and others have joined hands to get things moving and have forced the old guard reluctantly to follow suit. But as recently as five or six years ago, if you had taken a picture of New Orleans and compared it with one taken forty years previously, you would have been hard put to find many differences. And, in the mid- and late 1950's, word to the members of the town's principal social bastion, the Boston Club, that a Zeckendorf was approaching their city would automatically see them raising the drawbridge, standing to arms against the infidel. We were unable to buy property in meaningful continuous lots, and as for Title I projects, we might as well have been preaching racial integration.

Whenever I think of American cities, I always find myself comparing New Orleans, which had everything handed to it, and Houston, which made itself what it is. New Orleans had a one-hundred-year head start over most U.S. cities. Seventy years ago, Houston could not have been more than an overgrown village. True, Houston found oil, but so did New Orleans. It was the dynamic leaders in Houston who made their town the true top city on the Gulf Coast. And they weren't even on the coast, they were many miles inland in the hot flatlands. What Houston did was cut a canal to the Gulf to become a seaport. Then they built a chemical center and, later, a space-age technological center. Houston has now safely bypassed Galveston and undercut Beaumont, Port Arthur, and Orange, Texas, which once might also have been rivals. And farther down the gulf, New Orleans, for all its free gifts of nature, will not catch up to Houston in our lifetimes.

In contrast to towns such as New Orleans, Pittsburgh, where a new Democratic mayor, David Lawrence, formed an alliance with all those deep-dyed Republicans to make a better town, is a grand example of a creative response to challenge. What's more, Pittsburgh's major companies have resisted the enormous centripetal pull of New York, and built new headquarters in Pittsburgh. Chicago, in spite of great troubles, has also kept its dynamism. Atlanta is another city where an enlightened and forceful local citizenry took responsibility for their own town. Robert Woodward of Coca-Cola and a great many other men were involved there.

Taken together, our successful projects and our aborted nonprojects prove that a prime requisite for a successful program is a mayor strong enough to control the local demagogues and predators who inevitably rise up to attack or to fatten off a great development. It is not enough, however, that a mayor be politically powerful; he also has to have strong backing from the truly important business leaders of his town. And this leadership group must be sufficiently sophisticated so they do not insist that what is best for their city can only be homegrown.

In cities where the mayor did not have the will or the muscle to protect our flanks, even though we might have backing from certain local interests, our projects succumbed to factional politics. In Boston, for instance, where we proposed an excellent plan for revival of the area around South Station, we found ourselves getting absolutely nowhere in that political Congo. Again, in Cleveland, our ally, Mayor Celebrezze, was so deeply embroiled in feuds with elements of the City Council that he was severely handicapped in getting the proper business backing and, in the end, was also unable to get the public's agreement to taxes needed for city improvements. Meanwhile, in Cincinnati, though it was the publicity and the prospect of our participation in the program that did much to make a construction bond issue acceptable to the voters, we, over the course of several years, were in effect eased out by the interests of local developers.

Title I projects take time, and during this time some quite powerful local forces can develop to challenge the newcomer who, when first on the scene, meets no real competition or resistance to his plans. In the case of Hartford, for example, we generated an economically and aesthetically well-balanced plan for a shopping-mall, high-rise office, hotel, and apartment complex to reknit the town's raveled core. Our project, however, with its plans for new stores, disturbed the sleep of the Aurbach family, who owned Fox's, Hartford's main department store. A man named Putnam, whose hopes for Hartford were even greater than his years, gave us the prestige of his backing. As long as he was alive, so was our plan, but when he died the Aurbach and other interests were able to block our development effectively. Webb & Knapp dropped the project.

We were quite hopeful for our St. Louis proposal and fully expected to get the job. However, another out-of-town developer, James Scheuer, from Area B in Washington, also came to St. Louis.

He developed various local contacts, made a proposal, and, to our chagrin, also made off with the prize. As it turned out, Scheuer was not able to follow through in St. Louis. Webb & Knapp, I should note, did have a way of somehow or other seeing through those projects it started, and every one of our projects wound up making money for its eventual owners.

Some years after this surprise flanking maneuver and rejection on the Mississippi, I was invited out to St. Louis. I was asked if I had any advice for this stalled city. When I flew in, St. Louis looked as if it had been bombed. Aside from the great open cut of acreage around Mill Creek, the center was scarred with half-block- and block-sized parking lots using the space formerly occupied by buildings. Touring the town by car, I found that the slums razed to clear the Mill Creek area had merely spread to other parts of town. There had been some redevelopment near the river, but when you see federally subsidized housing for retired people in what was originally intended to be a luxury area, you know a city's redevelopment program is dying. St. Louis in the late 1960's was a monument to a 1950's political regime that had no vision and to a complacent business elite who would not act forcefully or generously to save their city. For all its brave talk and hopeful bicentennial plans for 1967, I was looking at a sad, dry husk of a city surrounded by a politically insulated and presently healthy, but soon to be contaminated, ring of independent townships.

There was and is one major exception to my generalizations about American cities. This exception was New York City. Though New York might lack a constitutionally or politically powerful mayor, or a cohesive business elite, it had Bob Moses. Moses, all by himself, is worth two dozen blue-ribbon citizens' commissions and is personally responsible for more urban redevelopment than any other man in the world. Between 1949 and 1960 he lined up a grand total of thirty-nine Title I projects and five billion dollars of construction for his city. While other towns, often under Webb & Knapp prodding, were still trying to decide what, if anything, they could do with Title I, Moses had buildings coming out of the ground and tenants moving into them. He cleared land for cooperative housing projects, for privately sponsored conventionally financed projects, and for FHA-backed developments. As head of his own superagency, the New York Slum Clearance Committee, he was Mr. Redevelopment. Admittedly, as Mr. Redevelopment, Moses made new enemies and eventually worked himself into trouble. A growing citizens' clamor about his bulldozer tactics, the low aesthetic or "human" quality of many projects, the very high rents in some developments, and various alleged as well as actual scandals among some of the sponsors of various projects eventually created so much political heat that Moses stepped down from this office. Moses, however, did that which he set out to do: he put up housing, and we helped him to do it in three key developments—Park West Village, Kips Bay, and Lincoln Towers.

An important element of Moses' phenomenal speed-up of the time-devouring Title I process was his method of allocating and clearing land. Most cities did their own relocation of tenants and clearing of land before turning it over to the designated sponsor. In New York, however, after a sponsor had signed for his land, he had to do his own moving, relocating of tenants, and clearing of the land. Moreover, when a sponsor took over an existing slum for redevelopment, he took over as a taxpayer and paid taxes throughout the clearance process. In this way the city never lost any of its desperately needed income, and the taxpayer-sponsor, once he had cleared his land, had an extra incentive to keep moving, to put up his new buildings and receive income with which to pay taxes.

However, with so many conventional investors already wary of Title I, the prospect of their having to do their own evicting proved a powerful deterrent. The last thing in the world that Metropolitan Life, for instance, would want to see would be a series of newspaper and magazine stories on their putting poor old people, women, and children out of their homes, however miserable these homes. There were a number of investors, however, who spotted a special sweetener in this "New York System." As "temporary" landlords, since they need do little or no maintenance on buildings slated for demolition, they would have very few expenses. As landlords, however, they would for a time receive rents which in aggregate were impressive. Considering the knockdown prices at which they would be acquiring the condemned but occupied buildings, the short-term return on their actual cash investment would be fabulous. However, because of the usual delays in Title I projects, owners would often have to stretch out the relocation and clearance process. If, in the meantime, they kept collecting rents, and if they could funnel off this income to salaries and other "special costs," the sponsors and their friends could wind up quite a few dollars ahead.

A number of men-about-politics-and-business, who were as interested in the short-term, slum-landlord aspects of redevelopment as in the long-term rebuilding effort, joined together to sponsor various developments. But some coincidence, a number of these particular projects began to fall seriously behind schedule. A 1954 congressional investigation brought forth evidence that, though their projects were stalled, some sponsors and their business associates were doing rather well financially from their slum properties. A full-blown newspaper scandal that lasted intermittently for three years was under way. The two most notorious projects were Manhattantown Project, a six-block section of tenements just west of Central Park and north of Ninety-sixth Street, and NYU-Bellevue, between First and Second Avenues on the Lower East Side. By 1957 the questionable Manhattantown Project had been taken over by the city for nonpayment of taxes and NYU-Bellevue was similarly about to go under. At the invitation of Robert Moses, we took over both these stalled projects by buying up majority control from the original sponsors and paying the back taxes. At this time we also arranged to be the sponsors of the Lincoln Towers Apartment project. Overnight, Webb & Knapp became the major redeveloper in New York.

At Manhattantown, which we renamed Park West Village, we found ourselves committed to the existing architects and their basic building design. Pei, however, was able to greatly improve the site planning, and we wound up with a quite decent project. But the Bellevue site, which we renamed Kips Bay, was pure Webb & Knapp. Here we created something new in city housing—a sense of place and unity with buildings, gardens, and play areas—and have ever since been proud of what resulted. Kips Bay, being something new, had its flaws, but it was the prototype for any number of other developments.

The third project, Lincoln Towers, with its many buildings set out like cut-out sections of a giant beehive, was the largest project we ever built. Our financial backer in this venture was Lazard Freres, and this, from a New Yorker's point of view, had regrettable results. Lazard Freres, aware of our exceeding our original budget at Kips Bay, was determined to keep costs down and profits at a maximum for this next development. They resisted our use of Pei as architect. They fought with him over every major and minor design item and possible expense. Eventually they forced us to take him off the job and brought in an "expert" at putting up the pseudo-luxury, builders' housing that blankets so much of Manhattan and parts of Long Island. Lincoln Towers was a big job, where we handled the relocation of tenants with dispatch and fairness, but I'm not proud of the final product; I am ashamed of it. For a relatively very minor increase in costs, Lincoln Towers could have been one of the wonders of Manhattan, but this was not to be. When these towers are torn down, no one will mourn their passing, but the builder or politician who moves to tear down Kips Bay will have some angry citizens' groups on his hands. Kips Bay was no surrender, but a genuine advance in quality of city living, which is what Webb & Knapp's finest projects were really all about.

I was a guest at a Columbia University dinner honoring Le Corbusier. In due time Corbusier rose to make some remarks and at some stage paused and asked, "Is Bill Zeckendorf here tonight?"

I put up a hand, "I'm here, Corbu."

Stretching out a long arm to point a finger at me, Corbusier said, "There is the man who has done more than anybody else for architecture in America."

This was enormously flattering. Unfortunately, it was also true. In commercial architecture, Webb & Knapp was a lone and lonely pioneer for many years. In 1951, before we had yet launched our great building programs, *The Atlantic Monthly* printed a speech I had given at the Harvard School of Design. The speech was titled "Baked Buildings":

> *We may well be entering upon a golden era of construction, when the merger of the real-estate builder-economist and the artist and designer can be so skillfully integrated that we shall bring forth residential, industrial, and commercial architecture which will stand the two important tests of time: economic soundness, and beauty*

and functionalism. If we continue as we have been going, letting the devil take the hindmost—the builder builds for as little as he can and borrows as much as he can and runs, and the architect follows him —then the rebel who would design only things of great beauty can find no clients or only a few clients who are as crazy as he is because they do not understand. In that case, I say, we still have to wait for our golden era. But it is not necessary to wait. Not at all.

. . . There are many instances of buildings which combine beauty, functionalism, and economic soundness. But wherever you find them, the percentage in proportion to the total number of buildings erected is infinitesimal. Therefore, I do not address myself to the few but to the many.

. . . [Say] you go to a speculative builder—speculative builders build about ninety to ninety-five percent of all the things that are built in this country for rent—and you say, "Why do you dare to build that terrible-looking six-story apartment house that looks as though it came out of an oven, baked, according to a stenciled plan?"

He will say, "Well, maybe I like that, and maybe I don't. Maybe I would like to build something more beautiful, and maybe I wouldn't. But that's not my business. My business is to build within the framework, concept, and spirit of the FHA."

Well . . . that means designing as cheaply as possible, borrowing as much as possible, building as inexpensively as possible, and never mind the rest.

The builder says, "I'm not going to take a chance and build something more beautiful, something revolutionary. Maybe I do like a more modern design. But when I take that into a lending institution and they say to me, 'What is this . . . ? We've never seen that before. We'll discount it by twenty-five percent in the amount of a loan you've asked for'—well, that puts me out of business. I'm not that kind of a builder." And he speaks for ninety-five percent of the boys. "I have to borrow from the man who will lend me the maximum . . . and that man is the fellow who will lend me on what looks exactly like what every predecessor building of the same character looked like and was all the way back in time. Don't blame me. Blame the fellow I borrow from. Someday I'll build something more beautiful . . . But . . . I'm no contributor to the general welfare of the community. If I want to give charity, I'll find my own way to give it. But not in my business."

I am oversimplifying . . . but basically the philosophy of the

*speculative builder is exactly as I've said. So, you go to the man . . .
who finances him, who limits his horizon, his vision, and his potential.*

*Who is he? He is the insurance companies, the big ones and the
small ones; he is the savings banks; the building and loan companies
—the impersonalized corporations that people visualize when they see
a great tall building with a beacon on the top of it. But basically,
those beacons are supported by a little group of self-perpetuating
trustees, mainly of the same social strata, and you go talk to them.
You say to a typical one, "What is the idea of financing these baked
buildings that look like everything that was ever built before? What
is the idea of perpetuating these monstrosities? You're the fellow who
calls the tune, and the other fellow dances because it is your money
that makes these buildings go. And if you say X song, they will dance
X dance, over and over again, until they're dizzy. How come? Why
have you made so little contribution to the furtherance of thinking
in design and execution?"*

*Now, here is the answer you'll get from the typical trustee. He
will say to you, "I am a manufacturer, I'm a chemist, I'm a banker,
I'm a retired industrialist, I'm a professor, or I'm something—something completely unrelated to the subject specifically involved, the
subject of lending money. I'm a trustee of this institution or that
institution." He will say to you, "I'm interested in beauty. Come to
my home and I'll show you beauty. But when it comes to lending,
I want to bake them."*

"Why do you want to bake them?"

*"I want to bake them because I know that they've been baked
for twenty-five years and they've never failed. The . . . [twenty-two
story] flat is a good thing. You know I don't work here. I come here
without pay. I do not even get a director's fee for attending a meeting. I'm only here because I think it's my duty to run this institution."*

*Of course, he doesn't add that he enjoys being in association with
a lot of other fellows like him who finally got up there, or that he
is filling his father's seat, in the chair that his father and his father
before him filled. But he says, "I'm here and I am going to make
sure that this institution doesn't go broke. I know there's one thing
certain," he says; "I never can be criticized for doing something new,
something that was never done before—it might succeed; but the
Lord won't spare me if it doesn't—and I am not going to take that
chance."*

That is the attitude of perhaps eighty to ninety percent of the trustees of the eleemosynary and mutual institutions that are financing the vast bulk of the construction in this country. Add to that the FHA and its own completely unimaginative and limited scope in thinking and design, which is understandable, because they are trying to protect themselves by the most minute specifications against the chicanery of the builder who is interested only in borrowing the most and building for the least. There you have the double hazard, these two, the builder and the banker, on their high stools. And right between them, our architecture and design fall flat.

There are exceptions. There are provocative thinkers among the boards of trustees, and every once in a while you will see a great new thing come out which finally brings us a notch forward and lifts us up, because the power of emulation is something that is always with us. But it comes from such a minute number of those who are in control of the purse strings, and is given to that very small percentage of those who would build and who are interested in doing something more progressive and more important, that progress is painfully slow. We are now building new slums, for old slums, anachronistic conditions following upon the horrors of years before, so that notwithstanding the billions of dollars that are at our disposal, we are still building approximately the same thing that we have had in the years gone by. . . .

What I said at Harvard holds true today. Things have gone up a notch or two. By entering many design contests, Webb & Knapp upgraded the quality of, and opened new doors to, architecture. In commercial office projects, such as Mile High Center, Place Ville-Marie, and L'Enfant Plaza, we are showing that power and beauty in architecture can pay. In our housing projects in Chicago, Pittsburgh, Philadelphia, and New York, at Kips Bay and at our UN Towers development, we have shown that very remunerative housing need not be monstrous. Unfortunately, these great projects were not money-makers for Webb & Knapp; we were spread too thin in too many places to be able to hold these properties through an unexpectedly hard time, but the flaw was in me (I was trying to do too much too quickly) rather than in the projects.

Architects, as a group or guild, are at least as restrictive in their trade practices as doctors or plumbers, while as artists they are at least as jealous of each other as painters. Le Corbusier and Frank

Lloyd Wright, for instance, could not abide each other, but I was friends with both. Corbu I met during the UN development. Wright I met as a supposed antagonist on a TV discussion panel where I (the builder) was supposed to be his meat. All I knew about Wright was that I liked his work. When my aides compiled a dossier of his speeches and writings, I discovered the man made profound good sense. As a result, during the TV show we sang in duet and had a great time. After the program, in order to further admire each other and ourselves, we went out to my place in Greenwich for dinner plus a few drinks. The company was so excellent that we had a few more drinks, but in the course of maneuvering down into my wine cellar for a fresh bottle of brandy, Wright caught his heel on a step and fell, giving himself a nasty gash on the scalp. The next stop was the emergency ward of the hospital, where this fierce old man, refusing an anesthetic (he already had enough in him), sat on the operating table swinging his legs and singing bawdy songs as the intern stitched his scalp.

From then on we had an undying friendship, and I was very pleased, during the time of our Chicago redevelopment work, to save Wright's famous, 1909, prairie-style Robie House from destruction. The Chicago Theological Seminary, by dexterous compartmenting of its sense of values, was planning to raze the building in order to put up an apartment house for married students. We bought the building for $125,000 to use as a temporary headquarters. The eighty-seven-year-old Wright planned to take it over with his foundation, but he died. We then deeded the building to the University of Chicago, which eventually refurbished the landmark structure as its president's home.

I have worked or dealt in one way or another with a great many of the major architects of this era, but with the exception of Wallace Harrison, nothing very much ever came of these efforts. The fact is, I was so enamored of Pei, of how he thought and the kind of work he could do, that no other architects could really interest me. At first, because he was a newcomer and worked with a commercial builder, Pei encountered hostility in parts of the architectural fraternity and press, especially as regards Washington, D.C. But when everyone was able to see the kind of work he could do, and that we encouraged him to do, there was a complete reversal. The architectural fraternity became Webb & Knapp allies.

Webb & Knapp became a noted architectural research and training center. Pei and his associates, for instance, pioneered the techniques of poured-in-place, natural-finish structures to the point where they have become economically competitive with curtain-wall construction in many applications. As a result of my 1953 tour of Korea, made at the behest of President Eisenhower, I brought back many Korean architects for training at Webb & Knapp. We gave them quarters at the old Marguery Hotel, where they could cook up their own "kimchi" from time to time. In 1967, when I flew out to Korea to receive an honorary LL.D. from the University of Seoul, I found my trainees had become the leading architects in Korea.

Research is expensive, and the rewards, if they develop, tend to be far down the time line. Poured-in-place concrete, for example, is only now coming into architectural prominence, but I urged Pei to reach out for new things (he did not need much urging), and I encouraged him to spread his wings, take on outside projects, such as a design of part of the University of Taiwan or a housing project in Korea.

Pei is so gifted a man that even if he had not come to Webb & Knapp, he would eventually have attained or come very close to the eminence he now maintains, but we gave him and his partners the gift of time, with an accelerated boost up the ladder, plus some developer's insights on the use of land.

Once I asked Julian Bond of Bond Stores, "Do you give your architects much leeway in the design of stores?"

He snapped back, "Does your secretary dictate your letters?"

With Pei and Henry Cobb, we came to such a point that all I had to do, as in the case of Montreal, was lay down the basic guidelines of what I needed. The rest I could leave to them, because they had sat in on strategy and economic conferences and knew our needs. We had reached a point where we learned together and taught each other on every project we turned to.

There was too much going on at Webb & Knapp for the Pei group to handle everything. Thus, one great project that Pei had nothing to do with was a spanking new city Webb & Knapp ushered into being in California. This billion-dollar baby, Century City, born of Twentieth Century-Fox, through Spyros Skouras, had a full five years' gestation period and is now in healthy early life.

• 18 • Century City and Two Other Land Deals

SOMETIME IN LATE 1958, several years after our abortive attempt to purchase the Howard Hughes empire, I got a call from Spyros Skouras. He wanted a lunch. I knew what he had in mind. I accepted with an air of innocence, however, and was having a good time trading news and gossip until, about halfway through the meal, with studied casualness, Spyros said, "Have you heard about our Century City project?"

"Why, yes, I have. . . ."

About a year previously, Spyros had put Twentieth Century-Fox's Los Angeles studio properties on the market. He had realized that this 263-acre tract of land along Wilshire Boulevard would be worth more as real estate than as a movie lot. The architect, Welton Becket, had prepared a master plan indicating how high-rise offices, a hotel, shopping centers, and apartment buildings would fit on this acreage. Armed with this proposal, Spyros had gone looking for builder-developer-financiers to take over his plan and property. His asking price was one hundred million dollars, including oil rights.

The first I knew of the venture was a front-page story about it in *The New York Times*, but I decided not to make any bids. I knew Spyros would sooner or later come around to Webb & Knapp. He might shop that deal all over the country, but this was at least a half-billion-dollar conception, and I knew nobody else in America would tackle it; all we had to do was wait. Now, a year later, the old pirate was trying our door, which is why, when he asked if I had heard of his project, I said: "Why, yes, I have. It was in the papers. I'm surprised you haven't built it by now."

"Oh . . . but we are not builders. What we want is somebody like you. In fact, we want you more than anybody in the world."

"Come off it, don't kid with me, Spyros. You tried this thing out with every builder in America and struck out. They wouldn't take it. Do you want to know why?"

"Why?"

"Your price is too high. Your terms are no good. The project is overly ambitious, and it is overplanned."

"Would you buy it?"

"I'll take a look at it."

A few days later I flew out to Los Angeles and drove out to the studios. I had never studied the site with an eye to real estate. Here were 263 acres of rolling prairie land, located just south of Beverly Hills, only fifteen minutes from the Santa Monica beaches and eight minutes from UCLA's campus. In the 1920's and 1930's, when not shooting films, people used to shoot partridge, wild fox, and coyote on the acreage, but now I was after a different kind of game. I walked through and around various old stage sets with street scenes from Chicago, the Wild West, London, and Hong Kong, visualizing what could happen to the area with the addition of roads and new high-rise buildings.

Nearby Beverly Hills has stringent restrictions on heights of buildings, but the Twentieth Century lots were in Los Angeles and free for the high-rise kind of building that was our specialty. The more I looked around, the more I liked the concept; its very size attracted me. Given space and strategic location in an urban area, you can create and extend your own environment. The economics of the proposal, however, bothered me. It is wonderful to have something big, but this was too big; it could not work. I went back to see Spyros and said, "What do you want for this thing without the oil rights?"

"Around sixty million."

"Well, you're out of your mind. The studio properties alone will cost several million to demolish."

"But I don't want to tear them down," he said. "We'll turn over all the land around the studios, but we want to keep seventy-five acres for Twentieth Century."

That rang the bell. I quickly said, "If you would be willing to pay a decent rent for the studio stuff, maybe we could do something."

"How do you mean?"

"Well, if we buy the property we'll want to lease your studio property back to you for one and a half million dollars a year in rent."

"That's not too bad," said Spyros.

"In that case, we'll take it," I said, and we had a deal in the making. After a good bit of horse trading, we settled on a fifty-six-million-dollar sales price, but what I had realized as we first talked was that I really wouldn't be paying that much. I was actually paying only thirty-one million, because that 1.5 million rent, at six-percent interest, would be worth twenty-five million dollars to some insurance company. Of course, we would still have to raise thirty-one million dollars, which in 1958, with Webb & Knapp spread thin across America, was a staggering amount. But if we took it in small bites, maybe we could do it. We finally settled on a 2.5-million-dollar down payment and various sequential payments, rights of extensions on time, and so on. The essence of the deal was that Webb & Knapp would acquire the property, not in one lump, but in separate parcels over a ten-year period. What I had in mind, of course, was selling off parts and portions of the property to different investors. If the Hawaiian Technique could work for fractional parts of and rights in a building, why not a super-Hawaiian Technique for Century City?

We had much fun trimming, tacking, and sculpturing that deal, and when it was finally done, Spyros put on a proper Hollywood show. We met on the site of Twentieth Century's studios. Spyros, of course, had a bevy of starlets in attendance, a number of old-time movie greats, and several current stars present by "invitation." He had set up a reproduction of the Zeckendorf Store in Tucson, where my son and I had our picture taken, and he had a prepared speech. Spyros is a jovial man, but was born equipped with all the wariness of millennia of Greek traders; he is as hard as nails when it comes to a trade. He is also damnably persuasive. One of his directors once told me, "He speaks in the gravel voice and uses such broken English that we can hardly tell what he is saying. He is so earnest, though, that the directors vote yes without being sure just what he wants." Well, in the Century City deal Spyros had pulled off something nobody had thought could be done. Production costs on the movie *Cleopatra* had sucked Twentieth Century dry of cash, but here was a multimillion-dollar injection on the way. It was a great coup, but Spyros, a trader to the end, was complaining all the way to the bank. In his speech, he said, "Here is a Jew, Zeckendorf. He comes out here and outtrades me, a Greek. He steals the finest piece of real estate in all America." At this point the contract was not yet signed, but Spyros went on in the past tense, saying what a great deal we had pulled and that it was only through cunning and skillful flattery that we got the terms we did for the greatest piece of property in the world.

Then it was my turn. I had no prepared remarks, but I did have an opening. I said, "I am flattered by Mr. Skouras' remarks on my astuteness and how I am stealing this property: if, and when, I sign the contract, which yet remains unsigned. But I want to set the record straight:

"If I recall correctly, the United States paid Napoleon fifteen million dollars for the Louisiana Purchase, which includes five states and most of Texas. We paid just over seven million dollars for Alaska. We paid ten million dollars for the Gadsden Purchase, which picked up half of Arizona and southern New Mexico. We gave the Danes twenty-five million dollars for the Virgin Islands. Now I am paying almost as much as all these for 263 acres on the wrong side of the tracks here in Brentwood. . . . I wonder who is doing the better trading."

Spyros gave a great roar of laughter. Actually, we were both pleased with ourselves, with each other, and with the deal. We signed, and Webb & Knapp was under way with Century City.

For the vital, 2.5-million-dollar down payment we first put up our own cash, then brought in Lazard Freres by borrowing against other property of ours. Lazard Freres had the option of a "put" to us. "Put" is a financial term; it means that at any time of their choice Lazard had the right to walk out of the deal and we must give them back their 2.5 million dollars. In any event, we turned over the down payment to Spyros in April, 1959. Our deal began to cook through the rest of that year and the first part of 1960, but it didn't get done before we began to run out of gas. Colonel Crown, to whom Spyros had first peddled the property, was interested in joining; so were other developers and money men, but nothing was moving quickly. Meanwhile, the time for closing the deal and making a second 3.8-million-dollar cash payment had come and been twice postponed. Lazard Freres, anxious about its down payment, decided to call for its 2.5 million. At that time I was much committed to building a new Zeckendorf Hotel in Manhattan. This hotel was going to take up all the cash we had on hand, and I had to make a choice: either we could drop the hotel or fade at Century City. The very fact of our entry into Century City had done much to bring this project from the realm of fantasy to the world of the probable. People could now see that this was an area of great potential. So what I did now was arrange a sale to another developer. First, over a series of negotiations with Spyros, we agreed on new terms for the project: it would now be an all-cash deal for forty-three million. Then, in May, 1960, I sold our contract to buy the property at forty-three million to developer Marvin Kratter. We sold this contract for 4.5 million dollars but kept twenty-five acres for Webb & Knapp. Short of cash, we were bowing out, but only part way, and at a good profit. Kratter stood to make a lot of money from the further fractioning of the land, but, all things considered, I was content.

A month after this agreement, however, Kratter became suddenly afraid of taking on such a great commitment and, at the last moment, walked away from the deal. Now, to my horror, Webb & Knapp had another time bomb on its hands. Lazard Freres had called for their money; we had to have 2.5 million for them by August. A further 3.8 million dollars was now due on the Century City contract. If we did not come through with something pretty soon, we stood to lose the land and the down payment Twentieth Century-Fox already held.

A number of sources turned us down but hung around hungrily to see what we might do and what they might pick up cheaply in case we slipped. Somehow, somewhere, I was going to have to pull a solid-gold rabbit out of a hat I didn't own, or Webb & Knapp would be out of business.

Now, it happened that earlier in the summer, at a businessmen's luncheon, I had met Frank McGee, top man at the Aluminum Company of America. We got to talking, and I said, "You fellows are sure falling behind the times; you are doing nothing in real estate."

"What do you mean?"

"Well, Reynolds is going into the housing business to demonstrate products; so are others. But the biggest aluminum company in America hasn't done a thing."

"Well, we might be interested someday. If you have something good in mind, let me hear from you."

Of course I had in mind the forthcoming "put" from Lazard. I said, "Frank, don't say it if you don't mean it."

"Oh, I can't commit myself, but I'd be glad to hear from you."

"I've got nothing in mind right at the moment, but if something should come up, I'll call you and come down to see you to tell you about it . . . if you wish. But don't fool around. I don't want to waste your time or mine."

"That's all right, no harm done. Come on down sometime."

A couple of weeks went by, the commitment to Lazard was coming close. The Kratter deal flowered and died, and I decided, "Well, I'll make my pitch." I picked up the phone, called McGee in Pittsburgh, and said, "Frank, remember that conversation we had some time ago?"

"Sure."

"Well, I've got something."

"Fine. Let me know sometime when you'd like to come down."

"I'm letting you know now."

"When do you want to come?"

"Tomorrow."

"Tomorrow?"

"Yes."

"Well! That's kind of short notice."

"I asked you if you were serious last time, so this is not short notice. If you are busy, I'll come the next day."

"No, I'll find time for you."

"Good. The reason I want to come down tomorrow is that I have a date for lunch with Westinghouse, and I can come over and see you before lunch."

He said, "What time?"

"Ten-thirty."

So at 10:30 I arrived. I was ushered into Alcoa's executive suite on the thirty-second floor. McGee had a very large office, but it was well filled; most of Alcoa's top officers were there. McGee sat on a divan with his legs crossed, and after introductions said, "Well, tell us the story."

I had brought a map of the site and gave them an idea of what one could do with 263 acres of open land in Los Angeles. "The price," I said at the end, "is forty-three million dollars, but it need cost only eighteen million."

"Why do you say that?" asked McGee.

"Well, as you remember, Fox is leasing seventy-five acres back for its own use at a million and a half rent, and that million and a half can be sold for twenty-five million. So if you want to sell that off, your exposure is only eighteen million. With that eighteen million you can get the best of the land. I recommend that you take this deal.

"It will mean a great deal to worldwide public relations of Alcoa. Apart from that, you will make a lot of money in real estate. You will spend eighteen million dollars for land, plus another eight or ten million in developing the land with roads, utilities, sewers, bridges, and other things. Then you are going to sit back and make a big land profit. Because if you take the eighteen-million cost, plus, say, seven and a half million in expenses, this brings you up to twenty-five and a half million. For this expense you'll have six million square feet left, but it will be fully developed for land use, at a cost of roughly four dollars a square foot.

"It is easily conceivable that that land could be worth, in time, fifty dollars a square foot; you might even have a fifty-dollar-a-square-foot profit."

McGee listened to all this and more, and sat there, then said, "When do you want an answer on all this?"

"Today."

"How can we give you an answer on a thing like that today? This is so revolutionary!"

"Well, Frank, if you won't give it to me today, I'm going to have to go somewhere else. I told you before I came down here that you shouldn't ask me down unless you really meant to do business. That doesn't mean that you are committed to buy this deal, but I thought you wanted to give it serious consideration, and that means immediate consideration.

"Why don't you fellows think it over. I'm going to have lunch over at the Westinghouse Company, and I can be free this afternoon after lunch. I'll come back."

McGee said, "All right, if that's convenient."

"I'll be here," I said.

At 2:30 I came back, and the same group were all assembled. Nobody was saying a word; McGee sat on the same divan. I tried to seat myself near the center so I could keep my eye on everybody; then McGee began to speak in a quiet monotone. He talked endlessly. Actually, it was not a long time; it only seemed that way. He talked and talked, and of course I had to assume that he was explaining why they would not go into real estate, because what he was saying was that Alcoa had never varied from the pattern laid down by the founders of the company: this was to confine themselves and their capital entirely to the production and sales of aluminum.

He said, "We build ships, but we use them for our own cargoes. We just came through with an agreement to build a power dam, but that is to make aluminum at the site of our bauxite production in Surinam in Dutch Guiana; we'll put out 150 million dollars for that dam. We understand financing aluminum extrusion plants. We can understand putting money into our own office building where we occupy fifty percent of the space, but we don't understand going into real estate. Nevertheless, we are going to do this."

He said this last in the same monotone, and kept on talking. It was like President Johnson's famous 1968 announcement that he would not run for another term; one heard it but did not grasp it for several seconds, and by then wondered if he had heard right in the first place. No one in the room besides me had even seen the Twentieth Century property, and they had no full idea of the multitudinous things that had to be done. They just committed themselves right there in that room.

"Now," McGee said, "what do you want us to do?"

I said, "A check for two and a half million dollars."

"Who do you want it payable to?"

"Webb & Knapp."

He called over to the treasurer, saying, "Matt, you got two and a half million anywhere?"

"Yes."

"Give Bill a check. What are you waiting for?"

Now, we didn't have a contract, not a scrap of paper, and I had never met any of those men before in my life except for McGee, and I didn't know him very well. I got the check and I took my leave as quickly as I could politely do so, went downstairs in the elevator, got to a telephone booth, and called the office. With my son and the others on the phone, I said, "Fellas, we just got a great deal, we are out from under Lazard and we are off and running in a wonderful deal with Alcoa."

Earlier McGee had asked me what basis I would want to go on. I said, "You put up two-thirds of the money, and we'll put up one-third of the money. We'll take two-thirds of the profit, you take one-third of the profit. You get your money . . . we all get our money back before profits are divided." And that was the original basis of the deal. It was the beginning of a relationship which, without exception, without a single incidence, was the finest relationship any company could wish to have with another.

Eventually there will be close to a billion dollars' worth of improvements in that area, and the rise in value has been so great and so evident that Alcoa doesn't have to invest any more of its own capital; it can find plenty of banks and insurance companies to give it all the mortgage money it needs, with no liability to the parent company. The land is presently worth more than forty dollars per square foot and will continue to accrue in value. Alcoa can eventually expect to make at least a quarter of a billion dollars on this one property, and it will long stand as one of their finest investments and as a great contribution to architecture and building.

The dominant stockholder group in Alcoa were the Mellon interests. I got to know General Richard Mellon during our Pittsburgh venture. Some years after, returning to the United States aboard the S.S. *France,* we chanced to be shipmates. He remarked that the purchase of Century City was one of the greatest milestones in the company's history, and one of which they were very proud. It was indeed a milestone, for this first step led to others. Alcoa became partners with us in our greatest urban-redevelopment projects and eventually took them over completely. They also took over all of Century City; we sold out for fifteen million dollars, this money going to our British partners during Webb & Knapp's time of troubles.

The Twentieth Century-Fox deal was one of the first efforts of the entire Zeckendorf-family team. My son, my son-in-law, Ronnie Nicholson, and I worked on it, beautifully backstopped on the legal side by Maurice Iserman. Spyros, of course, played the lead role for Twentieth Century. Working with him were Don Henderson, the treasurer, and Joe Moskowitz, also a financial man, who was also much involved in the purchase of film properties. Their lawyer, Otto Kagel, was a practical man and a deal-maker rather than a deal-breaker, which is what some lawyers try to be. Henderson was also *simpático*, and Joe Moskowitz was the bulldog at the gates.

Getting Twentieth Century to come down from the original fifty-six-million-dollar, ten-year deal to a forty-three-million-dollar, all-cash contract took an extraordinary number of sessions. We met in New York. We met in Los Angeles. We bargained in offices. We bargained in supper clubs while watching good-looking starlets swish by the table. Throughout all these sessions, short, round, cigar-chewing Joe Moskowitz, a cartoonist's caricature of a Hollywood mogul, kept a perpetual bargainer's scowl on his face and questioned anything and everything in suspicious detail. I got so sick and tired of watching his grimacing that at some point I called across the table, "Well, let's see first . . . Hey, how does Laughing Joe Moskowitz feel about this?" Up till then Joe had never so much as smiled. Now he burst into a laugh. I called him Laughing Joe from then on, and no matter how he tried, he could not help, at the least, smiling back. This helped our sessions and set a precedent; "Laughing Joe" will go to his grave with that name.

At about the same time as our early Century City negotiations, we became involved in yet another potentially fabulous conversion of city-side acreage to urban square-foot values. This next deal was in Cuba, which, having replaced Mexico as Marion's and my vacation headquarters, provided us with fun, games, and a touch of adventure.

Before Castro's takeover, Marion and I often went to Havana for long weekends. It was a joyous town for tourists. The Habañeros were a friendly, accommodating people. The Tropicana and Sans Souci, in quality of food and service, and the spectacular precision of their shows, all outdoors in the glorious weather, were the two best nightclubs in all the Americas. Besides the clubs and beaches, there were gambling casinos, the horse races, and jai alai. I never played the horses but religiously went to the jai-alai games. Through betting on these games I was able to earn my expenses on every Cuban excursion except one. I earned my way in jai alai, not by gambling, but by recognizing that the game was rigged.

I won for years, but finally I must have been betting too often or too much, because the bookies recognized and caught up with me. When I would try to make a bet, the bookies were blind and ignored my signals. This was their way of saying, "You're on to our racket, but now we are on to you, too, and won't let you win." So, for a few nights they really hooked me; I probably gave them back one thousand of the five thousand dollars I had taken over the years, but it was all in the spirit of good crooked gambling and took nothing from my vacation pleasure. Marion and I could still enjoy ourselves at the Floridita, which was world-famous for its daiquiris—I am one of the few people who have their recipe; and the delights of their black-bean soup and Morro crab on a balmy night are still with me.

The only property we ever owned in Havana was the Hotel Nacional, which was put up in the twenties by the Fuller Construction Company and in my view is possibly the finest hotel in Latin America. It was owned by the Plaza Hotel Operating Company, which owned the Plaza and the Savoy Plaza in New York, as well as the Copley Plaza in Boston. The Nacional and a number of other hotels were acquired by a shrewd trader named Arnold Kirkeby during the thirties. We acquired the Nacional, the Gotham in New York, and the Beverly-Wilshire in Los Angeles and a couple of other hotels from Kirkeby in the 1950's; a few years after its acquisition, I sold the Nacional to Juan Tripp and Pan Am's Intercontinental Hotels for a couple of million dollars' profit.

During our visits to Cuba, we had come to meet a number of moneyed and influential visitors and residents, such as Southenes Behn of ITT and Julio Lobo, the Cuban and international sugar king. Lobo, who had made a career of cornering and riding the sugar market, owned or controlled sugar lands, mills, deep-water docks, the Hershey candy-bar business in Cuba, and much more that I never knew about. He was the biggest fish in the Cuban pond and quite friendly, of course, with General Batista, who ran the country. To copper his bets, Lobo was probably supplying a bit of backstairs help to Castro as well.

The largest sugar-mill operator, after Lobo, was the Aspura family, who owned the Toledo mills. The Aspura lands, once on the outskirts of Havana, had been partly engulfed by Havana as the city grew, and now accounted for something near one-third of the city. The ownership was plagued by what are called *colonos*, squatters who settle on land and after a period of time get title by adverse possession. This meant that real title would be hard to clear, though not impossible. More important, there were great tracts of city-side cane land, free of squatters, only awaiting proper development. I had met Aspura at one or two social functions and brought up the question of buying his lands. A little to my surprise, he offered to sell for 7.5 million dollars, and we agreed to buy.

I called up Lobo and said, "Julio, we are buying Aspura's land."

Lobo, who went to Lawrenceville and Princeton and speaks perfect English, said, "Oh, that's a great deal, I've been trying to get hold of it for years. How did you do it?"

"Well, just one of those things."

I knew that Lobo was glad to be rid of a competitor. He was also aware of the real-estate aspects of the Aspura land, and liked to be in on anything big in Cuba. I knew what reply I'd get when I said, "It occurs to me that we might be well advised to have a Cuban like yourself in a powerful position as a partner. How would you feel about taking a half-interest with us?"

With great warmth he said, "Yes, of course I'll take it."

That, then, was the combination. I called on Rafael Oriomuno, who was South American lawyer for the Rockefellers. Instead of taking a few weeks, it took months to draw up the necessary papers. Everything was very slow, very technical. Aspura obviously was in no hurry to make the sale, but Oriomuno assured me that things were moving ahead.

Many months had gone by, when one day Lobo called me. He was in New York and wanted to have lunch.

At lunch he said, "I think we should do this thing by one-third shares."

"What do you mean?"

"This is such an important property, and you'll have a great deal of trouble with the *colonos:* you'll need government help. The Big Boy ought to be a partner."

"You mean Batista?"

"That's right."

"Well..."

I was wondering if this was a typical muscle job where the local chief was going to take one-third without paying, but Lobo said, "He'll pay his full share."

"I'd like to meet him," I said.

"He wants to meet you."

A date was set up. I arrived in Havana and drove to the palace, through the gates, past the submachine-gun-carrying guards, under the muzzles of the machine guns on the roof, and walked into the President's office. Batista was stocky, ruddy of face, and obviously had a good bit of Indian blood. He was most jovial, and didn't talk about our deal as such. What he wanted to talk about was large-scale housing for the people of Havana and what we could tell him about urban redevelopment. He spoke benignly about upgrading the status of his people. Finally he said, "You have a fine prospect here in Havana."

I agreed, saying, "... in respect to that, I assume we deal through our friend Julio."

He said, "That is right," and that was all. He had given his official blessing to the deal, and not too long after, I heard that the long-delayed papers were in order.

I had not seen Aspura since we first shook hands on our deal a year previously, but he did not want to sign the contract in Cuba; he wanted to sign in the United States. He and his family came up over a weekend. That Monday he and his lawyer–son-in-law had a very convivial lunch at our office. At that time I had an abstract painting on a stand at the back of the room which seemed to catch Aspura's eye. He asked a few questions about it. I could tell he liked it, and knowing a little about Latin customs, I had it wrapped up and sent to his hotel that afternoon. That evening we took his entire family, including his two beautiful daughters and wife, to dinner at Le Pavillon. Naturally, no business was discussed during this time, but neither was the painting. The contract papers were to be signed on

Wednesday. Tuesday, we heard nothing from Señor Aspura. Wednesday, he could not show up for the closing. On Thursday I got my painting back with a flowery note saying he could not permit himself to be obligated for such a handsome gift, and by now I was getting the message. I said, "Boys, this fellow is going to welch; otherwise he would never have broken the date on Wednesday or sent back that picture."

Getting Oriomuno on the phone, I asked, "Rafael, what do I do in a case like this?"

Rafael came right back, "This case would be under Latin law. You can sue. Under our code, a contract is a contract when all points are agreed to. Signed or not signed, there is a contract if there are no open points."

There were no open points. The contract had been completely agreed to and only needed signing. But, Oriomuno cautioned, "You can sue, but you would never be able to serve him in Havana; you'll have to catch him here before he leaves. Be sure to get a photo of his being served, or he will deny it ever happened."

I called in Jim Millard, an aggressive young Irish lawyer on our staff, and said, "Draw up an affidavit of service. We are suing Aspura for ten million dollars. Get a photographer, get over to the hotel, and give him the summons before he skips town."

Millard and his photographer hopped over to the Plaza, asked for Aspura at the desk, and were told, "He left for the airport ten minutes ago."

My men raced in a cab to the airport, and there, at the terminal, smiling for a squad of newspaper photographers, the Aspuras being something in the way of Latin socialites, were my friend, his admiring family, and various hangers-on. Millard, photographer in tow, walked up and asked, "Are you Mr. Aspura?"

"Yes, I am Mr. Aspura." Seeing the photographer, Aspura kept a pleasant face, because he enjoyed being in the society columns.

"I have this for you, Mr. Aspura," said Millard, handing over the summons.

"Oh, thank you very much, we already have our tickets."

"It is not that kind of ticket, sir."

Aspura took the papers. Flash! went the camera. A few moments later: Crash! went Aspura. When he read the summons, he fell in a faint. They revived him, got him aboard, and flew from New York to Havana at two thousand feet of altitude. We had the goods on him, and a badly shaken Aspura knew it.

Our lawsuit was then filed in Cuba. It had not yet gotten to trial the next time I was down there on a weekend. Julio Lobo invited me to lunch, during which he asked what I was going to do about the lawsuit.

I told him I'd never been involved in this sort of lawsuit, that I liked to limit my appearances in court to speeding tickets. I told him I'd like to drop it if Batista agreed.

"I think that might be the best thing."

I am not sure what prompted Lobo's anxiety for peace, but I had no appetite for a forced deal and said I would drop the suit immediately.

Julio was obviously pleased and immediately announced that he would give a dinner party, invite Aspura, and we would all be friends again.

Aspura showed up at the party to give me an embrace and pronounce me a great *caballero*. It was his daughters, he said, who had talked him out of selling the property; they wanted their sons to have it. For his part, he would rather sell to me. Within a year of this dinner, Castro had taken over Cuba. The first major property he took over was Aspura's Toledo mills. Castro would have been even happier to take it away from Mr. Zeckendorf, and if I'd shown up and could have been proved to be a partner with Batista, I might have lost more than property.

For more than two years, under Castro, Lobo continued to hold sway and was allowed to keep his lands. When I asked about this among knowledgeable exiles, I was told that the government needed Julio's professional abilities in the world sugar market, but in due time they would undoubtedly swallow him up for dessert. This indeed happened, and Lobo barely escaped with his life to safe haven in the United States.

Once here, he again went into sugar speculating and manipulating and came within a grain of cornering the market and making a fantastic killing, but he overplayed his hand. The market got away, and he was cleaned out. In old Cuba, where the cards were marked for him, he could corner the market and squeeze the short buyers dryer than a cane husk. Away from his own base, he almost did it—but not quite.

Yet a third vast land deal, one that created the basis for a great subempire in the Webb & Knapp realm, came to us sometime near the holidays at the end of 1955 and early 1956. My broker called offering us a major block of shares in Godchaux Sugars, Inc. This company, with thirty-five thousand acres of petroliferous land along the Mississippi between New Orleans and Baton Rouge, owned and operated sugarcane lands and a sugar mill and refinery. Its annual sales were in the fifty-million-dollar range, but the return was only one percent, and the owners wanted out. It was not the sugar but the real estate that interested us. We agreed to buy. Other offers of stock came in, and we eventually wound up with a chance for eighty-five-percent control of the company for 8.5 million dollars. For this kind of financing we needed help. I called Bob Young, at the New York Central, outlined the deal, plus its possibilities, and asked if he would put up the money.

He said, "I don't think we have the money, but I'll give you a takeout by Alleghany—can you use that on a loan?"

A takeout is an agreement to buy a note on maturity; Alleghany, in other words, was lending us their credit. I called my crusty friend Jim Muir at the Royal Bank in Montreal and asked, "Will you take Alleghany's takeout and lend the money now on stock?"

"How much?" he asked.

I told him.

"What else goes with it?"

"I'll get you some compensating balances of at least as much money." These compensating balances would be unrelated, a sort of interest bonus to the Royal Bank.

"How long will you want it for?"

"A year."

"What rate will you pay?"

"Six percent."

"It's a deal." He hung up.

The next day the New York agent for the Royal Bank called to say I could come and get the money.

I got Bob Young to execute the papers, and Webb & Knapp had a

Southern plantation on its hands. Even before the deal was fully con-summated, however, I went downtown to see Horace Havermeyer of the National Sugar Company. He bought the sugar refinery from us for 14.5 million dollars. Some 8.5 million dollars of this money went to pay off existing mortgages and debts of the company, leaving us with six million in cash. Over the next two years we sold the sugar mill, plus seven thousand acres of land, to South Coast Corp. for 3.2 million dollars. After liquidating $700,000 of inventory and cash receivables, and paying off the remainder of existing debts, we were left with another 1.5 million dollars in cash. Godchaux Sugars now owned roughly twenty-eight thousand acres of land free and clear and had a few million dollars of cash in hand: it was a very sweet deal. We changed the name of the company from Godchaux Sugars to Gulf States Land & Industries and began putting the new property to work.

First, we sold six hundred acres of land to Du Pont for a new polyethylene plant at $1,250 per acre. This money helped finance some of our acquisitions of the Waggoner estate between Dallas and Fort Worth. Then we began development of a strategically located new town just north of New Orleans. We also acquired fifteen thousand more acres of land just to the south of New Orleans from Louisiana Citrus Corp., and we had Gulf States take over some very promising interests in the Strategic Materials Corp. from Webb & Knapp.

John Udd, a brilliant Canadian engineer, builder, and hotel operator, a man of many parts, had concocted a process for removing the thirty-three-percent iron ore left over in mining slag. The Koppers Company of Pittsburgh was involved in some of this work, which was somewhat comparable to removing the dry vermouth from a martini, but at the laboratory and early pilot-plant stage the process seemed most promising. Webb & Knapp had become interested in the venture, bought into it, and had gone so far as to acquire the ghost town of Clarkdale, Arizona, and a nearby forty-million-ton slag pile as a pre-liminary inventory. We turned this operation over to Gulf States, which had cash to carry it forward. Later there was a merger with Chemetals Corp., which would supply the chemical and mineral know-how to bring the process to fruition. We kept putting money into the development work for many years. There were other residuals—gold, silver, and traces of copper—which made it attractive, but in the final analysis we could not make the process economically feasible. We had to let the business go.

In the meantime, however, the company went into numerous other ventures. In 1958, partly to help glamorize Gulf States land, we became involved in the oil business. We wound up seeking oil off the coast of South America because a small group of suntanned and whiskey-reddened buccaneers strolled into my office one afternoon in 1958. They stood around speculatively eyeing the secretaries, the furniture, and everything else that was not nailed down while waiting to see me, then filed into my office behind their leader, Jim Wooten. Wooten, a fantastic character, was something out of Kipling. He had flown supplies into China during World War II, was for a time president of Alaska Airlines, and had since wandered around parts of the Orient and South America delivering planes, selling arms, dabbling in revolutions, and gaining and losing money and influence from one adventure to the next.

He had great vitality, enormous charm, and a contagious sense of humor. Of a continual string of breakfast visitors who used to visit me, Wooten was the only one whom Marion would rouse herself to join because he told such fantastic and uproarious stories. Somehow or other Wooten and his friends had acquired the concession to search for oil off the coast of Dutch Surinam. They needed eighty thousand dollars in order to make the test drill necessary to keep their concession, and that is why they were in my office. Another similarly flamboyant but far shrewder man, John MacArthur of Banker's Life & Casualty Co., had sent them to me.

After Wooten and I had talked things over a few times, I half-decided that Webb & Knapp, through Gulf States, should take the whole thing over. I would rather do that than just drill one well. I called Ham Metzger at Standard Oil and asked if he would recommend we take the concession. He said, "We had it and we dropped it; it was no good." I decided to go ahead anyway.

Many a company has come in behind another one and found oil where others thought there was none. The investment would be a relatively modest one. The rewards, if we made a strike, would be fantastic. It would be great fun to take on something the greatest oil company in the world said was no good and maybe find oil. We bought out ninety-five percent of the Wooten deal. My piratical partners then scattered to blow their money and pray that we struck oil so their five percent could blossom.

Looking at a map, I realized that if we did find oil, Surinam's neighbors in French and British Guiana would start arguing about boundaries and we'd be in the World Court for twenty years. The answer, though it was a large order, was to tie the concession in with both of these two countries as well. The French, after numerous negotiations, proved to be interested and willing. We arranged a fifty-fifty exchange; they would have rights to half the Surinam area, we would have half of the French Guianan area. British Guiana, however, was then under the control of Jagan, the Communist dentist turned rabble-rousing politico. I met Jagan at the UN. He was polite enough, but neither he nor any of his coterie had any interest in leasing potential oil lands to a New York capitalist. We had to settle for a French-Surinam deal.

With Alcoa planning a power dam on the Surinam River as power source for a Surinam alumina plant, there was a possibility that, if we found oil or gas, we could supplement this power source and do away with need for a second power dam. With these and other possibiilties and negotiations pending, I flew out to Surinam to see the country and meet some of its officials. Part of the trip involved a two-day trip down the jungle-edged Surinam River in a dugout manned by two black men. I fished for piranhas all the way down and had a wonderful time in spite of the heat.

Meanwhile, we chartered a drilling rig in California, brought it through the Panama Canal, and put it to work fifty miles off shore in 450 feet of water. We drilled 4,500 feet down and found seven oil and gas shoals. None were commercial, but it heartened us enough to take more geologic soundings. Eventually Gulf States sold its concession rights to the Shell and British Petroleum companies for seven million dollars, keeping a percentage share of possible future oil finds. Our Surinam venture, all in all, was therefore profitable. In fact, up till the very end, Gulf States was one of the principal bastions from which we maneuvered for three desperate years to keep Webb & Knapp from falling, but more about that later. Before discussing the *fall*, there are some major parts and pieces to fit into the mosaic. For instance, there is the Wall Street Maneuver, which in turn helped lead to some further adventures on Sixth Avenue.

· 19 · Wall Street Maneuver

ALTHOUGH PRIVATE BUILDING complexes, urban-redevelopment projects, and massive land deals constituted the visible bulk of the Webb & Knapp empire, we had never given up our original business of assembling properties and packaging deals. In the 1950's and 1960's we continued buying and selling lots and buildings as we had in the 1940's, except, where we had once dealt in thousands of dollars, we now dealt in millions. We were the most noted and trusted dealer in the business, and it was through a reputation built up over the years that we were led into the single greatest project or series of projects of all, the Wall Street Maneuver.

In 1954 I was invited to a special meeting at the old Chase Manhattan Bank headquarters at 18 Pine Street. Arriving there, I was led down a paneled corridor to a deep-carpeted conference room where David Rockefeller and a group of his distinguished colleagues were gathered. I stepped into the room with these distinguished gentlemen, and we began to discuss the Chase's dilemma within a general Wall Street dilemma.

The Chase, like every other New York bank, was growing. Its offices were inefficiently scattered through eight separate buildings in the area. Their immediate problem was: should they build a new building downtown to bring everything under one roof or should they abandon their downtown holdings in favor of new quarters in midtown?

The Chase, like every other major financial institution downtown, was living with its hat on, ready to jump uptown. Mid-Manhattan was enjoying an office-building boom. More and more important corporate headquarters were being established in the midtown section. Nothing had been built in the financial district since the Depression. The decision was in balance. No one wanted to make the first move. No one wanted to guess wrong about what the other boys might do; so no one was doing anything. All it would take was for one major bank to make the leap, and the others would follow. The result, for midtown Manhattan, would be phenomenal congestion. The result in the old financial district would be nearly disastrous. Values would drop. By just how much values would drop would be anybody's guess. The deserted stock markets and investment community would come under pressure to move. In time, residential construction would creep into the area, but first there would be a period of relative decay.

When the gentlemen from the Chase said that they would like to preserve their thirty-seven-million-dollar investment in the area, I replied that while this saving was important, the real question was, could the Wall Street community be saved? If it could be saved, this would call for a truly bold maneuver. When everyone nodded, I said, "The whole community can be saved only if enough major banks agree to stay here, if not all of them, then a substantial number."

"Agreed."

I said, "The trick will be to stabilize Wall Street. You can't do it alone, but you can start. You have to start in a way that the others will follow. What you need is a musical chair, a place to move into. . . .

"There is only one logical musical chair open and available to you"—I pointed out the window—"and that is the Mutual Life site on the corner. Guarantee Trust was going to build a new home there, but they changed their minds and are restoring their old building at 140 Broadway.

"The Mutual Life site is under negotiation for sale, and you have no time. You have to bid for it today."

Somebody interjected, "What are you talking about, today?"

"Today is the day."

"What is the price?"

I said, "It is $4,670,000."

"We'll have to take that to the board."

"There is not a man in the room who cannot commit the bank to a maximum loan of fifty million dollars. Anyone of you can lend the limit without consultation from your board. I'm not talking about ten percent of your maximum lending power, just one percent. Your whole future is at stake; you can't wait to go to your board with a silly thing like that. Here's what you do. I suggest you call Guarantee Trust and verify that they are about to sell off the property."

The call was made and it was verified that Guarantee were about to close.

All this time David Rockefeller had been quietly directing the meeting. He did this *sotto voce*, because that is his manner and because many of the older men in that room were more powerful than he within the bank, but it was David who personally guided Chase's gamble on the stabilization of Wall Street. The Chase now owned a musical chair. I undertook to liquidate their surplus buildings and to persuade other banks to stay downtown by providing them with proper quarters.

Some of the Chase properties adjoining the Mutual Life site became part of the new project, but I promised to get the thirty-seven-million-dollar book value of all their properties from sale of the remaining properties. We wound up getting sixty million. It was these other properties, which the Chase would vacate, that would create the open chairs in the game of musical banks I was planning.

To find the next player in the game, I called Harold Helm, chief of the Chemical Bank, and said, "Harold, I would like to see you and your colleagues for an important discussion of a relocation idea."

He said, "Fine. When?"

"At your convenience."

"Let's say tomorrow at ten."

"I'll be there."

The next day Harold Helm and three other heads of Chemical were waiting for me at their offices on 165 Broadway. I sat down, put the flat of my fingers on the edge of the table, and said, "The idea is that you should move to 18 Pine."

Helm said, "That's the Chase Bank."

"Yes."

"We move there, let them go uptown, and we're left holding the bag!"

"No, Harold, you move there, and we will have it written into your contract that you are not bound to that property unless the

Chase puts up a building that does not cost less than sixty million dollars in the immediate neighborhood. They have committed themselves to buying the Mutual Life site to do this."

The Chemical Bank agreed to a deal in principle, and now we began talking price. The Pine Street building, I told them, would cost 17.5 million dollars. This was acceptable, but in part payment they wanted us to take two properties that were surplus to their needs. One was on Williams Street and the other across the river in Brooklyn Heights. Now we were in the used-bank-building business, but that is what makes deals. I agreed, took the proposition to the Chase, and our first step was set.

We had successfully popped the first olive out of the bottle. Everyone was delighted at how smoothly it had gone. Then, two weeks later, I got a call from Helm: "I'm sorry, Bill, but the deal is off. We are on a very short lease here at 165 Broadway; we have three years to go. The Chase won't get their new building up for at least six years. Our landlord is a very tough guy named Norman Winston, and he won't give us a lease of convenience. In fact, he is aware of the situation, and he wants to hit us for a twenty-one- or thirty-year extension, or it's out in the street for us.

"This puts us in a terrible bind," he continued. "Should we stay here for twenty-one years? That wouldn't be very good. Should we go uptown? Should we do something else? We don't know yet, but we can't make that deal with the Chase. We'll have to move before they can give us 18 Pine Street."

I said, "Give me a little time, I'll see what I can do."

Ten days later I called Helm: "I've got you a lease of convenience."

"How did you do it? We couldn't."

"Well, I just did it."

"How?"

"I'm your landlord."

I had gone to Winston and bought him out. We had to pay more than the building was actually worth, but I figured a wash on one deal might be overcome by profits on others, and we went ahead.

The next place in the mosaic was 40 Wall Street, the tallest building in the financial area, a typical product of the crazy, hectic financing of the 1920's. It was built with speculative bond issues, the common stock thrown in for free, and very ingeniously dovetailed out of three properties. There were actually three fees. One fee, or piece of the land, was owned by the Chase, because it had originally been the site of the old Manhattan bank, which the Chase absorbed. Another fee was owned by the Iselin estate. The third fee belonged to the building corporation that put up 40 Wall Street. The ground rent payable to the Chase for its ownership of one of the fees was $500,000 per year. The Chase had a bank and offices in the building, for which they paid one million dollars a year in rent. The Chase wanted to be relieved of paying that rent and also wanted to get back the cash value of $500,000 land income. I promised the Chase that at current rates of five-percent interest I would get them ten million dollars for their fee. (Actually, by the time of the sale, interest rates had climbed to six percent.) That $500,000 income was worth only 8.35 million dollars, but I had said ten million, and I kept my word. The next job was to get our money out by selling that fee to someone else. Now, selling only part of the fee of a great building would be very difficult to do. There was only one way to turn the trick: we would have to pour in more money in order to buy the other two fees from the Iselin estate and from the publicly held company that owned and leased the building.

The first move was to buy from the Iselin estate. My contact here was Graham Mattison of Dominick & Dominick. He had once been a member of the firm of White & Case. The trustee of the Iselin estate was Robert Youngs, chairman of the Louisiana Land & Exploration Company, who was also a one-time White & Case man. Mattison brought us together. I met Youngs in Paris for dinner. We supped at the Au Caneton, a fine restaurant near the French stock exchange, and there we sealed an agreement. Next came the job of buying up the shares of the third company. Most of the two classes of bonds and bonus stock of this company was in the hands of Wall Street secondary-money types, scavengers who had picked up the property during the Depression. We gradually bought up close to half of the shares from the larger holders, then opened market purchases for the balance. We knew that we could not get more than two-thirds of the stock, but under New York State law, if two-thirds of the stockholders of a company vote to sell the assets and liquidate, they can do so. When we had two-thirds, I moved for liquidation that would put the property up at auction, with the highest bidder taking it. I knew we could outbid anyone, because two-thirds of almost anything we bid was our own. We had a lawyers' holiday, however, getting this thing through. Every strike lawyer in town, and some lawyers that were not supposed to be strike lawyers, hurried to get his oar in, in hopes of getting a little extra money through an out-of-court settlement designed to buy his cooperation. Finally, however, the court gave us the right to auction, and the affair was held in the main hall of the Wall Street Club, which was a tenant in the building. We won our auction, against competition, at a price where the old bonds were paid off one hundred cents on the dollar and the stockholders got twenty-two dollars per share for bonus stock it had cost them nothing to acquire. Our total cost of this acquisition was ten million dollars to the Chase, 4.25 million to the Iselin estate, and some 17.75 million for the remainder of the property, for a total of thirty-two million.

The Chase was now free to move out. Meanwhile, there was an excellent building at 15 Broad Street which the Chase would also be emptying, and I had to find a buyer. I called on Henry Alexander, president of Morgan Guaranty Trust, explained what we were trying to do with this total Wall Street maneuver, and how the ideal part for Morgan would be to take over 15 Broad.

Henry wasn't buying. He said, "We're not real-estate people. We already have this beautiful little corner here. We play a special role in finance; we are not big, but we are powerful and influential, we have relationships. Furthermore, we don't want to be big and don't need the space."

I said, "Henry, you are going to get married."

"What?"

"Someday you are going to merge with another bank, a big one. When you do, this property will be in the nature of a dowry coming with a bride; you will be able to make a better deal with your new partner."

"Morgan will never merge."

"Well, that's just my prediction," I said, but I kept pointing out to Alexander the advantages to Morgan of the new property, and eventually they decided to buy it for 21.25 million dollars.

Five years later I called Alexander and congratulated him on Morgan's coming merger with Guarantee Trust Company. He said, "You know, I've often thought of that conversation we had and how right you were."

"I wasn't right Henry, I was wrong."

"How so?"

"You're not the bride."

Having moved the Morgan and having moved the Chemical, I was beginning to run a little low on possible tenants for the vacant slot we would have for a bank at 40 Wall Street. In fact, this situation was becoming crucial.

Metropolitan Life was interested in 40 Wall. Fred Ecker said they'd buy it for twenty million dollars.

I said, "Fine, we'll lease it back at six percent, and that means we now have only twelve million in the building in the form of a leasehold."

"But," Ecker said, "you'll have to find a tenant to replace the Chase Bank. That million-dollar-a-year rent is too important for us to take it on speculation."

I went down to see my friend Jeff McNeill at the Hanover Bank and said, "Jeff, how about moving over to 40 Wall?"

"What about my buildings here at 60 and 70 Broadway?"

"Jeff, you know we are the biggest dealers in slightly used bank quarters in America; we take them in like secondhand cars."

"My book value is six and a half million dollars."

"What are you telling me?"

"That's what I've got to get."

"Oh, Lord, that's a terrible rabbit warren. God only knows what we will do with it when you get out."

"Bill, I can't give you anything better than that. If we take the lease over at 40 Wall for one million a year in rent, that's the deal."

We argued a little and bargained a lot, but on basic price McNeill was unshakable; he had to get book value for his buildings, so finally I said, "You've made a deal," and we shook hands.

McNeill made a memo of the meeting. I never make memoranda

—I try to use my own memory and rely on people's word. Sometime later the bank drew up preliminary papers; I looked them over, and the price read 6.8 million dollars.

I told Jeff he'd made a mistake in the papers.

He said he was sure they were right.

There had been a lot of conversation that day, and it was entirely possible he was right. I told him if that was how he remembered it, it was O.K. with me. The business of drawing up the papers then went on, but after a few days I got a call. It was Jeff McNeill: "Bill, I got that memorandum out. You were right. It is six-million-five, and I'm changing it. And I'm telling you right now, you are a wonderful sport."

The Hanover then passed title of the building to us, took back a mortgage and a lease of convenience. That gave us three years to move the property, but there were problems. The buildings were old, there were three different floor levels in what were actually three buildings. In fairness to the Hanover, they were beautifully maintained, but the interiors were a Minotaur's maze of offices and hallways that only the Hanover or somebody like them could use. What's more, they were down at the end of things, near the tip of Broadway. The Wall Street area was still shaky. Number 2 Broadway had not yet been built, and few companies would want to move in down there at the perimeter. The only logical and possible buyer was the Irving Trust Company, whose offices at 1 Wall abutted the Hanover properties.

The Irving Trust already had a beautiful building, a well-designed, soaring tower. This great tower was not efficient; because of its great height and small ground area, it was really a test tube; you were running up and down all the time. So I tried to sell Irving Trust on the idea of buying the Hanover buildings, using them, or putting up a new structure on the site. They showed interest from time to time as I talked with them, but I was asking something over nine million dollars for the properties. There are no secrets on Wall Street, so they knew we had paid over 6 million for the Hanover properties and balked at my figure. I took the position that our cost had nothing to do with what we would sell for. After all, I still had the problem of selling off our lease at 40 Wall. I still didn't know how

I'd get out of 40 Wall. If we sold the Hanover properties at cost and had to take a loss on selling 40 Wall, we would be in trouble. Nobody cares too much whether it is profitable or not for the other fellow, but I had to look out for our interests. We were not a non-profit foundation dedicated to putting out our capital for the benefit of the banking industry. Finally Irving Trust offered us seven million, then seven and a half million, and I was advised to take it, but I said no, I was asking nine and I was going to get nine.

"How are you so sure you will?" I was asked.

If the Irving Trust had already crossed a certain bridge in their own minds and were planning to go uptown, I could offer them the properties at a fire-sale price and not get a nibble. But when they began bidding 7.5 million dollars, I knew they had crossed a different type of bridge; they were not going uptown. I knew then they would have to pay the nine million or change their policy, and 1.5 million dollars was not enough to force a change in that kind of policy; 1.5 million in the total land cost might have constituted five percent of the total cost of a new building and I felt this was pretty good ground on which to stand pat. I stood my ground, and we got nine million.

The negotiators for the Irving Trust handled themselves beautifully. In that sense it was a classic series of negotiations, but after a certain point they knew and I knew what the land was worth to them, and we settled at a worthwhile figure; land values are only a relatively small portion of the total cost of a new structure. For instance, take the new Chase building: it ended up costing 120 million dollars. The original land cost $4,670,000 (more land was added later). But, if the original land had cost eight million, this would not in the long run have mattered. Once a course of action is set, a wise negotiator knows what its parts and pieces are worth to him. If he can get it for less, fine; but he will not scuttle his plans on a matter of minor increments. You can lose that much money in the door knobs for a new building.

The Irving Trust deal was concluded in June, 1961, but I still had to find a buyer for the twelve million dollars we had tied up in the lease we held on 40 Wall Street. We got a ten-million-dollar mortgage on this lease from the Chase. This left us with two million in equity on a profitable property, but I needed a buyer to get out our sorely needed cash, and in time one came to me. A London-based real-estate financier named Charles Clore was merging with another Englishman, Jack Cotton. They were starting an American real-estate company. I had previously talked with Clore about 40 Wall Street, with no success, but now the phone rang; it was Clore in London.

"Do you still have 40 Wall?"

"We do."

"Do you want to sell it?"

"Yes."

"What will you take for it?"

"The same price."

"What's that?"

"Fifteen million for the leasehold."

There were more talks and conferences, but eventually he bought it. The 40 Wall Street chapter was closed, and our game of musical banks was ended with a grace note. Seven years had gone by. We had moved the Chase. We had moved the Chemical and Morgan banks. We had moved the Hanover Bank. We had persuaded the Irving Trust to take over the Hanover properties and sold off a half-dozen ancillary properties on the side. Webb & Knapp's profit of perhaps ten million dollars from these combined deals amounted to little more than music teacher's pay for our efforts. The Chase Bank financed many of our moves, but we put up Webb & Knapp assets over and beyond those of the subject properties as collateral; we were the prime risk-takers. The total volume of business involved directly and indirectly amounted to some 250 million dollars. Considering five percent is the average broker's commission, with no risk involved, our take at four percent was indeed modest. We were in business for profit, so why did we do this? We did it because it had to be done, and nobody else could do it. There is a tremendous satisfaction to individuals and corporations alike in leaving an important constructive mark in their trail. There was excitement and fun in putting the puzzle together, but, second only to our United Nations deal, the Wall Street Maneuver was the most important thing we ever did in the New York community, and we were happy to do it. Expanding the effects of these maneuvers, David Rockefeller and his associates have sparked an imaginative renaissance and reformation of downtown Manhattan which Webb & Knapp tried to further make use of and accelerate.

Throughout our Wall Street maneuver the very first building we had purchased, the Chemical Bank headquarters at 165 Broadway, had been burdening our books. We had had to pay Norman Winston such a surcharge for his stock in this fifty-story structure that the return on investment was negative. Over the years, however, land values in the area promised to rise, thanks to our maneuvers, and, thinking in terms of land values instead of building costs, I began to sense a possibility. If I could buy everything south of 165 Broadway for two blocks, including 111 and 115 Broadway, we would have a tremendously valuable plottage. Other buyers and sellers were thinking in terms of return on investment on existing buildings. But if we could buy the whole sweep of land, we would have enough underlying value to make it worthwhile to tear down the existing buildings, seal off or overpass the existing streets, and create a new superbuilding. West of this site, near the Hudson River, the Port of New York Authority, guided by Rockefeller, was planning an enormous World Trade Center. Our plottage, lying directly between the Trade Center and the new Chase Plaza, would become a people-magnet between these two areas. The more I thought about it, the better it looked. The New York Stock Exchange needed new quarters and would sooner or later have to move. The slot between the Chase Plaza and World Trade Center would be wonderful for them.

Actually, we had not bought full ownership of 165 Broadway from Winston, only a controlling interest. As in the case of 40 Wall Street, we then had to buy up two-thirds of the rest of the stock and bonds, go to the court requesting a reorganization, and in that way take over the whole property. This took about three years. This done, I set about buying adjacent properties. The biggest was the Singer Building, into which the company had just put 1.5 million dollars in automatic elevators and a general modernization. For reasons of his own, Donald Kircher, the chief at Singer, liked the idea of moving. He was in the process of trying to spark up and revive this old dinosaur of a company, and a move to new quarters might loosen some of the encrusted tradition that still befuddled the company. However, he wanted eight million dollars for his building; after all, there was all the money he had spent on elevators. Since we wanted to tear the structure down, the elevators, to us, represented a waste of money, but Kircher had his books to think about and was adamant. I argued and bargained again and again, getting nowhere, and we finally agreed to pay his price. Now we had two big buildings and respectable plottage, but because of the high cost of both structures, our average costs per square foot of land were still prohibitive; we had to buy more. I began buying in the next block south of the Singer Building and west to Church Street.

Though I negotiated earnestly and long, we never did get to purchase 111 and 115 Broadway. These buildings were owned by a man named Benjamin Miller, one of the most unreliable and difficult people in New York to deal with. He was an incorrigible delayer. He was trying to hold us up, and succeeded. I finally decided to go ahead without him. We had enough property, what with street closing and overpassing, to give us plenty of land at two hundred dollars per square foot of cost. We could put up our building and let him go his own way. In all, we spent twenty-eight million dollars acquiring 165 Broadway, the Singer Building, and other properties, but while all this was going on, of course, I had been working on the New York Stock Exchange as future tenant.

The man I went to see was John Coleman, who, though little known outside the Street, is one of its most influential members. He is head of the firm of Adler Coleman, who are specialists and probably have more seats on the Exchange than any other firm, except Merrill Lynch. Coleman's father was a policeman, and John Coleman had started as an office boy working for a man named Adler. He finally became a partner, and the firm became Adler Coleman. When Adler got in trouble, Coleman, who had an excellent reputation, carried on. He was a central figure in the Exchange, which is generally run by and for the specialists, and as we drove downtown in a cab one morning, I said, "John, here is a sketch of where I think the Stock Exchange should be."

"You mean we can buy all that property?" he asked.

"You can buy it or lease it, I don't care which. I'll give you everything from 165 Broadway down to 115 Broadway, and I can even buy 111 and 115 Broadway and bring you all the way down to Trinity Place.

"There will be the new Trade Center to the west. You have Chase Plaza to the east. One-forty Broadway will replaced by a new building. The axis between the Trade Center and Chase Plaza, with its access to parking and subways, will make for a year-round people-passage. We will have covered walks, malls, shops, and restaurants. Set the Stock Exchange on our site, and it will be the very heart and core of the entire financial district."

We talked further in his office, and Coleman finally said, "O.K., Bill, you deliver those buns, and we'll buy them."

I figured that conversation was enough to move the Stock Exchange. I thought Coleman did business that way; it is the way I did business. I walked away from his office and soon after agreed to pay Kircher his eight million for the Singer Building. Webb & Knapp then began buying south of the Singer Building. We formed a new corporation called Finance Place and set our architects to designing the greatest possible column-free area for a new Stock Exchange trading floor.

It is simple enough to build a giant auditorium or theater, which is what the Stock Exchange floor is, but it is something else to put an office building three-fourths the size of the Empire State over such a manmade cavern. I turned the task over to Pei and his partners, and Henry Cobb came up with one of the most ingenious building designs I have ever seen. One solution to the problem would be to create our "auditorium," then put a giant 25,000-ton, 270-foot-long truss or bridge of steel over the open space to support the skyscraper. This would be a brute-force and very expensive solution. What Cobb did, instead, was design a building that was seemingly conventional in all but two respects. First, the building would be sloped inward from a 270-foot width at the base to a 90-foot width above its forty-fifth office floor. In a sense, it would be something like a beautifully tapered Mayan temple. Across the 90-foot-wide top of the building, however, we would have a series of 28-foot-deep steel trusses. During the construction phase, the building would be put up with conventional steel girders rising through the center section to support the framework above. However, when the 28-foot-deep trusses were finally placed across the roof, all the great girders cluttering up the bottom-floor space where the Stock Exchange would go would be cut out with acetylene torches and carted away. Instead of being held up by center-floor girders, the office floors above this "auditorium" would hang down from the roof trusses, much as a nonmoving elevator hangs by its cables from a building's roof. The Stock Exchange area would therefore be entirely column-free.

It is dangerous to design a speculative building with only one prime tenant in mind, but I had decided to do so. We had a fabulous and distinctive design, and an ideal location. We also had, or thought we had, unofficial but powerful backing within the Exchange, so we went ahead. More accurately, we tried to go ahead—but didn't get very far. In fact, we lost out. As to the details of this story, I must be vague. I was, unfortunately, never entirely privy to what was actually going on. What I do know is that during the time of our planning of and assemblage for Finance Place, Keith Funston, president of the Stock Exchange, had been negotiating for a new site with another real-estate group headed by Sol Atlas and my friend John McGrath, a fellow trustee of Long Island University. Down close to the tip of Manhattan, near the Battery, Atlas and McGrath had a five-acre site, part of which they had offered to the Stock Exchange. The site had started out as an urban-renewal project, and the original assemblage was very cleverly done and neatly dovetailed. There had been some quite adroit use of city planning and street widening, so that by street-widening condemnation, original owners who might have held out against the assemblers were easily swept up and away at a relatively modest cost. Then, at the proper time, there had been a rezoning of the area, so the assemblers could charge top rates for later sale to the city. The area had originally been intended for some kind of housing project which the Wagner administration was increasingly attacked about. Therefore, the plot was turned into an office development. Moving the Stock Exchange to the Battery site would very neatly get the Wagner administration off an uncomfortable hook, so the whole thing was deep in local politics. Coleman was very close to the Wagner administration. Perhaps he was, or thought he was, tied into something he could not get out of. As I say, I still don't know the full story. I thought I had backing, but at the crucial moment it turned out not to be there. By this time, the infield who were running the Exchange had their own deal lined up and wanted no inside comment, and certainly no outside suggestion whatsoever. However, the logic of the situation spoke so strongly for Finance Place that I kept trying. I made calls, made presentations, argued and pleaded my cause. In time, individual Stock Exchange members also began to argue against the foolishness of moving the Exchange so far south. Even *The New York Times* wrote a strongly worded editorial to the same effect. Over many months the ensuing dialogue generated a great deal of heat. It also brought a certain amount of light on a matter that the Exchange managers would have preferred not to debate, and for which they gave me no thanks.

One immediate result of all this was that Webb & Knapp and Finance Place lost out: the Exchange managers flatly refused to consider our site.

Part of what happened was that the Stock Exchange, a free-ride monopoly controlled by a small group of insiders, is a very sensitive and defensive institution. Like the old-time barons in Europe who charged a handsome toll for all boats using the stream by their castles, the Stock Exchange membership charge fees out of all proportion to the services they actually perform. Aware of and nervous about this, they habitually overreact to any outside interest or criticism of their situation. As a case in point, when Mayor Lindsay suggested a transfer tax on Stock Exchange transactions. The reaction was an immediate threat by Funston to move the Exchange out of town. The truth of the matter is that in spite of Funston's thundering, no Exchange members ever thought seriously for more than half a minute about moving the true heart of their operation out of New York. However, as happens at a time of pressure, politics, and propaganda, the Exchange, which officially was still committed to move to the Battery site, used this situation to extricate itself from the Battery move which so many of its members were now opposed to. Claiming the need for flexibility of action in their contest with Mayor Lindsay, they publicly rescinded the planned move to the Battery.

Shortly after the above incident, Funston left the scene. That the Stock Exchange might yet decide to move to the site we suggested to them was a very faint possibility, but the loss here was to the Exchange and not to Webb & Knapp. By then we had sold off that property, at a modest profit, to the U.S. Steel Corp.

During our assembly of the Finance Place properties and earliest wooing of the Exchange, the cash demands of the assemblage were relatively low. But, come law day, when we would pick up the various deeds and pay out over twenty-four million dollars for our purchases, we would need cash. The assemblage was good enough so I could borrow eighteen million dollars on the properties. If I could sell, lease, or borrow another ten million, we could get all our cost out, and some profit; if not, we would have one more potential disaster nipping at our heels. The difficulty was in finding a big enough and strong enough buyer or combination of backers to come into the thing with us. For months I had been casting about in my mind, and finally came up with the name of the single, most logical one of all possible entrants: the U.S. Steel Corp.

U.S. Steel, in spite of its size and ramifications, is an introspective company with very few outside interests. They might not immediately recognize that they were the logical buyers of Finance Place, but I planned to remedy that. By now we were working very closely with Alcoa on a great many fine projects. I called Leon Hickman, Alcoa's executive vice-president and chairman of the finance committee, and asked him if he knew Roger Blough, head of U.S. Steel.

It turned out that Hickman and Blough were great friends. As a matter of fact, it was Hickman who proposed Blough to the United States bar.

That phase of the bar is much like proposing a man's name to an exclusive club, and when Hickman said, "Would you like to meet him?" I replied, "I would, very much."

A few days later I got a call, and a voice announced, "This is Roger Blough. I understand you want to meet me."

"I do, Mr. Blough."

"Well, I'll be in town Saturday. I'm officiating at a Pennsylvania

Society meeting; we are going to give Jim Simms of the Penn Railroad a medal as 'Man of the Year in Pennsylvania.' "

Blough then said, "I could be in your office at twelve o'clock."

"Would you like me to call on you, Mr. Blough?"

"No, I'll be there."

I had our architects and staff alerted. We had a beautiful model of Finance Place set up in our upstairs conference room, and at twelve o'clock the next Saturday, in walked Mr. Blough, accompanied by one other gentleman. Blough introduced the second man, Tyson, as chairman of Steel's finance committee. I thought to myself, "That's the guy I really want to see." We shook hands all around, and we took them upstairs to see the model. Though other metals had lately been entering the picture, steel's great competitor in construction was concrete. Steel, however, had great advantages over all its competition, and one advantage I wanted to point out right then was its use in the truss. Only the truss, by overpassing the streets, could free architects from the design limitations imposed by city street patterns. Most architects, I remarked, are little more than zoning lawyers. The truss, however, could help architects break into new areas, I said, and pointed to the intriguing detail of our model as a lively example of what I meant.

Blough and Tyson were quite interested and pleased by the idea (we all like to see our product well used), and as this little exposition came to a close Blough said, "I want to thank you very much, for showing us all this."

They both got ready to leave, and I said, "Gentlemen, I didn't exactly go through this for my health or because we are running a school; I had a purpose in telling you what I did.

"The purpose of this discussion was to point out that the concrete industry is taking the cream of the building business right away from you.

"When I was a boy, all these buildings around here were going up with nothing but steel. Concrete was for one- and two-story structures only. Today, structural concrete is doing the job in sixty- and seventy-story structures. In fact, it is becoming the rule to use concrete and the exception to use steel. You people are dying in the high-rise market. You are losing ground every day to concrete.

"I'll tell you what your real difficulty is: you've got mastoid trouble."

They were turned back and listening now, and Blough said, "What do you mean by that?"

I said, "Think of this: when you were a boy, mastoid disease of the inner ear was very common—it was a threat to every child, and a most important specialty in the surgical profession. As a matter of fact, a hospital known as the Manhattan Eye, Ear, Nose, and Throat Hospital, of which I am a trustee, was built around the mastoid operation. It was the hospital to go to for mastoid, just as some other hospitals are the place to go for cancer, open heart surgery, or some other specialty.

"But the mastoid operation has gone out of style; penicillin has put it out of business. The number of surgeons familiar with this operation has been cut by at least ninety-five percent. The mastoid specialist has retired somewhere along with the horse and buggy. ... God forbid there should be a sudden new kind of mastoid epidemic; you would have no people around to handle it. Nobody studies it anymore.

"In building, it's the engineers and architects who determine what materials and techniques will be employed on a job. In years gone by, all structural engineers studied structural-steel design—in great depth; it was a primary course. Today, the only fellows who do that are the bridge builders. Young doctors don't bother studying the mastoid operation; they have penicillin. In your case, the engineers have concrete. The schools are turning out more and more brilliant young designers in concrete, and this is a self-feeding thing. I'll grant you, steel can't go all the way out of business like the mastoid operation has. And your industry is so big and such an important buyer that you can persuade a lot of companies always to choose steel over concrete—but you can't persuade enough of them. You are losing the market!"

Up to this point I had encountered nothing but stunned silence, and I kept right on talking.

"What you've got to do is go out in the field and develop some imaginative uses that show how steel does jobs concrete can't even begin to match. I will name some for you right now. Steel is unexcelled for overpassing. It can be used in treacherous subsoil conditions. Steel is quicker to erect. Steel lends itself to a design change of pace, where, for a change of horizons, you may want an open auditorium at one point, a closed theater in another, or apartments or offices in juxtaposition. With steel you can create flying bridges at the upper levels of high-rise buildings. Steel has so very many advantages, that I don't believe you really need to lose relative position to concrete. But nobody is going to pull your chestnuts out of the fire; you've got to do it for yourself.

"And it will take ten million dollars," I said.

"Ten million for what?"

Pointing to the model, "That's how much we need to take title to this property."

Tyson said, "We're not in the banking business, we're in the steel business."

"You are in the steel business, all right, but you are archaic and reactionary, and it's time you fellows woke up. All you have to do is look over beside you and see the trail that's being blazed by the aluminum companies. The whole aluminum industry have gone out into open-field demonstrations of their product by going into real estate. Other industries are doing the same thing. But I didn't see the steel industry doing anything that counts. The cement industry is far more progressive. Gentlemen, you've got to take some steps to get in line and get up there with the best."

This frank discussion of what their best friends wouldn't tell them was new to my visitors, but if I was being harsh, I was also being sincere, and they knew this. They also knew I was the man who had put Reynolds and Alcoa into real estate and construction, so I spoke as far more than a visionary. We talked a bit more, and then they left. They left making no promises, but about ten days or so later they agreed to put up the ten million dollars we wanted to buy our land, and that got us out of our problems at 165 Broadway and points south. Finance Place was not built as we first visualized it. U.S. Steel designed a most conventional structure. The First National Bank of Chicago did later put up a building very much like our Finance Place conception. They wrote us a letter of apology, saying that this was purely coincidental, they had arrived at the idea on their own, but since our conception was written up in every technical journal in the country years before their project started, none of us took this protestation very seriously.

By now we were through with the Wall Street Maneuver. We were out of the woods with 165 Broadway, but the tie-in of one deal to another in a city like New York can, in time, spread out like a network of roots in a rose garden. From Broadway and Wall Street, we soon enough found ourselves adventuring at Sixth Avenue near Rockefeller Plaza, where we planned a giant new Zeckendorf Hotel.

· 20 · The Webb Begins to Tangle

THROUGH THE 1950's, midtown New York was going through an enormous office-building boom. And yet, in spite of this redevelopment between Forty-second and Fifty-seventh Streets, one key section remained untouched. Sixth Avenue, unaffected by its fancy new name, "Avenue of the Americas," remained a seedy fortress of nineteenth-century brick and brownstone buildings with busy bars, small shops, and restaurants on the ground floor and old apartments above. The side streets to east and west of the avenue on Fifty-first, Fifty-second, and Fifty-third streets contained a variety of nightclubs and restaurants, many once speakeasies during prohibition. These nightspots and tourist traps, like those in the Forties between Sixth Avenue and Times Square, were an established part of New York's night life. The only structures of any note on the avenue were parts of Rockefeller Center, whose buildings rose above their surroundings like well-trimmed hedges above the crabgrass.

All this has since changed. Sixth Avenue now boasts a collection of corporate crystal palaces rivaling anything on Park Avenue. It was Webb & Knapp that started the trend to corporate offices on Park Avenue. It was also Webb & Knapp that cleared the way for the first corporate beachhead on the west side of Sixth Avenue. We did so by assembling the land where the Time-Life Building now stands. I acquired this frontage from Eva Fox, widow of the ruined financier William Fox. Mrs. Fox and her two daughters occupied a cavernous old apartment on the Marguery block which we owned on Park Avenue. It was a dark, rambling place filled with oddments, side tables, antimacassared chairs, and religious paintings featuring angels, devils, and endangered souls. One saw all this in dim light that was absorbed by heavy, red damask curtains. To step into the place was to step back seventy-five years in time and attitude. I stepped in as an agent for the future. I wanted to persuade Mrs. Fox to move so we could tear down the building for a Park Avenue office tower. Mrs. Fox's two daughters were studiously eccentric. Except when they went to the opera, I never saw either of them wearing anything except trousers and white shirtwaists. One daughter, Mona, dabbled in the occult and the other, Belle, was handsome and brilliant, but a very sharp and suspicious woman.

Eventually I became a friend and a help to the family. Their affairs were in great disarray, and their holdings, since their father's bankruptcy and death, had been under a cloud. I persuaded William Warren, dean of the Columbia Law School, and one of my directors, to advise them. Through brilliant work he was able to restore and improve their holdings. As an agent, I was able to buy some property for them. This also strengthened our relationship. By now, they had long since agreed to move from their apartment. But, even so, when I approached Mrs. Fox about selling her Sixth Avenue properties, she was most reluctant. It took great persuasion finally to get her to agree to sell some thirty thousand square feet for the record price of five million dollars.

Our arrangements agreed to, I brought Mrs. Fox a $500,000 check from the Chase Bank as a down payment. She took my check. She read it. Staring me in the eye, she then tore it into little pieces.

"Eva, what in the world is the matter?"

"The Chase Bank sent my husband to jail. This is another trick of theirs. You're just a collusive agent of theirs! I'm through with you, and them, and everyone else!" With this, she disappeared into the depths of her apartment.

It took me three days to get her to see me again. This time I brought a check from Bankers Trust. She took it. Sixth Avenue's west bank was now breached, Rockefeller Center would expand westward. Sixth Avenue was now certified boom country.

My next move on midtown Sixth Avenue, however, came courtesy of 120 Broadway, near the tip of Manhattan. One-twenty was the biggest building in the downtown area. Completed around 1940, before new zoning came into effect, it packed more square feet of office space over its landmass than any New York building put up before or since. This meant that when full it could realize great amounts of cash. The building was publicly held, with Wertheim & Co. as principal owners. We bought it for ten million dollars in cash, the market price of the stock, plus a bonus of 8.5 million dollars in Webb & Knapp debentures. These, the only unsecured debentures Webb & Knapp ever issued, were what would trigger our bankruptcy in 1965, but then the deal was all to the good.

Using the Hawaiian Technique, we were able, very profitably, to fraction off various parts of the property. Eventually, we wound up holding only the fee. This fee brought in $875,000 per year, with about $525,000 going to pay off a very low-interest mortgage, originally of fourteen million dollars, held by the John Hancock Life Insurance Co.

Meanwhile, back on Sixth Avenue, just to the north of my Time-Life assemblage, the Equitable Life Insurance Co. had acquired the west block of Sixth Avenue between Fifty-first and Fifty-second streets for a new headquarters building. Through agents they had also acquired and torn down all but one building on the block across the avenue. The plan was to put up a speculative office building on this land, but in 1958 things were being delayed by a holdout, Toots Shor's restaurant, which had a lease with seven years to run. Toots had scorned selling out for $750,000, spurned one million, and sniffed disdainfully at suggestions of 1.2 million. The Equitable's agents were preparing to build around Toots, wait until his lease was up, and then boot him out. But a new development took place: the New York State Insurance Department decided the Equitable was concentrating too much capital on one section of Sixth Avenue and was verging on speculation. It was one thing to build a headquarters building on one side of the avenue, but to put up a speculative building across the street did not look good to Albany. Insurance companies are not supposed to speculate. These quiet little talks with Albany meant Equitable would have to sell its fee or, at least, sell off a ground lease on its Sixth Avenue investment. If it sold its ground lease, somebody else would then assume the building risk, and Equitable would get an O.K. from its official consciences in Albany.

Meanwhile, I had come to the conclusion that New York very much needed a new hotel, no hotel having been built since the Waldorf went up. The Equitable's Sixth Avenue site, right next to Rockefeller

Center, was a perfect location, good for business travelers and tourists alike. What is more, a hotel here would help maintain a touch of night life in the area. I called up the management at Equitable and asked what they might want for their assemblage. They replied it had cost them sixteen million dollars. They wanted a 5½-percent return on this investment, which comes out to $880,000. This was as expected, and I next asked whether it mattered to them if their income came directly from the Sixth Avenue property or some other safe property. They replied that where the money came from did not matter as long as it was safe income.

I then suggested a swap. We would give them the fee to 120 Broadway, it earned $875,000, and they in turn would give us the fee to the block of Sixth Avenue; 120 Broadway was a going business and very safe; they agreed to swap.

By this time, the John Hancock mortgage on 120 Broadway's fee was down to twelve million dollars. So that the Equitable could get an unhindered $875,000 from the fee, I would have to give them twelve million dollars to clear the mortgage. We raised this money, and more, through a visit with the Prudential Insurance Company.

When I explained to Prudential what we planned to do with the Sixth Avenue site, they agreed to give us a purchase and construction loan. All I had to do was buy out Toots Shor, and we were in business. Toots dealt with us through a very able lawyer named Arnold Brant. We bargained and argued until, on September 8, 1959, we all met at the Chase at nine P.M. for a closing, but the bargaining started up again. Finally, at three the next morning, we gave Toots a check for 1.5 million dollars, and he gave us his lease. Shor had never seen that much money in his life. That night we went over to "21." Toots laid down the check and said, "Please cash this. I need a drink."

Within a year, what with one thing and another, Toots was, as he put it, "Strictly c.o.d. again," but that is his style. By then, we had torn down his building and begun excavation for a great forty-eight-story, sixty-six-million-dollar Zeckendorf Hotel. In due time we had a 50-foot-deep, 200-by-450-foot hole in the ground reminiscent of our Court House Square excavation in Denver. We had also spent two million dollars in making this hole and were discovering that building-construction costs had taken off for Mars.

Our hotel's estimated costs, once figured at a maximum of thirty thousand dollars per room, had zoomed up to forty thousand. By now it was 1960. Webb & Knapp was spread thin over a variety of projects, all of which cried for cash. We just could not pull together the forty million dollars of equity money needed to flesh out our basic Prudential loan. I had to give up my hotel.

We went to Prudential, explained the situation, and suggested they confine themselves to a land loan. They were agreeable, but gave us our head to move either way. I knew the block could be used for an office building. Nevertheless, before abandoning the hotel idea, I decided to offer it to Conrad Hilton.

A meeting was arranged in the New York apartment of financier Colonel Henry Crown, Hilton's second-largest stockholder. Hilton, Crown, and some of their other people were present. Hilton, who had come up from Mexico for the meeting, was not well; he had a touch of grippe. I offered to turn the deal over to them for three million dollars, saying, "Gentlemen, I urge you to take over this hotel and build it. If you don't, you will lose New York and your preeminence in New York.

"As long as we keep working on this hotel, no other hotel will be built in New York. Having our hotel in the works is like having sixteen-inch naval guns trained on your enemies, because no insurance company will put a penny into a new hotel until they see whether this one really goes up. If our hotel is built, it will hold other hotels off for a time, because we will be launching two thousand new rooms. But if we ever drop our guns or unload them, you'll see a rash of hotels go up in this town. When that happens, Hilton, willy-nilly, is going to have to build here just to keep up with the parade. But you'll be late arrivals then, faced with newly entrenched competition."

Colonel Crown agreed with my analysis. He urged Hilton to step in. For the first time, according to those who know him, Hilton went against Crown's advice. He turned the deal down.

With the Hilton alternative closed, I had to try elsewhere. I knew I could sell to the Uris brothers for an office building, but they are not exactly internationally famous for fine office buildings. This site was right next to Rockefeller Center. It should have a fine building, and I turned to the Rockefellers. At that time Richardson Dillworth was handling such affairs for Laurance Rockefeller. It may be that the personal chemistry between us didn't work. Perhaps there were other reasons. In any event, even after I pointed out that Uris was a willing buyer and would be putting up a typical Uris office building, I could make no sale. I then sold out to Uris, not for three million dollars but for five million.

After this, the Rockefellers, *now* worried about the kind of building Uris might put up, bought a half-interest in the deal in order to have some control of the architecture. What resulted is the Sperry Rand Building.

As soon as our hotel project died, the Loew's Theatre people, who were diversifying into hotels, built the Americana Hotel on land we sold them, plus a rash of motels elsewhere on the West Side. As I had warned, Hilton a few years later had to come up with a new hotel in New York. He finally built one, in partnership with Uris and the Rockefellers, on Sixth Avenue between Fifty-third and Fifty-fourth streets. His construction costs, it developed, were some thirty million dollars above estimates, but this hotel helped make Sixth Avenue just that much more valuable as real estate.

Early in the game, we were aware of what was happening and going to happen on Sixth Avenue, and we tried to acquire as much frontage there as possible. Every morning I used to ask one financier or another to hike up and down Sixth Avenue with me. I would say, "This will be the greatest boom town in the world, right here! You must help me finance it." But I could not get anybody to move with real strength at that time. We did buy on the east side of the avenue from Fifty-second to Fifty-third Street, where CBS now had its headquarters, and we acquired land between Fifty-third and Fifty-fourth, where the headquarters for Central Savings Bank are now located, but it was uphill work and only a portion of what we would like to have done.

Part of the problem may have been that we were already doing so much in so many other places.

By 1960, Webb & Knapp, with five hundred million dollars in construction under way in the United States and Canada, was beginning to feel the pull and tension on the finances of its multiple operations. Most of the projects mentioned in previous chapters, each with its particular moments of risk, crisis, and overhead costs, had either peaked or were obviously on their way to fruition. Denver's Court House Square, thanks in part to backing from Robert Young's Alleghanys' Corporation, was finally completed. We held the flag raising for the hotel opening in April. In Canada we had shopping centers under construction, as well as a housing project in Flemington, near Toronto, plus several industrial parks. At Place Ville-Marie, our nasty, five-million-dollar steel crisis had finally passed. With our new British partners, and their twenty-two million dollars aboard, we would top out the steel work in 1961 and open our doors in 1962. Century City and the two million we had put at risk there had been pulled home by our timely partnership with Alcoa. At Roosevelt Field we were putting up a new store for Gimbels.

The list goes on and on. In Washington, D.C., we were finally building the first of our Town Center apartments. In Chicago we were putting up the two ten-story apartment towers of our townhouse-apartment project at Hyde Park. Park West Village, a seven-tower complex, was under way in New York; so was Kips Bay, and Lincoln Towers was in the planning phase. We were meanwhile getting ready to tackle our Lower Hill project in Pittsburgh and our Society Hill towers and townhouses in Philadelphia.

Our Gulf States Land company was developing a mixture of properties and projects, including our slag-recovery program and oil properties.

Like buds on a prize rosebush, all these and dozens of other projects had not fully, profitably blossomed as yet. It would take generous watering, careful pruning, and delicate spraying to bring them forth, but it was obvious that when they did blossom it would be a glorious show.

To keep our prime projects going, we sold off other properties, brought in new partners, and borrowed millions. The sell-off of properties in order to raise cash accounted for our premature sale of the Chrysler Building and 112 West Thirty-fourth Street, as well as our Mountain Park acreage in Los Angeles, Mile High Center in Denver, and many more of our finest income properties. In this way we gained capital for new investments. Our expectation was to more than make up this temporary loss of present income through great future income.

Besides, I had a record of generating impressive amounts of income from deal to deal.

It was our new partners, the British and Alcoa, who brought in the most important money to specific projects, but as urban development ate up more and more of our cash, we borrowed more and more on our properties and prospects. We took first, second, and third mortgages and any other kind of indebtedness possible. It was about this period that the press picked up a quote of mine they used again and again: "I'd rather be alive at eighteen percent than dead at six percent." It was perfectly true. Nonetheless, with some of our finest properties sold off, our income was less secure and our debt and interest burden was growing.

On the bright side, our hotel chain was, in 1960, doing handsomely. I was convinced that New York's hotels were in for a boom. Spreading affluence, the rise in travel, and the introduction of jet aircraft all augured well for business and tourist travel. In New York we acquired a core group of six hotels—the Astor, Commodore, Manhattan, Taft, Drake, and Chatham. At one time or another we also owned the St. Regis and the Gotham. In Chicago we had the Sherman and the Ambassador East and West. Webb & Knapp at one point was the biggest hotel operator in the country. Hotels, like aircraft, can make spectacular profits if they run full. In 1960 our hotels were operating at a cut above the average occupancy rate, and there was promise of more business yet to come: the World's Fair was due. Naturally, we mortgaged and leased out these promising properties to the hilt in order to raise cash for the company.

The only project and property which we already had a few qualms about in 1960 was Freedomland Amusement Park, situated on the three hundred acres of Baychester swampland we had acquired in a swap for Ohrbach's store. We got into Freedomland the way the United States got into Vietnam, back-sideways, without really intending to, and only to clean up the mess somebody else had left behind.

The idea of Freedomland, as fallout from the explosive success of Walt Disney's fabulous Disneyland, was wafted eastward by one C. V. Wood. Wood is a promoter's promoter, a terrific, enthusiastic idea man who could sell snow to Eskimos. Wood had worked with Disney on Disneyland. He was at some point eased out by Disney, but not before convincing himself and a number of other people that Disneyland's success was really a matter of Wood's rather than Disney's ideas and management. Wood put together a masterful presentation of his Freedomland idea. The idea was to create a star-spangled amusement park, an America-in-miniature, to which hordes of Easterners would flock. It was a great idea, beautifully presented. Sober outfits such as Paine, Webber, Jackson & Curtis lined up to help underwrite the show. Rather early in the game the project proved to be overpromoted, overexpensive, and underfinanced. Too late for us to do much about it, it turned out to be misconceived, grievously mislocated, and utterly mismanaged, but Webb & Knapp, at the outset, was perfectly safe. We were merely the landlords. We didn't have a penny in the project. All the publicity and traffic Freedomland generated was bound to increase the value of our real estate. How could we lose? We leased them the land.

After a time it turned out they didn't have money to pay their rent. We accepted stock in the business in lieu of rent. Meanwhile, some of the underwriters had backed off, and the company was in hock to the contractors who were building the shows. The builders and suppliers were threatening to close things down before the show even started. Freedomland still seemed like a good promotion: to get our money out, we put more in. We took forty percent of the company's stock and advanced them money to pay off a few million in due bills. This process continued: we ended up owning Freedomland. Show-business productions tend either to make it big or to flop very expensively. Freedomland, with its enormous fixed costs, never got near the break-even point. Year after year, till it closed, it siphoned away Webb & Knapp funds and credit, for a total drain of maybe twenty million dollars. There was one silver lining. Freedomland attracted attention to our acreage, and we did, after closing Freedomland, sell the lease to the land to Abraham Kazan's United Housing Foundation. Co-op City, with its seventy-five thousand inhabitants, now rises over the site of Freedomland. Freedomland, however, with its promise of a better season next year, seriously debilitated our firm at a crucial time.

For a time, in 1962, it seemed we might once and for all clear ourselves of excess debt and stabilize operations. The British investors who had previously joined us in Place Ville-Marie through Trizec Corp. now joined Webb & Knapp in the United States through the Zeckendorf Property Corp. Like Trizec, Zeckendorf Corp. was essentially a fifty-fifty company, half-owned by Webb & Knapp and half-owned by the British group with Alcoa owning 10 percent of the stock. The new company's properties consisted of Lincoln Towers, Park West Village, Kips Bay Plaza, Society Hill, and Lower Hill, as well as Southwest Washington—our urban-redevelopment projects that were still under way. It also consisted of United Nations Plaza, the Alcoa luxury development we had under way on the East River, as well as Century City, our Russian Hill property in San Francisco, our air rights to the New York Central yards on the West Side of Manhattan, our Baychester land, and various other pieces of real estate, including 165 Broadway, which we later sold to U.S. Steel. In return for rights in these properties, our partners supplied some 42 million dollars in capital and credit. As part of the deal, the British also acquired five million shares of Webb & Knapp stock and put three men on our 12-man board of directors, which consisted of four outside directors and five Webb & Knapp officer-directors.

As one of the British group then stated, "We hold the jewels of the Webb & Knapp empire." This was quite accurate. In nature, however, jewels are created under conditions of intense heat and pressure. The Webb & Knapp jewels were not yet fully formed. Before they did finally form, some of us would be burned, but that is another book.

· 21 · The Demise of Webb & Knapp and the Rebirth of William Zeckendorf

I HAVE NOT SPACE in this volume, nor the heart at this time, to go into a detailed description of the last days and final foundering of Webb & Knapp. To do so properly would take a separate book and, perhaps, another author. I was and still am too close, too intensely and emotionally involved in those events to give a proper blow-by-blow account. From 1962 on, as we sailed into increasingly difficult weather, the Webb & Knapp story is that of a ceaseless series of sharp tacks, sudden jibes, and difficult reaches by an increasingly waterlogged ship. It is a tale of conferences, exchanges, and minor ventures devised to stave off disaster while we prayed to put together one or more major projects that could finally begin to pull the company back together. But exactly when we moved from a hopeful position into a desperate situation, I cannot say. I was doing what I had always done. If any alarm bells rang, I did not hear them. In 1962, as we created the Zeckendorf Property Corp., things were serious as usual but very hopeful. There was new money in the company, not as much money as we wanted and needed, but as much as we could get. With shrewdness and a bit of luck, we would make it home to a safe port.

When you cross the ocean on a steamship, you will notice that on some days, though there may be a prevailing wind, the ocean waves may actually come from five or six different directions at once. As these waves move by and through one another, they sometimes cancel each other out. At other times they augment each other and can create high crests and low troughs in the ocean. When the proper combinations of waves come together, these peaks and valleys on the ocean's surface can be enormous. To a passenger in a modern, high-speed steamship, such waves are merely an interesting phenomenon. To the skipper of a low-in-the-water sailing ship, however, the sudden appearance of the wrong combination of waves in such a gusty sea can spell disaster.

Something like the above is what could be said to have happened to Webb & Knapp. An unexpected combination of trends and events, coupled with our own actions, caused us to founder. Any two or three of these developments, we could have ridden out, but the total combination and sequence of happenings swamped us.

That a great many of our urban-redevelopment projects, as in Southwest Washington, were running late and costing us money was by now an old story. Less obvious, but in the end more painful, these projects had fallen out of phase with local markets because of their delayed construction cycle. Though in case after case we had been among the first to see the demand for quality housing in city cores, the delays we ran into in our pioneer efforts, and our own financial difficulties, permitted a wave of follow-the-leader builders to finish rival structures about the time we came to market. This competition meant great difficulties in getting adequate first rentals for many of our projects. As a result, we had losses, rather than income, on our books during these stretched-out beginning periods.

In New York, a third great wave rose to augment our problems. The city passed new zoning regulations having to do with the height and necessary setback of new buildings. The long-range effect of this new zoning was to create more plaza space at the street level, and this was highly desirable. However, construction costs per square foot of rentable space would be higher for the new structures than for the old, tiered construction common in New York. The immediate effect of the new ruling was a rush into construction by every speculative builder with a plot to build on. Everyone raced to get his new buildings up under the old rather than the new, regulations. For the next few years, as more and more new buildings were finished, a glut of so-called luxury apartments developed in the New York market. Almost trampled in their own stampede, new-building owners offered two and three months' rent, trips to Europe, and any other incentive they could think of to get a few tenants signed up to help meet mortgage requirements. This glut in the New York market came to a peak just as the bulk of our own New York redevelopment projects came to market—and it hurt. It turned out that Webb & Knapp, instead of producing income for their developers, was burning away their financial resources instead.

Meanwhile, on another flank, the coming of the jet age was indeed changing American travel patterns, but not at first in the ways some of us had anticipated. The jets brought much more travel business to key American cities. I think they were a background factor in the continued growth of New York as the corporate capital of America. But the jets, because they were so fast, actually cut back a bit, at first, on New York's hotel business. It turned out a businessman could fly in from Chicago or St. Louis, do his business, and fly back home in the same day instead of staying in New York overnight. About this time, too, the Internal Revenue Service severely tightened its interpretations of expense-account items in businessmen's budgets, and this also hurt the hotel business. When the World's Fair did come, it was not the success New York had hoped for. Highly publicized racial demonstrations at the commencement of the Fair scared away a modicum of would-be visitors. Any one of these developments was incidental. Cumulatively, their effect on our hotel operation was calamitous. When hotels are full, as New York hotels are at this writing, they are money machines. When they operate below capacity, they drink away cash like a jet gulps fuel, and in 1962–1963 our hotels drained away cash we didn't actually have. Freedomland, meanwhile, was running losses, and Roosevelt Field was not making money. By 1963 Webb & Knapp was suddenly awash and, in fact, breaking up in rough waters. To keep just the Zeckendorf Property Corp. above water called for millions of dollars in cash and credit. Webb & Knapp, losing money elsewhere, could not meet this need. Fortunately, Alcoa, originally a minor partner in Zeckendorf Property Corp. and a partner with us in Century City, had cash in depth. We had brought them into real estate. They had faith in the long-term prospects of our projects, plus deep pockets and other income against which to write off losses. In the fall of 1962, Alcoa bought parts of Zeckendorf Property Corp.'s holdings with future conversion rights that would make them one-third partners in Zeckendorf Property. Zeckendorf Property Corp. was designed to be insulated from Webb & Knapp proper. It was tacked on somewhat like the prow of a modern tanker is attached to the rest of the vessel. But as our losses continued to mount, the strains of keeping the two companies in association were more and more evident. Webb & Knapp board members representing the British group became more and more unhappy. Finally we decided to break things up, each group to go its own way.

In the summer of 1963 Webb & Knapp, as its share of Zeckendorf Property, took unto itself five of the less-developed Zeckendorf Property Corp. holdings. These included Southwest Washington, Baychester, and air rights over the New York Central yards in west Manhattan. Webb & Knapp then severed itself from the Zeckendorf Property Corp., which changed its name to Covent North American Properties, Ltd. This severance was very much like the breaking up of a ship into parts. The British and Alcoa drifted off. The British, to their later sorrow, I suspect, sold out to Alcoa. Alcoa, in due time, wound up with some wonderful money-making properties.

Meanwhile, back with what remained of Webb & Knapp, we tried to make our own way to a safe shore. We still had substantial holdings. Our principal assets were our position in Gulf States Land and Southwest Washington; but we held numerous other properties. These later we sold off as best we could, but now I was running into an ironic reverse of what went on during the first years of my Webb & Knapp career. In the 1940's, when we were handling the Astor estate and our own accounts, the very fact that we owned a property gave it a certain name and glamour which appreciated its market value. But in the 1960's, that a beleaguered Webb & Knapp owned a property was a signal to some potential buyers to hold back or bid low, in the expectation that, in our eagerness for cash, we would hold a fire sale. I resisted this downgrading in every way possible. The sharks, sensing the distress of our situation, kept circling closer but remained wary; there was still strength in Webb & Knapp, and always the possibility of a surprise move from us. For instance, I had sold 165 Broadway to U.S. Steel. We sold over seventy-five million dollars' worth of other properties. We also initiated the sale of the Savoy Plaza Hotel to General Motors, which they would use as New York headquarters. We had first offered them a tower on Times Square, but they chose the Fifth Avenue and Central Park location instead.

The GM deal was actually an offshoot of Webb & Knapp's last great real-estate effort. We had conceived plans for developing a great double block, a master block, from Forty-fourth Street, overpassing Forty-fifth Street, to Forty-sixth, on the west side of Seventh Avenue. The tower would encompass the Paramount Building and our old Astor Hotel site. When finished, it would be another Place Ville-Marie, with shops, arcades, and tremendous pedestrian traffic at the street and subway levels. I had the key land elements lined up, numbers of interested lessees in waiting, and Colonel Crown committed to finance the basic deal. Papers were drawn up ready for signing; all that remained were a few details. My son, Ronnie Nicholson, and I met with the Colonel. I was planning to go to Mexico for a few brief days of vacation and asked, "Now, is there any question about this, Colonel? If there is, I don't want to leave here."

"No, the boys and I will straighten out anything that comes up, and there's really nothing to do; we have an agreement: we divide the profits up, after I get my money back, and you're putting up $100,000 of your own. . . ."

We shook hands, and I left. And during the short time I spent in Mexico, Crown changed his mind. When he did so, he killed any hope of a masterful, sensible development in Times Square, because property there is now going piecemeal. I tried in every way to salvage the project, and came close, but it never quite worked out. Webb & Knapp, shortly after that, was tumbled by the Marine Midland's calling in our old 165 Broadway notes, which I mentioned in the beginning of the book.

▪ Epilogue

THE FALL OF Webb & Knapp, when it came, was an upsetting, ego-devastating event, but in a way it was also a relief. I was like a man let out of jail. The ordeal was over. The increasing pressure of the last three years was finally off. I had gone down honorably, fighting to the last minute to save my company. I had no intention of donning sackcloth and ashes or of bemoaning the past. My son, Ronnie Nicholson and I, and a handful of old employees, never even moved out of 383 Madison Avenue. We leased back our old offices, bought back some of our own furniture, hung up our shingle as General Property Corp., and went into business. Within a year, we had control of our office building again, and as consultants, as packagers of and participants in various projects, we were making money.

The Zeckendorfs were alive and well and very much in real estate. True, we were severely limited in capital, but we had brains, experience, and contacts, and we kept making new contacts.

Somewhere in the midst of our new projects, I began to realize that I was having a marvelously good time. Marion's death was a stunning blow, but I recovered from that, too, in good time, and have come to realize that since the fall of Webb & Knapp I have, in effect, been privileged to live and to savor a second life and second career. How many other men get such an opportunity, I do not know, but I am grateful for mine. There are many fine, useful projects and developments waiting only for the proper push and financing to be brought into being. Chief among these is our fabulous water-displacement construction system for the creation of docks, buildings, and airports in rivers, lakes, or the sea itself. Meanwhile, other projects keep popping up in the form of my own or somebody else's new ideas. The job is to select among the possible choices and get to work.

Index

Abbott, Richard, 97
Abercrombie, James, 53
Abrons, Louis W., 83, 84
Acapulco, Mexico, 59
Affleck, Desbarats, Dimkaopoulos, Lebensold & Sise, 181
Air Canada, 178
Air rights over New York Central West Side terminal and yards, 140, 293, 297
Alexander, Henry, 130, 269–70
Allegheny Corporation, 126, 136, 290
Allen & Company, 161
Allied Stores Corporation, 57
Aluminum Company of America, 67, 180, 249–53, 263, 282, 291, 296
Aluminum Limited, 177–78
Americana Hotel, New York City, 289
American Broadcasting Company, 81, 93, 153–55
American Export Isbrandtsen, 12
American Institute of Architects, 73
American Superpower, 100–01, 106
Anderson, Robert, 151, 152
Apache Indians, 16
Architectural Forum, The, 204
Arizona Territory, 15
Army Corps of Engineers, U.S., 205
Aspura land deal, 256–59
Associated Dry Goods Company, 148

Astor, John Jacob, 44, 170
Astor, John Jacob, II, 56
Astor, John Jacob, III, 49
Astor, Lady Nancy, 44
Astor, Vincent, 44–47, 49–50, 57, 93, 149
Atlanta, Georgia, 99
Atlantic Monthly, The, 204, 238–41
Atlas, Sol, 277
Auchincloss, James C., 213
Aurbach family, 234

Bankers Trust Company, New York City, 79, 94, 100, 153, 159
Bank of England, 179
Bank of Europe, New York City, 28
Bank of Montreal, 173, 175, 177
Batista, General Fulgencio, 141, 255–56, 257, 259
Bator, Franciska, 52
Bator, Victor, 52
Batten, Barton, Durstine & Osborn, 9
Baychester, New York, 150–51, 291–92, 297
Becket, Welton, 245
Behn, Southenes, 154, 255
Bell, John Price, 76, 204
Best & Company, 53
Beveridge, George, 224
Blough, Roger, 279–82
Blumenthal, A. C., 60
Blumenthal, George, 40–41, 42, 48
Blythe & Company, 161

OTHER INSPIRATIONAL AND METAPHYSICAL BOOKS FROM PARKER PUBLISHING COMPANY

- The Cosmic Power Within You, Joseph Murphy

- Infinite Power for Richer Living, Joseph Murphy

- Miracle Power for Infinite Riches, Joseph Murphy

- The Mystic Path to Cosmic Power, Vernon Howard

- The Power of Miracle Metaphysics, Robert B. Stone

- The Power of Your Subconscious Mind, Joseph Murphy

- Secrets of the I-Ching, Joseph Murphy

- Secrets of Mental Magic, Vernon Howard

- Telecult Power: Amazing New Way to Psychic and Occult Wonders, Reese P. Dubin

- Your Infinite Power to Be Rich, Joseph Murphy

www.parkerpub.co